D1124512

Wildlife Management and Subsistence Hunting in Alaska

Wildlife Management and Subsistence Hunting in Alaska

Henry P. Huntington

University of Washington Press,
Seattle

First published in the United States of America by the University of Washington Press, PO Box 50096, Seattle, WA 98145-5096

Library of Congress Cataloging-in-Publication Data
Huntington, Henry P.
  Wildlife management and subsistence hunting in Alaska / Henry P. Huntington
    p.   cm.   —(Polar research series)
  Includes bibliographical references.
  ISBN 0-295-97218-1
  1. Eskimos—Alaska—Hunting.   2. Eskimos—Alaska—Fishing.
3. Wildlife management—Alaska.   4. Subsistence economy—Alaska.
5. Game-laws—Alaska.   6. Conservation of natural resources—Law and
legislation—Alaska.   I. Title.   II. Series.
E99.E7H974   1992
333.95′4′09798—dc 20   92-14143
                                           CIP

Printed and bound in Great Britain

To Mom and Dad

Contents

Contents

List of figures

List of tables

Abbreviations

Note:
I have tried to keep abbreviations to a minimum, and to confine each to the section that discusses that particular subject. For reference, here are the abbreviations I have used.

ADF&G	Alaska Department of Fish and Game
AEC	Atomic Energy Commission
AGC	Alaska Game Commission
AEWC	Alaska Eskimo Whaling Commission
AIBWC	Alaska and Inuvialuit Beluga Whale Committee
ANCSA	Alaska Native Claims Settlement Act of 1971
ANILCA	Alaska National Interest Lands Conservation Act of 1980
ANWR	Arctic National Wildlife Refuge
ATV	All-Terrain Vehicle
BLM	Bureau of Land Management
EIS	Environmental Impact Statement
EWC	Eskimo Walrus Commission
FGMC	North Slope Borough Fish and Game Management Committee
FWS	U.S. Fish and Wildlife Service
IGC	Inuvialuit Game Council
IPCC	International Porcupine Caribou Commission
IWC	International Whaling Commission
MBTA	Migratory Bird Treaty Act of 1918
MMPA	Marine Mammal Protection Act of 1972
MMS	Minerals Management Service
NOAA	National Oceanic and Atmospheric Administration
NMFS	National Marine Fisheries Service
NPS	National Park Service
NSB	North Slope Borough
PCH	Porcupine Caribou Herd
RurAl CAP	Rural Alaska Community Action Program
SAC	North Slope Borough Science Advisory Committee
Y-K Delta	Yukon-Kuskokwim Delta

Preface

Regulating and studying the impacts of hunting is a major part of wildlife management. The subject of this book is a particular type of hunting in one specific area – local subsistence hunting in northern Alaska. I examine the ways in which subsistence hunters, primarily Iñupiat Eskimos, are affected by various management regimes and initiatives, and the ways in which the regimes have or have not adapted to accommodate the needs of those hunters. It is an issue in wildlife management, and also includes aspects of anthropology and political science. In Chapter 1 I elaborate on these themes, but here I would like to discuss subsistence hunting in terms of conservation.

As efforts to conserve natural resources increase in scope and prominence, it becomes increasingly important to examine resource use and resource users. Hunting wild animals is a consumptive use of a renewable resource. But as consumptive does not necessarily equate with destructive, renewable does not mean either limitless or permanent. The task of wildlife management is to conserve animal resources – in the sense of making sure that they are able to continue to renew themselves – while allowing for sustainable use of those same resources. While such uses can include commercial or sport hunting or fishing, hunting for subsistence adds another dimension to the idea of use, namely dependence upon the resource. This is particularly important in terms of conservation, since it is natural that those most dependent upon a resource will be its staunchest defenders.

This compatibility of hunting and conservation is often overlooked (though not by most hunters!). Subsistence hunting, especially, is dependent upon long-term conservation, since subsistence involves continuous use of many natural resources, often passed along the generations in communities where the material and spiritual culture is based on the hunt and the animals that are hunted. The object of conservation is not to protect one animal or save a representative slice of nature from extinction. Protecting animals where their habitat is being destroyed conserves nothing, and a remnant population saved from extinction is little more than a specimen in a bottle. True conservation requires keeping ecosystems intact to preserve the full diversity of the natural world on a large scale and for the long term. Only under such conditions can the healthy populations exist upon which subsistence hunting depends.

In addition to requiring conservation for its own ends, subsistence hunting can itself greatly benefit conservation efforts. The needs of communities of hunters are a tangible and forceful argument against adverse impacts to populations of hunted animals. The difference between a herd of 100,000 caribou and one of 400,000 caribou is most apparent when villages, unable to meet their needs at the lower population level, can thrive at the higher. An impact that would reduce the herd, even without any threat of extinction, would be unacceptable to dependent hunters whose harvests would be reduced either by regulation or by scarcity.

Such changes in abundance can, of course, occur naturally. In hunting societies people living off the land became an integral part of the local environment, and their patterns of resource use reflected this. If the population of one animal declined, others could be taken instead while the first recovered to harvestable levels. This was often a conscious strategy made formal by the establishment of hunting areas where individuals and families could husband the land and its resources.

In former times, hunting weapons were likely to have been too primitive to drive species to extinction. Scarcity and the availability of other animals as substitutes for food and clothing would protect an animal population that had declined. Starvation in times of great scarcity was also undoubtedly a factor in limiting the impacts of aboriginal societies, especially in communities where one species provided the bulk of the diet. The best evidence for the conservation effects of such a way of life is the state in which the land and the animals remained, even though people have been living in "wilderness" areas like northern Alaska for upwards of 10,000 years.

Hunting, however, does not necessarily lead to sound conservation. In modern times, firearms, motorized transport, and alternative sources of food from outside the local region have given man the capacity for wiping out populations and species, and for getting around the necessary balance with his local environment. Large numbers of immigrants have exacerbated this problem. Passenger pigeons, North American bison, and Alaska muskoxen were wiped out – or nearly so – by the unchecked use of modern weapons by many people.

Incentive for hunting often contributed to these excesses. Hunting was for bounty, the market or sport, not just for subsistence. Even so, the lesson is clear: through hunting, as through other means, man now has great destructive capacity. No societies and no ecosystems are completely free from such impacts, and for this reason management and regulation of hunting, including subsistence hunting, have become necessary.

The forms taken in northern Alaska by such regulatory efforts are the subject of the rest of this book. Clearly they are necessary to ensure proper conservation of the natural world. By effecting conservation, wildlife management can also protect subsistence, or at least the resources used by subsistence hunters. This is the importance of conservation. Now I would like to turn to the importance of subsistence societies.

Subsistence hunters spend a great deal of time hunting, observing animals, and learning about their surroundings. In aboriginal societies, many stories, dances, beliefs, and other manifestations of culture concern hunting, treatment of killed animals, proper behavior of hunters towards their prey, and other aspects of the hunting way of life. This connection to and understanding of the environment has been gained over millennia of close contact and interaction, and has given individuals in those societies deep insight into animal behavior, population fluctuations, and the interrelationships that characterize an ecosystem. Though not infallible, this experience can help wildlife biologists and managers achieve a scientific understanding of local ecology. Such knowledge should not be squandered by ignoring the keen hunter's eye, or, even worse, lost forever by trying to end traditional ways of life.

In addition to the benefit that subsistence hunters can provide to scientists and other outsiders, they have the right to existence inherent in all communities. The diversity of human experience and existence should not be held lower than the diversity and viability of the non-human environment. Separating one from the other is a concept alien to many aboriginal societies. The Iñupiat Eskimos have no word for "wilderness." What others may perceive as vast expanses of trackless tundra, the Iñupiat see as peopled land, where geographic features are familiar and named, and the means of sustaining life are all around. There is no conflict between such a society in its traditional way of life and the resources that sustain it. Protecting the opportunity to continue that way of life is no more than the right of a people to self-determination.

But times have changed. The conditions in which aboriginal societies thrived no longer exist in most of the world. New people have moved in, displacing aboriginal people, or competing with them directly or indirectly for the resources of the area. Traditional forms of conserving animals and other resources are no longer adequate. Continuing to live off the land requires awareness of the potential for harm and of the extent of other influences and impacts on the resources, such as, for example, habitat disturbance by mineral development or increased hunting in other parts of the range of migratory species. The search for a way in which sound management can be achieved is the concern of this study. The question remaining is, where lies the burden of promoting and achieving new forms of management?

In my opinion, that burden must be shared by all those whose interests are served by sound resource conservation. This book addresses the share of that burden that lies on the management agencies – to promote conservation while providing subsistence hunters the opportunities they need to harvest animals. But a share of the burden lies also on the hunters. It is their livelihood, their resource, their culture and way of life that is at stake.

If hunting regulations are to reflect local needs and conditions, hunters must help develop those regulations, and must work to achieve the goals of conserving the resource for continued use. Overuse of resources despite evidence of their scarcity threatens both the resource and those who use it. Subsistence hunters must be aware of the status of the animal populations they hunt, and must be willing to take the necessary steps, including harvest reduction, to ensure that those populations are not harmed.

The details may be subject to discussion, negotiation, and disagreement, but conservation requires cooperation among managers, hunters, and other interested parties. Well-managed hunting is no threat to resource conservation, and by enhancing understanding, appreciation, and use of a resource, it can play an effective role in promoting and achieving conservation goals. Conversely, through appropriate hunting regulations and controls on other impacts to a resource, conservation efforts can help preserve subsistence hunting and the communities and cultures such hunting sustains. Turning such an ideal into reality is difficult, frustrating, and slow. But it is also necessary if we are to preserve both natural resources and human cultures. I hope this book will help make this possible.

Acknowledgements

This study is essentially my doctoral dissertation, written in the Polar Studies program at the Scott Polar Research Institute, University of Cambridge. My interest in the area began in the spring of 1988 while working on the census of the bowhead whale for the North Slope Borough Department of Wildlife Management. Following master's research on the Alaska Eskimo Whaling Commission, I decided to look at other examples of managing subsistence hunting in northern Alaska. This book is the result. I hope it is a constructive contribution to the effort to provide sound management for the wildlife resources on Alaska's North Slope and beyond.

Many people and organizations have given me generous and valuable help during my research and writing. The North Slope Borough Department of Wildlife Management in particular gave me logistical and moral support during my year of research in Barrow; without their assistance this study would not have been possible. In addition, I thank the following: Ben Nageak, Tom Albert, Craig George, Mike Philo, Charlie Brower, Clarence Itta, Deano Olemaun, Robert Suydam, Dolores Vinas, Noe Texeira, and Liza Delarosa of the North Slope Borough Department of Wildlife Management; Geoff Carroll, Jim Magdanz, Kathy Frost, Lloyd Lowry, Sverre Pedersen, Doug Larsen, John Trent, Jim Davis, Hannah Loon, and Larry Jones of the Alaska Department of Fish and Game; Jerry Stroebele, Victor Karmun, Charles Hunt, Dana Seagars, Donald Voros, Alan Crane, and Jon Nickles of the U.S. Fish and Wildlife Service; Steve Zimmerman and Howard Braham of the National Marine Fisheries Service; Kate Rooney and Bruce Collins of the National Park Service; Bishop Buckle and Mary Leykom of the Bureau of Land Management; Jerome Montague, Cleveland Cowles, and Jerry Imm of the Minerals Management Service; Charlotte Brower of the Alaska Eskimo Whaling Commission; Matthew Iya of the Eskimo Walrus Commission; Sidney Huntington of the Alaska Board of Game; Pete Schaeffer of the Kotzebue Advisory Committee and the Arctic Regional Council; Gunther Abrahamson of the Beverly-Kaminuriak Caribou Management Board; Doug Urquhart of the International Porcupine Caribou Management Commission; Randall Weiner of Trustees for Alaska; Jack Hession of the

Sierra Club; Doug Heard and Dyan Grant-Francis of the Northwest Territories Department of Renewable Resources; Charles Greene and Dennis Tiepelman of the Northwest Arctic Borough; John Bockstoce of the New Bedford Whaling Museum; Milton Freeman of the Boreal Institute for Northern Studies; Mark Fraker of British Petroleum, Alaska; John Burns of Living Resources, Inc.; Dale Stotts of Ukpeagvik Iñupiat Corporation; Don Gordon of the World Conservation Monitoring Centre; Bud Burris of the Alaska Outdoor Council; Senator Ted Stevens; Rose Fosdick; Bob Uhl; Sarah Horn; Flip Stander; Marie Adams; Karen Brewster; John Clain and Liz Kenny; Trinity Hall, Cambridge; and Bernard Stonehouse, my supervisor at the Scott Polar Research Institute.

I have benefited greatly from the advice and input of those mentioned above, but the opinions expressed herein are my own, and any errors are solely my responsibility.

1

Background to the study

The problem

Current management of local subsistence hunting in northern Alaska is widely regarded as inadequate (Langdon, 1984; Schaeffer *et al.*, 1986; Brewster, 1987; Osherenko, 1988; Pinkerton, 1989; Case, 1989; Loon and Georgette, 1989). Some animal populations are poorly monitored, leaving large population swings possibly undetected. Under certain regulations, subsistence hunters – primarily Iñupiat Eskimos – are unable to provide for their nutritional, cultural, or spiritual needs or to continue customary patterns of resource use. As a result, management regimes are often widely ignored. In much of rural Alaska the conflict between traditional patterns of resource use and Western management practices is heightened by problems of allocation between commercial, sport, and subsistence uses of fish and game. Uncertainty about the long-term roles of the federal and state governments further complicates the management picture, since management priorities at each level of government are not always the same.[1]

In terms of local subsistence hunting, successful management of wildlife stocks would both allow local people to provide for their needs and ensure that game populations remain healthy. Despite many attempts to protect local interests and needs, by this standard there have been few management successes in northern Alaska. A change in management emphasis is required, similar to the one Marks describes in writing about Zambia:

> wildlife managers require information about the nature of political, social, economic, and cultural conditions on which to base new programs of wildlife management in Africa that will avoid the failures of the old programs with their

Background to the study

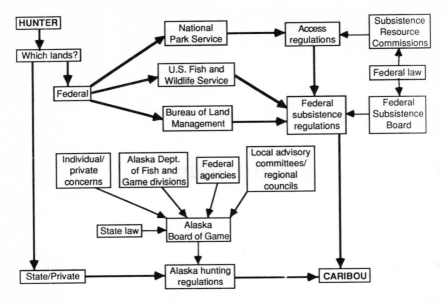

Figure 1.1 Schematic diagram of the regulation of caribou hunting as an example of the complexity of the regulatory and management system affecting a northern Alaska subsistence hunter. This diagram shows the situation following the *McDowell* decision, when a subsistence hunter hunting on federal lands encounters a new set of regulations established by federal agencies. Although the Federal Subsistence Board has not been fully established, it is expected to have similar inputs to those of the Alaska Board of Game.

> emphasis on the biological resource . . . wildlife management must, of necessity, become more situationally relevant in rural areas. (1984: 35)

To examine the current situation in northern Alaska, this study examines currently active management and regulatory regimes in the region to discover what characteristics are shared by effective regimes. The goal is to produce a list of criteria, based upon the experiences of the regimes that are examined, that are important in providing effective management as defined above. As Figure 1.1 shows, the regulatory system facing the hunter can be highly complex, with overlapping jurisdictions and shared responsibilities between various agencies. The varied responsibilities of the different regimes make a comprehensive model of an effective regime impossible. Instead, the criteria are intended as a tool for examining existing or proposed regimes.

What is "effective management"?

This study examines one particular aspect of the function of management regimes, that of the interaction between the regime and local subsistence hunters. In northern Alaska this is a crucial link, and one that has not been examined in detail before. While individual regimes have been looked at in a variety of studies (*e.g.*, Langdon, 1984; Caulfield, 1988; Freeman, 1989), no attempt has been made to analyze systematically the regime–hunter interaction. The list of criteria I have developed proposes a new means with which to analyze and understand the role of the management regime in relation to subsistence hunting. Strengthening the regime–hunter interaction can significantly improve scientific understanding of the resources and their ecosystem, as well as enhancing understanding and support of the regime and its goals among hunters. Many subsistence hunters spend a great deal of time in the field, and their observations of animal populations and behavior can greatly enhance the accuracy of monitoring changes to those populations.

Subsistence hunting is not the only, nor even the primary, purpose for which most management regimes exist. Other constituents of the regimes that I examine include (but are not limited to) sport hunters, conservationists, developers, users of other resources such as oil and gas, and the expression of public intent, usually described as the "national interest." These interests often compete for allocation of and access to resources and which gains priority in a particular case will depend upon its relative political strength, the orientation of the management agency with respect to the interests of that constituent group, legislative and constitutional limitations to the actions of the management regime, and the nature and extent of the impacts that a particular course of action will have on the various interested parties.

In examining only the interaction between the regime and the local subsistence hunters I have left aside the other responsibilities of the management regime and the agency charged with its administration. In other words, this study focuses solely on improving one particular aspect of management. In practice, the various and conflicting responsibilities of a management agency may make it difficult to improve the shortcomings that I identify with regard to management of subsistence hunting. However, by isolating the regime–subsistence hunter interaction, I am able to identify more clearly the specific needs of that relationship and to compare more accurately its expression among a variety of existing regimes.

In addition to the limitations on a regime's actions imposed by other interests than subsistence hunting, other constraints may be legal restrictions to its authority, the priorities of agency leadership, the professional culture and perspective within the agency, the availability of funds to carry out its goals, or other factors beyond the control of the agency implementing a particular regime. Furthermore, the nature of the resource being managed affects the difficulty of the task of management. Geese, for example, migrating to California and Mexico in the winter, require extensive monitoring as well as coordination with management agencies outside Alaska. By the same token, although biological information about bowhead whales is difficult to gather, management of the harvest is simplified because it is limited to Native hunters in nine whaling villages and can be easily and accurately monitored.

Although I note some of the constraints limiting the actions of various management regimes, in developing the final criteria I do not attempt to compensate for the difficulty of the management task facing them. In my conclusions (Chapter 7) I review the implications of such constraints for the application of the criteria that I develop. It is unlikely that each criterion can be applied to every management regime but a clear understanding of the shortcomings of a regime in its interactions with local subsistence hunters may still be useful in helping to promote effective management.

Within this study, I have defined "effective management" as that which accomplishes two things:

1. Protecting animal populations; and
2. Allowing local people to provide for their needs.

Clearly, this definition of "effective" applies only to local hunters, although the interests of other constituent groups may or may not be adversely affected by actions taken to improve management effectiveness under my definition. Development may be possible without threatening animal populations or reducing the ability of local hunters to get what they need. High animal populations may allow all types of hunters to harvest the resource.

Elaboration on the two objectives of my definition of effective management is necessary. First, protection of animal populations. Animal populations are susceptible to over-harvest and to adverse impacts from such activities as habitat destruction, disruption of migration routes, and competition for food (between fishermen and seals, for example). An obvious minimum standard is to preserve the population from extirpation, yet this is scarcely adequate for a resource upon which people depend. Maintenance of a high and stable population, on the other hand, may be impossible. Caribou populations have fluctuated greatly both in historic and in prehistoric times. A simpler test, and one that is used in legislation such as the Marine Mammal Protection Act of 1972, is that adverse impacts to animal populations that arise from human activity should be minimized. This does not preclude, although it also does not require, management actions such as those designed to avoid population crashes associated with natural factors such as an exceptionally severe winter or deterioration of range quality.

Second, allowing local people to provide for their needs. With the possible exception of isolated villages in times when bad weather prevents planes from coming in, harvesting wildlife is not necessary to prevent outright starvation. That definition of "absolute need" is contained in Alaska's hunting regulations. The definition I have adopted for this study is broader in scope: a "need" is a nutritional, cultural, or spiritual requirement that cannot be readily or adequately replaced. Quantifying this need presents a real problem, and one which this study does not address (see Uhl and Uhl, 1977; Pedersen, 1979; North Slope Borough, 1980; Jacobson and Wentworth, 1982). Recent studies (Stephen R. Braund & Associates and Institute of Social and Economic Research, 1988, 1989a, 1989b) have quantified current subsistence production in Barrow and in Wainwright; it is unclear how current production relates to current need. Another study (Braund *et al.*, 1988) has attempted to quantify the need for bowhead whales in the nine whaling villages by defining it as the average production for the period from 1910 to 1969. Incomplete records make this method difficult for bowheads and impossible for other species.

More complex than defining need is defining how a management regime allows local people to provide for that need. This problem is at the heart of this study. Because the need is more than merely nutritional, it is not simply a question of ensuring that a certain number of seals and caribou can be taken. Requiring Iñupiaq hunters to obtain a tag before hunting brown bear does not allow hunters to satisfy the spiritual need to show respect to the bear, which includes not discussing their intent prior to hunting. Individual bag limits may restrict the cultural need of a successful hunter to share his catch with members of his family and community. To achieve the goals of management, they must be viable in the field. The best-conceived regime cannot be effective if it is ignored by local hunters because they feel that it is inappropriate. The attitude of local hunters to management regimes and their willingness to cooperate to achieve the goals of management are crucial parts of the regime–hunter interaction.

In the analysis of regimes in this study, I identify some specific shortcomings each regime has in its ability to satisfy the requirements for effective management. Such shortcomings include placing an unnecessary burden on Native hunters by limiting methods of harvest, or failing to establish an adequate management plan to prevent overharvesting. It is not my intent to provide a lengthy analysis of how each regime might be improved. Rather, I draw on the experiences of the various regimes in order to improve our understanding of the interaction between management regimes and local subsistence hunters.

Background to the study

The academic setting

This study is linked to a large body of previous work and a wide range of current issues. It involves aspects of many academic disciplines, including economics, political science, anthropology, natural resources management, and wildlife biology. Previous studies have examined Arctic management regimes in the context of Native rights, anthropology, political science, and cultural interaction (Langdon, 1984; Berger, 1985; Freeman, 1985, 1986, 1989; Usher, 1986; Case, 1989). Others have looked at the economic basis of subsistence hunting and fishing in rural Alaska (Kruse, 1986; Wolfe et al., 1986; Schroeder et al., 1987) and the questions of government policy it creates (Lonner, 1980, 1981; Kelso, 1982).

Related management regimes, problems, and initiatives relevant to the subject exist elsewhere in the state and the country, and across the Arctic in Canada, Greenland, and Scandinavia (Cohen, 1989; Busiahn, 1989; Doubleday, 1989; Kapel and Petersen, 1982; Usher, 1986; Bjorklund, 1988; Gunn et al., 1988; Wheeler, 1988; McDonald, 1988). In southern Africa several methods are being attempted to improve wildlife management strategies by including local people in both planning and in receiving the benefits of consumptive and non-consumptive use of wildlife resources (Marks, 1984; Cumming, 1990).

The body of the text focuses on empirical observations of the interaction between the hunter, the resource, and the management regime. The following is an introduction to some of the questions and issues implicit in this study as they relate to wildlife management, political science, anthropology, and polar studies. It is hardly an exhaustive list, but I hope it will give specialists in those fields an idea of what they might find of interest in examining this book and its subject.

Wildlife management

Wildlife management is the science and practice of controlling wild animals and wild animal populations for human purposes. Such purposes include, among others, enhancing numbers of trophy-sized animals in big game species, allowing populations to fluctuate without interference to preserve aesthetic values of wilderness, maintaining animal populations to provide large sustained yields, and protecting endangered species from extinction. Combinations of these goals and the many other potential goals of wildlife managers gives a wide range of possible management initiatives. In any area, people have differing and sometimes conflicting or competing interests in wildlife resources. Often such interests are vocally expressed, with the result that wildlife management is often a visible and controversial undertaking.

Determining the goals of wildlife management for a particular area is a political concern, reflecting the influence of various groups in persuading the management agency or agencies to give priority to one goal over another. This aspect of management will be discussed more thoroughly below in the section on political science.

Achieving the desired goal or goals of wildlife management depends on accurate information and the ability to control either the animal populations in question or the human users of the animals and their habitat. For the majority of species in northern Alaska, direct control of the animals is impractical at best. Instead, managers have exercised control through hunting laws to achieve desired goals of population enhancement, predator control, or trophy-animal yield. This approach still requires accurate information about the status of animal populations, and additionally requires compliance with hunting laws by the people in the area.

Compiling accurate information about wildlife populations, dynamics, and behavior is a difficult and lengthy process. Many factors may affect population levels, migratory patterns, and animal distribution, making accurate long-term predictions next to impossible. This lack of certainty, especially when coupled with occasional erroneous predictions, may undermine the credibility of wildlife managers and of wildlife management among certain interest groups. If the professional managers aren't sure, why should their views be taken any more seriously than any other group? Where acceptance of the concept of wildlife management is in doubt, this problem can be critical. If the accuracy of even basic information, such as population levels, is suspect, wildlife users may come to question the relevance of wildlife management to the problems they face.

These observations may appear too harsh, and they do in fact, represent an extreme view. Nonetheless, versions of these concerns often surface in rural Alaska when the subject of wildlife management is discussed. Simply put, in Alaska as elsewhere traditional wildlife management approaches have focused too narrowly on the biological aspects of the field. Native hunters have detailed firsthand and extensive communal knowledge of animal behavior, population fluctuations, and other information relevant and necessary to the science of wildlife management. Respecting and using such knowledge can enhance both the accuracy and the acceptability of wildlife management in rural communities.

Native people also have patterns of resource use that are often highly complex, flexible, and intertwined with other aspects of their social, spiritual, or material culture. For example, separating out waterfowl hunting and binding it with seasons and limits has caused considerable mistrust and conflict between managers and hunters in parts of Alaska. Neither group can afford the effects of such feelings of ill-will. Managers need the cooperation of the hunters to understand the extent and impact of hunting on a particular species. Hunters need the cooperation of the managers to promote management initiatives that are responsive to their varied and changing needs. As noted in the quote from Marks (1984) above, "wildlife management must, of necessity, become more situationally relevant in rural areas."

This study presents many examples of the struggle to achieve such relevance. I hope that examining the experience of such efforts will help both managers and users understand the nature of their relationship, enabling them to improve the effectiveness of wildlife management initiatives.

Political science

As a science, wildlife management requires quantitative information collected by the rules of science. However, turning such scientific information into regulations, seasons, methods restrictions, bag limits, and the like, takes managers out of the realm of science. Wild aminals are a common-property resource, and regulating their use is a matter of public policy. Determining the goals and expression of public policy is by definition a political process.

In the case of northern Alaska, this arena is vast. Management agencies and regimes discussed in this study range from international treaties to local voluntary agreements, with federal, state, and local governments in between. Pervading many of the regimes are questions of Native rights, preferential allocations to certain users, and the effects of activities such as mineral development. In addition to its obvious implications in the area of resource allocation, this material is rich ground for case studies in empowerment, representation, government intervention, and bureaucratic behavior. The previous section concerning "effective management", addresses the nature of the management regime in terms of its constituents and constraints. This section outlines other areas of political science that are involved in the study of wildlife management.

The Marine Mammal Protection Act of 1972 grants a subsistence exemption for Native Alaskans only, while the Alaska State Constitution prohibits racial discrimination, effectively abolishing any Native rights in areas and issues controlled by the state, such as hunting terrestrial mammals. The Alaska National Interest Lands Conservation Act of 1980 attempts to compromise, giving priority to rural residents, among whom the ratio of Natives to non-Natives is much higher than in urban areas, without specifying special treatment for Natives. In all cases there is no explicit mention of the question of whether there exists a moral imperative to recognize any special rights held by Native people. Although clearly beyond the scope of this study, this is an pervasive issue and one often in the background in the debates and lawsuits concerning special allocations of resources.

Although often identified with Native rights, a separate question is that of preferential resource allocations among different uses and users. For rural residents subsistence hunting may provide a cultural and spiritual need, as well as representing the most cost-effective way of placing food on the table, but big game hunting, especially by people from outside the state who must pay large fees, may do more to stimulate the state's economy. For some animal populations this poses additional questions, such as whether it should be managed for maximum harvests or for large numbers of quality trophy animals. While there currently exists a preference in favor of subsistence hunting in Alaska, the state's definition of "subsistence hunter" has broadened to include most of the state's residents, while the federal definition still includes only rural residents. This issue has not yet been settled in Alaska, and will continue to contribute to uncertainty over the relative importance held by subsistence hunting within the regulatory system.

Another form of competition between users is less direct. Developing mineral resources, such as oil and gas, may affect both animals and hunters. Allocation between hunters is a controversial area, and so is the problem of allocating impacts between hunters and, in this case, industry. Is it more important to leave caribou calving grounds undisturbed or to tap potential sources of crude oil? In the public imagination, where the issue is usually viewed as oil versus wilderness, subsistence hunting may be a minor issue. Many pieces of federal legislation, however, require that industrial development minimize or eliminate adverse impacts on subsistence hunting. Establishing that such impacts will occur and determining their extent leaves a wide region of uncertainty, nonetheless, it is an important interaction between users of different resources. In this particular case the interest is heightened by the contrast between perceptions of the wealthy and powerful oil industry and the few and remote hunters.

Efforts to bring rural subsistence hunters into some sort of equality in terms of political influence have appeared in both federal and state legislation. Establishing local advisory committees, regional councils, and subsistence resource commissions has attempted to give rural residents an effective means of influencing the decision-making process via the same mechanism used successfully by urban hunters. The immediate reasons for the success or failure of these bodies are discussed in the text, but it would seem that they have less influence in practice than was intended by their creators. The influence of the bureaucracy with which they interact may help or hinder the expression of the concerns of members of the committees, or it may prevent implementation of their recommendations. Additionally, representation may be a problem on the committees, if certain groups are over-represented or if some members are not effective representatives of their communities.

The structure of the management regime, too, reflects the priorities for which it is established, and determines how it responds to management issues. Similarly, the staff of the agency responsible for the regime influences it greatly, especially in the smaller and newer regimes. A wildlife biologist will approach a management problem differently than an anthropologist, who will in turn approach it differently than a Native hunter. An agency staffed primarily by one group will have a different perspective than an agency staffed by another group. The expression of this professional culture manifests itself in the interaction between the regime and the hunters, and affects the ability of both parties to accomplish their goals.

Finally, there is the question of the lengths to which government or other management regimes are obligated to go to obtain public participation. If public meetings are held but no one attends, is the agency responsible for finding another way to determine public opinion? Or, to what extent is it the responsibility of the agency to inform the public, and what is it reasonable to expect people to find out for themselves? For example, should new hunting regulations be delivered individually to all hunters and explained, or can they be left in the village office or store where people can pick them up? This may seem a minor question, but without a tradition of written hunting regulations there may be little perceived need for going to the trouble of obtaining and reading them, especially if enforcement is low. By the same token, public hearings may not be the best way to obtain public input, especially where experience with the process is limited.

These questions are interesting and, in the long run, important to the future of wildlife management both in northern Alaska and elsewhere. As the scope of wildlife management widens, understanding the politics of management will become increasingly important in providing effective long-term management of natural resources.

Anthropology

The nature of the interaction between Native hunters and wildlife managers is an anthropological question. This question contains elements of cross-cultural communication, acculturation, cultural change, and cultural domination. Looking at the history of this interaction in northern Alaska provides some useful background in understanding today's issues. At the same time, because wildlife management addresses issues of great concern and importance to Native society, its history provides a rich source of information for anthropologists. Chapter 3 outlines the major events in the history of Iñupiat–Western interaction, but many current issues are touched upon in the body of the study.

Of primary concern to the wildlife manager – and anyone else who works in a cross-cultural environment – is the question of communication. This involves both the basic process of transferring information from one party to another, and also the more complex problem of gathering, interpreting, and applying that information. The perceived roles of hunter and hunted are crucial to understanding how people view the natural world and their part in it. The Native view that animals give themselves to worthy hunters, shedding their "outer parka" of hide, meat, bones, sinew, and returning as another caribou, seal, or whale, colors their perception of the role of wildlife management in affecting that relationship. A quota or a hunting tag may require the hunter to break his part of the compact between himself and the animal. Understanding such differences as this is necessary for a manager to communicate effectively with his Native constituents.

Establishing advisory committees to help regulatory agencies create equitable regulations may work fine, except that the formal representation implied by membership on such a committee is an alien concept in Iñupiaq society. Having one member of the community speak for the others, and expecting the others to follow what has been agreed upon, has no traditional cultural basis. Similarly, asking a long list of questions of an Iñupiaq hunter may be considered rude. For a manager working in several parts of the state, this problem will be intensified by the differences between different Native groups. What is acceptable in Barrow may not be in Bethel or Angoon.

Learning to overcome this barrier is a process of acculturation. This works in both directions, as Iñupiat learn the ways of Western society and government, and Westerners learn about Iñupiaq society and culture. The bulk of the shift, however, has fallen on the Iñupiat. In part this is a reflection of the cultural domination of Western society, both direct – such as in past efforts to eradicate the Iñupiat language – and indirect – such as in the need for Iñupiat to fight for their rights in the courtrooms and legislative halls of Western society. Many Native-controlled institutions are organized and run on the Western model of a representative committee, which may help them bridge the gap between the two systems.

Iñupiaq society, like any society, is constantly changing. Because of contact with Western society, this change has been greatly accelerated in the past century and a half. Many Native people are attempting to preserve the strengths of their traditional culture while adopting what is useful from the Western world. However, many legal definitions are static, so that some new practices would technically no longer be considered aspects of traditional Native culture. How to define Native culture in such a way that still allows for development and change is a difficult problem. In wildlife management, it is centered on the question of traditional practices in hunting and animal use. Such phrases as "customary and traditional use" are common, but attempts to define them are cumbersome and difficult to apply when many things are changing at once.

Anthropology no more holds the answers to current problems than does any other discipline. However, like the concerns discussed so far, it has much to offer those who try to understand the broader picture of events. Conversely, the successes and failures of wildlife managers and management institutions have shown many facets of Native society that might otherwise have remained obscure. Studying what has happened between the two groups may offer insight to the anthropologist.

Polar Studies

Polar studies is itself an interdisciplinary field, tying many issues together with the common thread of high latitude. In the circumpolar Arctic, there is more overlap than geography and climate. Indigenous peoples are faced with the pressures of immigrants and the immigrant society. The relationship of man to his environment is evolving, especially with the pressure to develop natural resources such as coal, minerals, and oil and gas. Remoteness has long protected the Arctic from such exploitation, but that very factor now often makes it an attractive place to explore for minerals, away from population centers and their opposition to nearby industrial activity. Others view the Arctic not as a remote wasteland best suited to exploitation, but as a wilderness of great beauty and value, deserving full protection. This conflict over economic development, especially when it involves indigenous cultures who may also be beneficiaries of that development, is a common problem to Arctic regions. Subsistence hunting is often neglected as a vital part of Native cultures, and is seen as either an obstacle to development or as a threat to the wilderness values of the region. This study attempts to put subsistence hunting in perspective as an issue of management. It concentrates on one portion of the Arctic, but the issues it addresses are found right across the North.

Study parameters

The region

The study focuses on the North Slope of Alaska, a region covering approximately 88,000 square miles (see Figure 1.2). The North Slope Borough, established in 1972, is the local government of the region; its boundaries are roughly those of the Arctic Slope Regional Corporation, established under the Alaska Native Claims Settlement Act of 1971. With the exception of the area around Point Hope in the southwest, the region is designated as Game Management Unit 26 by the Alaska Department of Fish and Game. The geographic boundaries of the area are the Brooks Range to the south and the Beaufort and Chukchi Seas of the Arctic Ocean to the north.

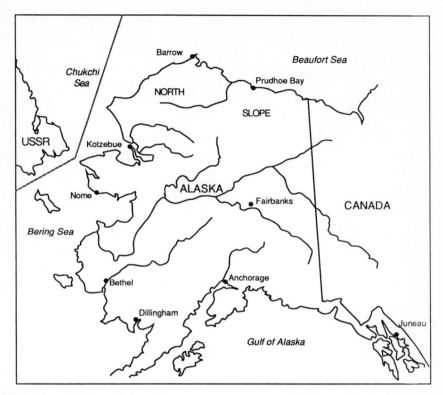

Figure 1.2 Alaska. Figure 6.1 (page 102) is a more detailed map of the North Slope Borough.

There are eight villages in the region: Anaktuvuk Pass, Atqasuk, Barrow, Kaktovik, Nuiqsut, Point Hope, Point Lay and Wainwright. Prudhoe Bay is the center of the oil and gas industrial complex (see Figure 6.1, page 102). The population of the North Slope is approximately 5,700, roughly 80 percent of whom are Iñupiat. A further 5,000 oil field workers are at the Prudhoe Bay area. With 3,500 residents, Barrow is the largest settlement and is the administrative center of the region.

Most of the management regimes examined in this study are active on the North Slope. However, some relevant management and regulatory issues are not currently receiving attention there. To make the study more complete, I will examine two regimes from other areas: the Yukon-Kuskokwim Delta Goose Management Plan from southwest Alaska, and the Beverly-Kaminuriak Caribou Management Board from Saskatchewan, Manitoba and the Northwest Territories. While some similar issues in management and cooperation between Native users and non-Native

13

Background to the study

Table 1.1 Species referred to in this study (in parenthesis are species not found in northern Alaska)

Common name	Latin name
Bearded seal	*Erignathus barbatus*
Beluga whale	*Delphinapterus leucas*
Bowhead whale	*Balaena mysticetus*
Brown or grizzly bear	*Ursus arctos*
(Cackling Canada goose)	(*Branta canadensis minima*)
Caribou	*Rangifer tarandus*
Dall sheep	*Ovis dalli*
Emperor goose	*Chen canagica*
Moose	*Alces alces*
Musk ox	*Ovibos moschatus*
(Northern fur seal)	(*Callorhinus ursinus*)
Pacific black brant	*Branta bernicla nigricans*
Pacific walrus	*Odobenus rosmarus divergens*
Polar bear	*Ursus maritimus*
Ptarmigan	*Lagopus lagopus* and *L. mutus*
Ribbon seal	*Phoca fasciata*
Ringed seal	*Phoca hispida*
Sea otter	(*Enhydra lutris*)
Spotted seal	*Phoca largha*
(Steller sea lion)	(*Eumetopias jubatus*)
White-fronted goose	*Anser albifrons frontalis*

managers exist in other parts of the Arctic – such as Greenland and northern Canada – the particular legal and political climate in Alaska make detailed comparisons difficult.

The Resources

This study focuses primarily upon birds and marine and terrestrial mammals hunted by North Slope residents (see Table 1.1). The actual management regimes may extend beyond or be based outside the region, but all the resources are used to some extent on the North Slope. Species examined in greatest detail are the bowhead whale, the beluga whale, walrus, caribou, four species of geese, polar bear and musk ox. Other species hunted in the region include several species of ducks and other waterfowl, ringed and bearded seal, ptarmigan, moose, brown bear, Dall sheep, and a wide variety of fish.

Methods

Information for this study has been collected through two primary means. First, I have examined the written records of management agencies and regimes. Second, I have interviewed people who play an active part in the conception, planning, and administration of various management efforts at work on the North Slope. This has involved a year's work based in Barrow, from September 1989 until August 1990. In addition to giving me access to information that is not available outside Alaska, and perhaps not outside the North Slope, I have had the opportunity to participate with local hunters in the seasonal cycle of hunting activities.

Terminology

Many of the terms in current use in Alaska may be ambiguous or unfamiliar. Following is a list of the terms that I use and the specific meaning of each.

Alaska: Can be used as noun or adjective. "Alaskan" refers to any person who lives in the state.

Athabascan: Native inhabitants of interior Alaska and parts of the Yukon and Northwest Territories.

Eskimo: Includes Iñupiat, St. Lawrence Island Yupik and Yup'ik, and is used when referring to more than one group at a time. When only one group is meant, I use the appropriate name (e.g., Iñupiat). While "Eskimo" is considered derogatory in some parts of the Arctic, there is no such connotation in Alaska. Groups such as the Eskimo Walrus Commission and the Alaska Eskimo Whaling Commission use the term freely.

Iñupiat: Native inhabitants of north and northwest Alaska. "Iñupiat" is the plural form; the singular form is "Iñupiaq." A more complete discussion can be found in Okakok (1989: 406, footnote).

Management regime: An organization, institution, or agency active in management. See "Management system."

Management system: A theoretical or practical approach to management, rather than a specific instance of management.

Marine mammals: As defined by the Marine Mammal Protection Act of 1972, this category includes whales, seals, sea otters, walrus, sea lions, and polar bears.

Native: Capitalized, refers to all indigenous inhabitants of Alaska, whether Eskimo, Indian, or Aleut.

St. Lawrence Island Yupik: Native inhabitants of Saint Lawrence Island.

Subsistence: Resource dependence that is primarily outside the cash sector of the economy. This term has a specific application in laws relating to Alaska wildlife, but has eluded a comprehensive definition. To Natives it describes their culture and their relationship to the land, and thus the economic definition seems inadequate (see Berger, 1985). To others, subsistence no longer exists in Alaska because the cash economy appears to predominate throughout the state, so that no one is truly dependent upon the land. For the purposes of this study, I accept "dependence" as either for cultural purposes or for nutritional need. It should also be noted that this definition does not describe subsistence users. Since I am looking at the way current management affects the ability of the hunters in northern Alaska to provide for their needs, I am not directly concerned with the status of hunters outside the region. Thus, subsistence users can be defined as those people who have no adequate means of replacing what they gain, culturally or materially, from harvesting subsistence resources.

Yup'ik: Native inhabitants of southwest Alaska.

Note

1. In December 1989 the Alaska Supreme Court ruled in *McDowell v. State of Alaska* that the provision of the state's subsistence law giving priority to rural residents violated the state constitution and could no longer be implemented. Failure to implement the law, however, brought the state into conflict with federal law under the Alaska National Interest Lands Conservation Act of 1980. In response, the federal government assumed management authority for subsistence hunting on federal lands in Alaska, which comprise roughly two-thirds of the state. In the fall of 1991 the U.S. Fish and Wildlife Service held hearings throughout the state on plans for the new Federal Subsistance Board, which would establish subsistence hunting and fishing regulations for federal lands in Alaska (see U.S. Fish and Wildlife Service, 1991). The State of Alaska may attempt to regain sole management authority by amending its constitution or by instituting a new system of classification for subsistence hunters. The situation is far from settled. To write in detail would be speculation on my part, and so this study does not discuss the implications or the effects of the *McDowell* decision. I have made reference in the text where management practices have changed as a result of the decision.

2

The evolution of game laws and wildlife management

Codified systems of game laws and of wildlife management were introduced to Alaska in the early 1900s by Americans of European descent. While new to Alaska, such regulations extended back nearly a thousand years in England. To understand the nature and extent of the conflict between Native wildlife use and western management, a review of the origins and purposes of game laws is important. Chapter 3 provides a similar background for the Iñupiat, the Native inhabitants of northern Alaska. McCandless (1985) and Lund (1980) provide concise summaries of the history and influence of English game law on North American practices. Lund, Nash (1982) and Tober (1981) give further insight into the questions of wilderness and wildlife use in the U.S.

England

Before the Norman conquest in 1066, recreational hunting in England was rare. Trench writes:

> They [the Saxons] seem, indeed, to have regarded hunting rather as pest-destruction: [King] Alfred's hunting is recorded with approval as a serious employment, a royal duty, like war and government. So deer were generally killed the easy way by driving them into nets or fenced paddocks; and boar, as often as not, were killed by professional huntsmen. (1967: 19)

On uncultivated lands – the forests – hunting was a much smaller issue than timber cutting (McCandless, 1985). With no recreational appeal to hunting, game had not nearly the importance of a valuable resource such as timber.

Game laws and wildlife management

The Normans changed things completely. Trench observes that William the Conqueror left intact most of the laws of Saxon England, with the exception of the game laws. William declared hunting to be a royal prerogative, and punished violators by "amputation, blinding and . . . castration" (Trench, 1967: 23–4). These laws were universally unpopular, largely because they were enforced by the corrupt and tyrannous king's foresters. Game now existed for the pleasure of the king, and hunting was limited to him and those authorized by him.

The Forest Charter of 1217 (in Stephenson and Marcham, 1972), two years after Magna Carta, codified the forest laws that had previously been subject to the whims of the King, made allowances for some hunting, and forbade the extortionate practices of the King's foresters. By defining and limiting the forests, and by removing that designation from some areas, the Forest Charter diluted the authority of the King. However, royal privilege was not lost.

John Manwood, a judge during the reign of Elizabeth I, defines a forest:

> A forrest is a certen Territorie of wooddy grounds + fruitfull pastures, priviledged for wild beasts and foules of Forrest, Chase, and Warren, to rest and abide in, in safe protection of the King, for his princely delight and pleasure, which Territorie of ground, so priviledged, is meered and bounded with unremovable, markes, meeres, and boundaries, either knowne by matter of record, or els by prescription: And also replenished with wilde beasts of venerie or chase, and with great coverts of vert, for the succour of the said wild beastes, to have there abode in: For the preservation and continuance of which said place, together with the vert and the Venison, there are certen particuler Lawes, Priviledges and Officers belonging to the same, meete for that purpose, that are onely proper unto a Forrest, and not to any other place. (1598: 1 recto)

He continues:

> Hauking and hunting in forrests are pastimes of delights and pleasure, ordained and appointed chiefly for the recreation of Kings and Princes, + therefore they are not to be used in forrests by every common person, but onely by such, as Earles, Barons + Noble men of the Realme, being thereunto licensed or authorised by the king, or, by his Justice in Eyre, or other officers of the forrest, or, by such, as have some good and lawfull authoritie thereunto. And even as the forrest is a priviledged place for the peace and safetie of the wild beasts, so likewise is it also a Sanctuary and Priviledged place for the peace and safetie of all manner of wild foules, but most especially for those, that are birds and foules of warren, and therefore every forrest doth containe in it a free warren. (*ibid.*: 105 verso)

Not only were hunting rights protected in the forests, but the game there was managed so as to continue to provide for the king's pleasure. Habitat was protected, and the game kept abundant (Lund, 1980).

18

By the time Manwood wrote his treatise in the sixteenth century, however, the forest laws were in a state of decay. Holdsworth points out that:

> The forest organization had never been popular with any class in the community. It was unpopular with the landowner because it fettered his rights over his land. It was unpopular with the farmer because the large powers of the forest officers led to much oppression. (1922: 102)

The reforms of the Forest Charter failed to control the abuses of the foresters and other officials. The royal monopoly on hunting and granting of privileges was also lost to a succession of statutes conferring hunting rights on members of the landed gentry (*ibid.*). By the seventeenth century, one needed property totalling £100 a year in order to hunt – fifty times the amount needed to vote for a knight of the shire (*ibid.*: 108).

Although the right to hunt now extended to the wealthy, it remained an elitist pursuit. Limitations on weapons and techniques emphasized the sporting character of the hunt rather than efficiency of harvest. Lund (1980: 7) writes: "Besides being too effective and thereby spoiling good sport, some hunting practices were abhorrent to persons of sensitivity." Hunting no longer had anything to do with providing food.

Lund (1980) describes four major goals of wildlife law exhibited by early English legislation. First, providing for sustained harvests. Second, regulating human activity, particularly by controlling weapons. Third, favoring particular groups, notably the wealthy. Fourth, protecting the animals themselves. Only the first and fourth goals have any ecological relevance. The second and third are political, designed to control one's opponents and to reward one's supporters.

In 1723, the House of Commons passed The Black Act, "creating at a blow some fifty new capital offences" (Thompson, 1975: 21). Thompson writes:

> The main group of offences was that of hunting, wounding, or stealing red or fallow deer, and the poaching of hares, conies or fish. These were made capital if the persons offending were armed and disguised, and, in the case of deer, if the offences were committed in any of the King's forests, whether the offenders were armed and disguised or not. (*ibid.*: 22)

Why the sudden severity of the new law? Thompson shows that the primary motivation was political. As McCandless puts it, "The Blacks became allied with the Jacobites, implacable enemies of the Hanoverians, so the law was aimed at quelling a local but potentially dangerous insurrection, and had little to do with deer" (1985: 11). Political or not, the law maintained the restrictions on who could hunt and made enforcement particularly harsh. Hunting was not an egalitarian pursuit.

Game laws and wildlife management

The general importance of game laws in eighteenth century England can be judged from a book by William Nelson, published in 1751. In the Preface he states:

> As Ignorance of the Law excuseth no Man, therefore it is absolutely necessary for every Person to be well acquainted with the *Laws of ENGLAND concerning the Game*; for there are scarce any laws of this Kingdom that require to be more universally known; all ranks from the Peer to the Peasant, not being exempted from Punishment for the Breach of them; on which account the Revisor of this Edition has endeavoured to shew, what is accounted *Game* in the Eye of the Law, their Proceeds and Seasons of hunting, &c. (emphasis in original)

With dire penalties awaiting those convicted of violating the Black Act, game laws were undoubtedly important to many more people than those who actually hunted. Establishing seasons and other restrictions on hunting meant that rebellious citizens had less excuse to be armed, and could be controlled by prosecution for crimes established by the Black Act.

In 1828 the Black Act was replaced by the Night Poaching Act, and in 1831 property requirements for hunting were abolished by the Game Act. Trench writes that, "By making a clean sweep of most of the old game laws, the Act abolished both the harsher punishments and the archaic qualifications to kill game" (1967: 154). By this time, however, the system in the New World had begun a course of its own.

The United States

The first Europeans in the New World saw an endless abundance of natural resources. Without the system of aristocratic privilege that characterized English society in general and hunting in particular, the immigrants considered wild animals to be free for anyone to take as they needed. Lund (1980) points out, however, that not all the colonies abolished the property requirement for hunting. Moreover, he writes, "settlers were empowered to disarm Indians who lawlessly carried hunting arms" (*ibid.*: 27). Remnants of the political goals of English game law carried over to the New World.

No one saw any need for conserving animals or habitat. Nash shows that early settlers saw uncultivated land as an evil that needed to be conquered: "When William Bradford stepped off the *Mayflower* into a 'hideous and desolate wilderness' he started a tradition of repugnance" (1982: 23–4). Far from extolling the virtues of the forest, the early settlers and the pioneers who spread westward sought to conquer the wilderness and replace it with fields and pastures. The idea of protecting wild lands came much later, originating on the heavily settled East Coast where such areas had become scarce. But protection of lands did not mean protection of game for the purpose of hunting. Unlike the forest in England, the National Park in the U.S. was for public, non-consumptive enjoyment.

Hunting practices in the U.S. before the mid-nineteenth century were utilitarian. Tober quotes William Cobbett, a visiting Englishman writing in 1819:

> And if poor [hunting] style were not sufficient indictment, the "general taste of the country is to *kill* things in order to have them to *eat*, which latter forms no part of the sportsman's object". (1981: 15) (emphasis in original)

The situation in the New World required a new approach to wildlife laws. According to Lund:

> As a reflection of the threats the colonists confronted regarding survival, the alterations [to the old-style laws] were expedient; as an expression of their democratic sentiments, the alterations were admirable; but as a means of preserving the remarkable wildlife bounty of the American continent, the alterations were a failure. (1980: 34)

In the face of new attitudes concerning game, a remedy for this failure was not easy to find.

That these attitudes took deep hold can be seen in an 1868 Report of the Commissioners of Fisheries of Massachusetts:

> People complain, and the legislature passes game laws, and nobody pays any attention to them after they are passed. Why? Because we insist on considering wild animals as our remote forefathers considered them, when men were scarce and wild animals were plenty. In a new country, the first settlers may properly have, not only liberty, but in some things license; license to till land anywhere, to cut wood anywhere, to shoot and trap game anywhere, to catch fish anywhere and in any way. All such things are then too plenty. (in Tober, 1981)

Having experienced the bounty of the land, people were unwilling to concede that use of game must be limited. Tober provides an example of the consequences of this vision:

> In 1857, the Ohio Senate quickly disposed of a bill which would have offered some protection to the passenger pigeon with the observation that the birds were so "wonderfully prolific" that "no ordinary destruction can lessen them, or be missed from the myriads that are yearly produced." The destruction that followed was extraordinary. Habitat was destroyed by lumbering and settlement, and birds, dead or alive, were shipped by the millions to market. The passenger pigeon was scarce by 1890, and Martha, the last known member of the species, died in the Cincinnati Zoo in 1914. (*ibid.*: 17)

Similar perceptions surrounded the demise of the buffalo on the Great Plains. While planned extermination of the animals in order to eradicate the Indians of the region may have played a large role (Lund, 1980: 89), the decimation of the buffalo herds in the 1870s came as a surprise to most observers (McCandless, 1985: 16). Loss of habitat to settlement and huge market harvests were not seen as potential threats to so numerous a species. Only when it was almost too late was there any reaction in favor of preserving wild lands and animals for the benefit of future generations.

Two late-nineteenth century developments played a major role in protecting animal stocks. First, the establishment of state and national parks, left in a primitive condition for the enjoyment and edification of the American people, introduced a wilderness ethic to American society (Nash, 1982), and protected the habitat of wild animals. Second, the creation of state wildlife laws generated revenues from licenses and empowered game wardens to enforce those laws (Lund, 1980). The importance of wildlife and of the hunting laws was underscored by creating a separate branch of enforcement officials. Lund writes:

> Particularly obdurate was the problem of law enforcement in a country as unsettled as the United States, where critical wildlife stocks were often found in remote areas. . . . That laws relating to wildlife should be dignified with an independent police force exclusively devoted to their enforcement is nothing short of remarkable, since few other areas of political interest have been similarly distinguished. (*ibid.*: 78–9)

The purchase of licenses generates the revenue to fund both enforcement and research. Lund continues:

> Through establishing the principle that tax revenues generated by hunting and fishing would be segregated for game purposes, wildlife interests precluded a continuing inquiry into the value of wildlife in comparison with other social goals. As a consequence, in periods of economic depression state fish and game agencies might enjoy a measure of economic health while other critical state services struggled along in penury. (*ibid.*: 79)

While early laws were designed for intensive use of game, the state system was designed to favor sport hunting, since recreational hunters purchased the licenses, and had sought the conservation measures that the state system provided.

Tober (1981) describes the development of a sports hunting elite. Priding themselves on knowledge of natural history, these hunters identified themselves by the use of specialized terms for game and by their hunting style. But, Tober observes,

> in spite of the best efforts of the sporting press to preserve a special place for these most highly principled American hunters, there were no grounds of either a legal or a customary nature for retaining control over access to the sporting experience. As the number of non-subsistence hunters grew, the lines between these gentlemen and other hunters blurred even before they came into focus. (*ibid.*: 46)

The idea of equal access has long been a key aspect of state wildlife laws.

While states are permitted to discriminate against non-residents – by higher license fees, stricter limits, or a complete ban on hunting – state constitutions and laws often forbid discrimination between state residents (e.g., *Lewis v. State of Arkansas*, 1913; *Bruce v. Director, Department of Chesapeake Bay Affairs*, 1971). This ideal reflects a fundamental tenet of American society: "In the American mind, equality meant equality of opportunity" (Tober, 1981: 18).

While specific game laws are usually under state jurisdiction, the federal government often plays a significant role. Huffman and Coggins write:

> the prevailing regulatory mode in the United States is "cooperative federalism," an intricate and delicate system of balancing and allocating governmental powers between state and federal governments. Because that intergovernmental relationship differs, depending on the resource and the statute at issue, the federal role varies widely. (1986: 53)

The Migratory Bird Treaty Act of 1918, for example, allows states to regulate bird hunting so long as state laws are not less restrictive than federal law. The Marine Mammal Protection Act of 1972 places all marine mammals under federal jurisdiction, although states can apply to regain control. For many game animals, however, no federal statutes apply, and so all authority is held by the states.

Within the balance between state and federal laws, issues of Native hunting and fishing rights remain ambiguous. Various federal treaties guarantee certain Indian tribes the ability to harvest fish and game preferentially or even without restriction, and these rights have been upheld in the courts (Cohen, 1989; Busiahn, 1989). Federal treaties, however, may only apply on federal lands. Lund writes:

> Although the first Indian wildlife treaty considered by the Supreme Court [in 1896] conferred an apparently perpetual right for Indians freely to hunt wildlife upon unoccupied federal lands, the Court inferred from the treaty a recognition of state power to impose generally applicable restrictions upon wildlife throughout the state. Subsequent decisions confirmed that while the states might not discriminate against Indians, they might impose common regulations upon all takers, Indian and non-Indian alike. (1980: 89–90)

Because of the orientation of state management to sport hunting, only the federal government, through treaty or legislation, has made substantial provisions for traditional Native harvests outside the sport hunting system of seasons and bag limits.

Alaska

Until 1975 game laws and regulations in Alaska were primarily applications and extensions of existing laws from outside the state. In 1975 the State of

Game laws and wildlife management

Alaska authorized separate regulations covering subsistence hunting and fishing. This was the first time that a statutory distinction was made between subsistence and other uses of wildlife, and it led to the development of a substantially different approach to regulating subsistence uses of wildlife. This section will examine the development of hunting laws and policies in Alaska and their application to specific cases of subsistence use.

During Russian administration of Alaska (1784–1867), only one law relating to animals was passed. Alexander Baranof, Governor of Russian America, issued an edict in 1792 that prohibited Natives from taking or possessing sea otters. Since the sea otter was the primary source of revenue for the Russian America Company, it is not surprising that the governor of that company sought to remove all competition for the valuable pelts of the animal. The edict was motivated solely by commercial concerns and was not part of any wider game management system.

Though a law passed in 1900 prohibited destruction and shipment of the eggs of certain species of birds, the first general regulations concerning wildlife use in Alaska were enacted by the U.S. Congress in 1902. The Alaska Game Law:

> defines game, fixes open seasons, restricts the number which may be killed, declares certain methods of hunting unlawful, . . . [and] authorizes the Secretary of Agriculture, when such action is necessary, to place further restrictions on killing in certain regions. (Wilson, 1903: 1)

These regulations follow the existing pattern of game laws in other parts of the U.S. As yet there were no game wardens in the Territory, so enforcement authority was given to all federal agents appointed to Alaska, such as customs agents, federal marshals and revenue officers.

The primary purpose of the law was to control the growing practice of trophy hunting. Wilson wrote:

> Owing to the fact that nearly all persons who go to Alaska to kill big game visit a few easily accessible localities – notably Kodiak Island, the Kenai Peninsula, and the vicinity of Cook Inlet – it has become necessary to protect the game of these localities by special regulations in order to prevent its speedy destruction. (*ibid.*)

However, residents of the Territory who might depend upon wildlife were specifically exempt from the regulations insofar as they hunted for personal use:

> The object of the act is to protect the game of the Territory so far as possible, but without causing unnecessary hardship; hence Indians, Eskimo, miners, or explorers actually in need of food are permitted to kill game for their immediate use. (*ibid.*)

What constituted "need" and what qualified as "immediate use" were not explained, but the intent was to allow local residents to continue their patterns of game use.

In 1908 the Alaska Game Law was amended to give authority for licenses to the governor of Alaska. In addition, the governor was authorized to register guides and to employ game wardens. The provisions for resident take of game contained in the original act remained intact (Wilson, 1908).

An interesting comment on the way in which these game laws worked or failed to work in Alaska can be found in the testimony before Congress of Charles Sheldon, vice president of the Boone and Crockett Club of America. Having visited Fairbanks in 1912, Sheldon found that there were no sportsmen in the interior of the Territory. He also found that game law enforcement was impossible due to the vastness of the region and the lack of funds available to pay for an effective system of game wardens. Sheldon's message to Congress is still relevant:

> They [the Alaskans] want something that is reasonable, and if you can get something that is reasonable for those people up there, and let them understand it and get behind it with a healthy local spirit, you will do more toward protecting game in Alaska than all the laws you can put on paper until judgment day that they do not believe in. (U.S. Congress, 1918a: 19)

In 1925 Congress passed a new Alaska Game Law, which established the Alaska Game Commission (AGC). The AGC had five members, one each from the four judicial districts of Alaska plus the chief representative of the Bureau of Biological Survey (later the Fish and Wildlife Service) resident in Alaska. Its functions were to recommend regulations to the Secretary of Agriculture and to oversee the administration of game laws in the Territory. For the first time, the game regulations of Alaska were subject to regular review by residents of the Territory (AGC, 1925).

The 1925 act also authorized the AGC to issue resident hunting licenses, although Natives were exempted from this requirement. Residents were defined as persons who have lived in the territory for at least one year. Under the new law, out-of-season hunting for food could only be done by Natives, explorers, prospectors, or travellers who were in "absolute need" of the resource, although the precise meaning of the phrase was not made clear. "Native" was defined as

> An Indian, Eskimo, or half-breed who has not severed his tribal relations by adopting a civilized mode of living or by exercising the right of franchise. (*ibid.*: 12)

The regulations were becoming more explicit and detailed, and were including more people.

The AGC existed until the State of Alaska took over responsibility for game regulation in 1960. In those 35 years, the AGC tried some new ideas and ran into its share of local problems. Sherwood (1981) describes the conflict between the AGC and military personnel who lived in the Territory for longer than the year required to establish residency, but because of a military exemption did not qualify as residents for licensing and hunting purposes. In 1939 the AGC began to require that Natives have certificates proving their status, in lieu of actual licenses (AGC, 1939). By 1943 this was no longer required (AGC, 1943), perhaps because it did not have the desired effect of encouraging Natives to report their harvests (Sherwood, 1981: 107).

The AGC was capable of responding to change in hunting conditions and practices, and of revising its past actions. An example of this can be seen in the regulations between 1947 and 1949 regarding use of aircraft while hunting. In 1947 when aircraft were first mentioned, the regulation read: "no aircraft shall be used for the purpose of driving, circling, spotting, or in aiding in the taking of any big game animals" (AGC, 1947: 11). But aircraft were a useful means of transportation, so in 1948 the regulation was altered to permit aircraft use for "transportation from a settlement or point of outfitting to a previously established camp" (AGC, 1948: 12). This, however, made it difficult to reach remote areas unless you already had a camp established. So in 1949 the regulation permitted use of aircraft to reach a "camp site on which a camp must be erected or established prior to hunting" (AGC, 1949: 12). Today you may not hunt until 3 a.m. on the day following the flight, with the exception that scheduled flights on jet aircraft are allowed (Alaska Department of Fish and Game, 1990: 9).

Although responsive to some concerns of resident hunters, the AGC was still oriented toward non-subsistence uses of game animals. The exemption provided for Natives, explorers, and travellers in need of food may be seen as a means of permitting subsistence uses without actually describing them as such. However, other provisions did not take into account practices common in some areas of the state. The regulations from 1925 onwards prohibit hunting swimming animals. At Onion Portage on the Kobuk River in northwest Alaska this has been done for thousands of years (Anderson, 1988) and remains common across the state. Schaeffer *et al.*, in a review of hunting regulations in northwest Alaska, write:

> Too many of these regulations, however, are value-loaded, having nothing to do with the biological well-being of the animals . . . . These regulations have to do with codifying a sport hunting ritual into the form of law. One is tempted to ask whether the duck dies with greater honor, once the ". . . motor has been completely shut off and the boat's progress from the motor's power has ceased". (1986: 18)

As a management tool, making the hunt more difficult may help limit harvests. To a subsistence hunter, however, a dead duck is a dead duck. Controlling harvests by the roundabout means of requiring motors to be shut off is inappropriate because it places an unnecessary burden on a hunter who is trying to feed his family.

Another example of such regulatory conflict concerns feeding game meat to dogs. The 1954 regulations contain the following:

> No person is permitted to feed any game animal, protected bird, game fish, or part thereof to a dog or fur animal held in captivity, except the waste parts, such as hides, viscera, and bones. (AGC, 1954: 9)

Schaeffer *et al.* comment:

> The prohibition against the feeding of game meat to dog teams provides an example of one of the great ironies in the wildlife regulatory system. On one hand, the biologists tend to view the use of snowmachines as somehow illegitimate, and have done everything possible to make it difficult to use snowmachines legally. On the other hand, the same biologists have deemed it illegal to feed game meat to dog teams, apparently expecting hunters from northwest Alaska to airfreight Purina dog chow to their camps. (1986: 23)

As the game regulations became more detailed, the potential for conflict between Native hunters and non-Native managers and agents was increasing.

At the Alaska Constitutional Convention, held in Fairbanks between November 1955 and February 1956, "the question of how fisheries and wildlife resources were to be managed gave rise to one of the deepest controversies of the convention" (Fischer, 1975: 134). At issue was whether the new state constitution should prescribe the structure of fish and game management commissions. Although the final decision was eventually left to the legislature, Fischer writes that:

> Before the resources article was finally disposed of, most of Alaska's sportsman and fisheries interests had been heard from in the largest outpouring of communications during the constitution writing process.
> . . . Behind these questions [of the structure of management commissions] lay the basic concerns over who would control and who would benefit from resources management. (1975: 135)

With no organization and little knowledge of the events in Fairbanks, the majority of the state's subsistence hunters did not participate in this debate. The structure of Alaska's regulatory system followed the design of the existing bureaucracy and had little room for accommodating the needs of subsistence hunters.

Statehood also brought another far-reaching change to the status of Natives. Article I, Section 3 of the Alaska Constitution forbids racial discrimination. Fischer writes that the National Association for the Advancement of Colored People (NAACP) urged the inclusion of this provision, which reads:

Game laws and wildlife management

> No person is to be denied the enjoyment of any civil or political right because of race, color, creed, or national origin. The legislature shall implement this section. [The word "sex" was added after "creed" in 1974.]

In addition to prohibiting discrimination against minorities, it removed any special status held by Natives in the eyes of the state government. While under federal law Natives can be exempted from such regulations as the hunting ban under the Marine Mammal Protection Act of 1972, under Alaska law Natives must be treated the same as all other residents of the state.

In terms of hunting regulations, Natives now need a license to hunt, and, like everyone else, cannot hunt during the closed season except in "dire emergency." One exception is that, on the grounds of religious freedom, Athabascan Indians are permitted to take moose out of season for funeral rituals (*Frank v. State of Alaska*, 1979). In lieu of the Native exemption for licenses, the 1960 game regulations – the first issued by the Alaska Department of Fish and Game (ADF&G) – allowed "anyone historically dependent on fish and game for subsistence" to purchase a license for $0.25 (ADF&G, 1960: 4). In 1963 this provision for historically dependent users was removed, although the annual income level which also qualified a person for a $0.25 license was raised from $800 to $3,600 (ADF&G, 1963).

After Alaska became a state, the Alaska Department of Fish and Game tried to improve the enforcement of game laws. This led, in Barrow, to the "Duck-In" incident in 1961 (see Chapter 3, page 42). In April, the Alaska House of Representatives urged the federal government to amend the Migratory Bird Treaty with Canada in order to allow the spring hunt, which is of great importance in northern and western Alaska (Kelso, 1981). Yet, the state still tried to enforce the Migratory Bird Treaty Act of 1918, which closes the migratory bird hunting season between March 10 and September 1 each year. In protest, nearly 150 Barrow residents, each with a duck in hand, presented themselves for arrest. The result was a policy of non-enforcement for hunting of birds (Blackman, 1989: 180–184).

Sadie Neakok, an Iñupiaq and the magistrate for Barrow, remembers the changes that occurred when the state took over management responsibility:

> we had lived so long under the federal government, under territorial law, that when Alaska became a state, the state promised that life for our native people would not change much. But it did. . . .
> . . . they started enforcing limits on how many [animals] we should catch . . . on ducks, fish, polar bear . . . They treated Barrow like down south, in Anchorage and Juneau areas, and disregarded our subsistence hunting up here. (*ibid.*: 184–5)

The application of existing laws and practices to the subsistence culture of Alaska was not successful in gaining the cooperation of the local hunters.

28

While some concern was expressed over certain aspects of subsistence use of animals, there was no institutional commitment to make a regulatory distinction of subsistence uses until 1975. Kelso quotes the legislative letter of intent accompanying the bill that authorized separate subsistence regulations:

> It is the intent of the majority of the House Resources Committee in reporting out HB 369 to have the Board of Fish and Game adopt regulations relating to subsistence hunting parallel to the regulations governing the existing fishing regulations.
>
> It is not the intent of the committee to deny subsistence hunting to any resident of the state of Alaska who is eligible to subsistence hunt. It is further the intent of the committee that the Board define subsistence hunting by regulation. (1981: 3)

The following year the state allowed local residents to petition for subsistence hunting areas. Kelso quotes a policy statement by the Boards of Fish and Game:

> While limitations on the productivity of fish and game must discourage continued increases in the numbers of subsistence type resource users, domestic utilization is still of fundamental importance to many Alaskans, and accordingly it is assigned the highest priority among beneficial uses. (*ibid.*: 4)

For the first time, subsistence uses had gained institutional recognition and priority, although the terms of its incorporation into the regulatory system were far from resolved.

In 1978 the State of Alaska passed a law creating a subsistence program for the state (Chapter 151, Session Laws of Alaska, 1978). This statute gave priority to subsistence uses of fish and wildlife, established mandatory procedures for the Board of Game when considering subsistence questions, created a new program within ADF&G to gather data on subsistence issues, and equated subsistence uses with "customary and traditional" ones (*ibid.*: 5). Langdon comments:

> It is important to underscore that in passing the subsistence law, the legislature mandated that if subsistence uses are present they must be authorized [by the Boards of Fisheries and Game]. This is a major departure from the previous operation of fish and game management. (1984: 24)

The creation of the new subsistence section of ADF&G (now a Division of Subsistence, equal in status to the other branches of ADF&G – see Chapter 5, pages 92–4) gave subsistence uses formal status within the state's management and regulatory system. Subsistence was given representation as well as priority.

Bobby v. State of Alaska (1989) underscored the extent to which subsistence uses must be accommodated in the regulatory system (see Chapter 5, page 95). A federal judge ruled that hunting seasons and individual bag limits for moose were inappropriate for residents of Lime Village. The opinion states:

> Bag limits and seasons are game management tools which have seen extensive use in Alaska and nationally. These restrictions have typically, if not universally, been used to regulate sport hunting. In this case, bag limits and seasons are being applied to a very different type of game use. . . .
>
> If bag limits and seasons are imposed on subsistence hunting, there must be substantial evidence in the record that such restrictions are not inconsistent with customary and traditional uses of the game in question. It must be clear in the record that subsistence uses will be accommodated . . . (*Bobby v. State of Alaska*, 1989: 777–8)

Whether this triggers a wave of similar suits across the state remains to be seen. In any case, the burden appears to be shifting from the subsistence hunters to the managers to prove that subsistence uses are not hindered by inappropriate regulations.

The primary difficulty with allocating subsistence uses has been identifying who qualifies as a subsistence user. The Alaska National Interest Lands Conservation Act of 1980 (ANILCA) required that rural residents of the state be given subsistence priority, or the federal government would exercise management authority on federal lands, which comprise some two-thirds of the state. If the state acted in accordance with federal law, it could retain control over hunting and fishing regulation throughout the entire state. In 1982 the federal government declared that the state's regulations were consistent with ANILCA, after the Boards of Fisheries and Game adopted regulations setting a subsistence priority for rural residents.

Following the pattern for the divisive issue of allocation of game, this policy wound up in the courts. In 1985 the Alaska Supreme Court found that the criteria used by the Board of Fisheries to determine subsistence eligibility were inconsistent with the intent of the 1978 subsistence law (*Madison v. Alaska Department of Fish and Game*, 1985). In 1986 the state amended the 1978 law so that only rural residents qualified as subsistence users. This did not settle the issue, for ANILCA's definition of rural was unclear. The state determined that most of the Kenai Peninsula in the southcentral part of the state was not rural. The Kenaitze Indian Tribe challenged this, and the U.S. Court of Appeals found that the state's definition of rural was inconsistent with ANILCA's definition and intent (*Kenaitze Indian Tribe v. State of Alaska*, 1988).

In 1989 the Alaska Supreme Court held in *McDowell v. State of Alaska* that distinguishing users according to their place of residence violated the Alaska State Constitution. In its opinion, the court wrote:

> One purpose of the 1986 act is to ensure that those Alaskans who need to engage in subsistence hunting and fishing in order to provide for their basic necessities are able to do so. This is an important interest. However, the means used to

accomplish this purpose are extremely crude. There are . . . substantial numbers of Alaskans living in areas designated as urban who have legitimate claims as subsistence users. Likewise, there are substantial numbers of Alaskans living in areas designated as rural who have no legitimate claims. A classification scheme employing individual characteristics would be less invasive on the article VIII [Alaska State Constitution] open access values and much more apt to accomplish the purpose of the statute than the urban–rural criterion. (*McDowell v. State of Alaska*, 1989: 10–11)

When the Alaska State Legislature failed to act to rectify the discrepancy between the state constitution and ANILCA, the federal government on July 1, 1990, took over management of hunting and fishing on federal lands throughout the state. It is unclear how this will be resolved.

Conclusions

The policy of giving priority to subsistence uses of animal resources has developed in Alaska in response to specific conditions and customs of resource use. In concept, this is a dramatic turnaround from the early forms of game law, which reserved hunting privileges for the wealthy and the elite. In practice, the regulatory system is adapting by fits and starts to the administration of patterns of resource use that defy easy classification. Since formal regulation of hunting originated in response to the pressures and needs of sport hunters, its methods and practices – such as seasons and bag limits – are more appropriate to recreational or part-time hunting than to year-round subsistence hunting.

The most significant difference between English and American game laws is the idea of equal access for all hunters, rather than access limited to the wealthy and powerful. To the extent that a subsistence priority creates a new privileged class of users, it runs counter to the egalitarian basis of American game laws. To the extent that regulation of subsistence must accommodate traditional practices and patterns of use that are often outside the customary regulatory framework, it requires substantial adaptation of management practices. Chapters 4 to 7 examine how well this difficult balance has been achieved in northern Alaska.

3

The Iñupiat and subsistence hunting

While not all local users of wildlife are Native, many of the divisive issues of wildlife regulation and management in northern Alaska reflect differing cultural values and perceptions between managers and Native hunters. The interaction between western and Iñupiaq culture has shaped perceptions and institutions on the North Slope, and an understanding of the origins and adaptations of Iñupiaq culture is important to understanding the key issues in wildlife management and regulation today. This chapter is a brief history of the Iñupiat of northern Alaska (see Figure 3.1), focusing on customs, and patterns of wildlife use.

The archeological record

Humans have lived in northern Alaska for at least 10,000 years (Anderson, 1972, 1988) and hunting on the wet tundra of the northern coastal plain dates from at least 6,000 years ago (Lobdell, 1986). Since the earliest occupation of this area, man's adaptations to the environment have been marked by a series of cultural and technological innovations; a pattern of development not of linear progress but of flexible adaptation to changing conditions. Various traditions of tool and resource use form the archaeological basis for determining successive cultures of the region. From the American Paleo-Arctic, the Northern Archaic, and the Arctic Small Tool complexes, to the Birnirk, Western Thule, and Historic Iñupiat traditions, improvements in design of knives, harpoons, arrowheads, and other implements show the history of man's efforts to thrive in the Arctic (Anderson, 1970, 1988; Bandi, 1969; Ford, 1959; Larsen and Rainey, 1948).

Birket-Smith writes:

Conditions in the Arctic have resulted in an almost extravagant perfection of

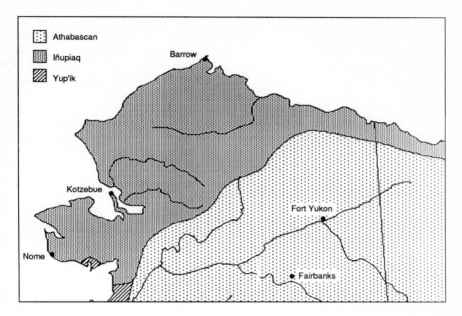

Figure 3.1 Native peoples of northern Alaska

Eskimo material culture, both directly by independent invention and indirectly by adoption from the outside such elements as were suited to their mode of life. (1936: 142)

Giddings and Anderson note:

The locations and types of settlements chosen by the Kotzebue Sound people were intimately connected to subsistence opportunities. (1986: 319)

Providing food and materials for clothing and construction – subsistence – was the driving force for the successive societies inhabiting northern Alaska.

Adapting to environmental change sometimes meant shifting the resource base. In the Cape Krusenstern area of Kotzebue Sound, for example, a whaling culture arose 3,800 years ago (Giddings, 1967: 245). After a short period it was replaced by the Ipiutak tradition, which shows little evidence of regular dependence on the bowhead whale. Giddings and Anderson (1986: 323) suggest that a change in weather patterns, especially in winds, may have made whaling a practical impossibility for several centuries, causing the Ipiutak people to return to earlier hunting patterns.

Alternatively, hunters could move to other areas to follow animals that were becoming scarce near home. Anderson (1988: 150) shows that in times of caribou shortages, Koyukon Athabascans moved into the upper

The Iñupiat and subsistence hunting

Kobuk valley, and the Kuuvangmiit Eskimos moved north to the upper Noatak. Such nomadism was common among the Nunamiut, or inland Eskimos, and lasted until the early 1950s when the village of Anaktuvuk Pass was founded by the last of the nomadic groups in northern Alaska.

Discussing the Natives of the Bering Strait region in the nineteenth century, Ray writes:

> The subsistence patterns had three important aspects: (1) the mobility of the inhabitants seasonally for food getting; (2) the flexibility of the food quests, and the variety of principal foods utilized within one subsistence area, which led to: (3) the many alternatives offered in all subsistence patterns. (1983: 175)

Hunting patterns existed in a general and fluid sense, characterized by resource availability, need, and opportunity. In the area of Cape Krusenstern National Monument, Uhl and Uhl describe the variant nature of the subsistence resource base:

> all living species utilized for subsistence purpose in the area of the Monument are nomadic, migratory and cyclic. Whether it be fish, bird, land animal, marine mammal or shellfish, none can be really classified as resident in the sense that applies in more temperate zones and milder environments. . . . Man and his subsistence activities have been an integral part of this ecological whole for a very long time. (1977: 9–10)

By necessity the inhabitants of northern Alaska developed a close connection to the resources of the area. This in turn created deep cultural and spiritual ties to the land, the sea, and the resources that remain fundamentally important to Native peoples today. The Iñupiaq sense of identity and well-being stems largely from maintaining those ties.

Iñupiaq society

Just as the material culture found in the archeological record demonstrates the development of tools and patterns of settlement and movement necessary to take full advantage of the resources of the region, the traditional social culture of the Iñupiat is an adaptation to a life of interdependence and cooperation. A few points are worth considering, because they are the basis of the Iñupiaq half of cross-cultural misunderstandings that have impeded management efforts by non-Natives.

Iñupiaq society is often characterized as highly individualistic. VanStone writes:

> Individuals usually do not give orders to others, at least outside the family, and resent such behavior. Even whaling captains are unpopular if they give too many orders to their crew members. (1962: 137)

Along with this reluctance to give orders is a reluctance to speak on behalf of others. According to Chance:

> Only rarely did a dominant village leader speak out authoritatively on behalf of those to whom he was not related by kin, and in such instances there was no assurance that his decisions would be carried out. (1966: 74)

There was in Alaska a definite sense of community, based upon the families which comprised each village. Burch (1974) shows that there were frequent battles between different villages and regions, provoked by real or imagined insults and threats. While the style of warfare was primitive, it shows the extent to which people were willing to defend their community. Settlements had traditional hunting areas (Spencer, 1959) which they would defend against outsiders. Strangers would sometimes be beaten or even killed (*ibid.*: 129; Brower, 1942; Hall, 1975: 303–4).

Even though there was conflict between regions, there was also extensive trade. The Tagiumiut, or coastal people, would exchange coastal goods such as walrus hides, whale blubber, and seal oil with the Nunamiut, or inland people, for caribou hides, wolf and wolverine furs, and dried meat (Spencer, 1959: 204). Trade also extended along the coast to the Bering Strait region. Spencer writes:

> Metal vessels, tobacco, trade beads, knives, and many other items of European manufacture came up to the northern coasts by these peoples and through the [trade] center at Hotham Inlet [near present-day Kotzebue].
>
> Trade, in short, was the factor which brought tremendously widely separated people together and which promoted the spread of ideas and culture elements from one center to another. (*ibid*: 199)

The northern Alaska Iñupiat were hardly an isolated group dependent solely upon locally available resources. They were able to get materials and ideas from distant areas. In fact, tobacco and other Eurasian goods reached northern Alaska via Siberia prior to the arrival of Europeans (Dr. John Simpson, in Bockstoce, 1988: 504–5).

European contact

Although European goods had already arrived, and British ships had passed by Barrow, the first sustained contact that Iñupiat of the Barrow area had with Europeans was with the *H.M.S. Plover*, commanded by Rochfort Maguire. Stationed at Point Barrow from 1852 to 1854, the *Plover* awaited the arrival of the Franklin expedition that had been lost searching for the Northwest Passage. *The Journal of Rochfort Maguire 1852–1854* (Bockstoce, 1988) describes first hand the interactions between the two groups, and what each learned from the other.

The Iñupiat and subsistence hunting

While that initial contact may have been mutually interesting and satis-factory, the contact period as a whole was extremely disruptive to the existing society. In a North Slope Borough study, Neakok *et al.* note that:

> The succeeding "Late Traditional Period" (1849–1875) marked the end of many traditional aspects of [Iñupiaq] culture. (1985: 14)

As a result of disease, alcohol, and competition with commercial whalers for whales and later for walruses, the Native population of the region dropped sharply. In 1800, the Point Hope population was 1,342. By 1849 it was less than 1,000, and in the 1860s disease killed half of the remaining people (*ibid.*).

Not all the changes were for the worse. Kilmarx writes:

> Euro-Americans may actually have helped the Inupiat become "better" Inupiat with the introduced goods; in other words, their efficiency in pursuing traditional activities was enhanced by contact. (1986: 223)

In a similar vein Chance observes:

> Nor do the adoption of Western technology and social institutions necessarily imply an important shift in Eskimo self-identification. Most Eskimos are quite pragmatic about the effectiveness of a given tool or idea, and accept or reject it according to their views of its usefulness. (1966: 92).

Nevertheless, while cultural identity remained strong, the patterns of life and the scope of the Iñupiaq world had changed dramatically. The next sections examine specific periods and incidents that illustrate these changes and the circumstances in which they occurred.

Commercial whaling

The first major change began in 1848 when Thomas Roys sailed the whaling ship the *Superior* through the Bering Strait and found a stock of bowhead whales that had never been commercially exploited. Over the next seventy years, as many as 18,000 whales were taken (Bockstoce and Botkin, 1980), reducing the Bering Sea stock to as few as 1,000 whales by 1920. As early as May of 1854 Maguire wrote that the Natives' whaling success

> hitherto has been very partial – Doctor Simpson has brought to my notice the fact of whether this may not in some way be accounted for, by the number of [whaling] ships that visit this sea every summer decreasing the number of whales & limiting this peoples supply without their knowing how to account for it. (Bockstoce, 1988: 376)

The competition for resources reached tragic proportions in the late 1870s. With whales becoming scarce, some whalers turned to harvesting walrus by the thousands for ivory. With few walrus left to eat, 1,000 out of the 1,500 residents of St. Lawrence Island perished in the winter of 1878–9 (Bockstoce, 1986: 139).

In addition to exploiting locally important resources, commercial whalers were also the first non-Natives to come north in substantial numbers. They brought with them new technology, new customs, new diseases, and a new way of life. By the 1880s many whaling companies had set up shore-based whaling stations at points along the coast. At Point Hope the commercial whaling community was known as Jabbertown, from the many languages spoken by the commercial whaling crews.

In Barrow, Charles Brower employed Iñupiaq crews in addition to leading his own crew onto the ice each spring. Blackman writes:

> By 1894 there were two shore-based whaling companies in Barrow controlling a total of twenty-eight whaling crews. Competition for native crew members was intense, particularly for harpooners and steersmen, and by 1908 some of the more affluent natives themselves were maintaining five or six crews. (1989: 12)

For the first time the Iñupiat were involved in a commercial activity, which brought the opportunity to obtain valuable new goods. Brower's presence also brought about a deeper change. He did not follow traditional customs that forbade such things as camping or cooking on the ice, yet he was successful in catching whales anyway. This example, as much as the new market for whale baleen, led to the abandonment of many of the old customs (Brower, 1942; Blackman, 1989).

The new technology introduced through the whale trade had no counterpart in traditional society. This period was one of incredible bounty for the people of Barrow. There was such an abundance of rifles, ammunition, cloth, and other desirable goods that Stefansson, perhaps with some exaggeration, wrote:

> you see rifles and shotguns, which our most fastidious sportsmen would consider good as new, lying around on the beach, thrown away by the Eskimo who have no realization of their value because of the ease with which they have always obtained them in the past. (1913: 61)

Although Maguire had noted in 1852–4 that such sought-after goods were hard to come by, by the turn of the century Barrow had changed considerably.

The trade of goods and ideas worked in both directions. Bockstoce observes that the Yankee whalers and the Iñupiat "for the most part coexisted peacefully and – in the perception of each – with mutual benefit" (1986: 13). The Natives had considerable experience catching whales in the Arctic environment and were able to teach the Yankees some of their techniques. The Yankees introduced the Iñupiat to the darting gun, shoulder gun, and exploding whale bomb, which were considerable improvements over the traditional lance (Thornton, 1931: 171; Brower, 1942).

The opportunity for employment in the whaling industry, and for obtaining Western goods, enticed many of the inland people to move to the coast. The patterns of trade that had sustained both the Tagiumiut and the Nunamiut were disrupted with the arrival of new materials and opportunities. Introduced diseases such as tuberculosis, measles, and influenza killed many people both on the coast and inland (Brower, 1942; Bockstoce, 1986; Blackman, 1989). Alcohol, too, made its first appearance in the region during the commercial whaling era, and proved highly destructive to the fabric of Iñupiaq life (Brower, 1942; Blackman, 1989).

The commercial whalers also brought with them missionaries. The growth of villages like Barrow and Point Hope, with the economic base of whaling and a trading post, meant that churches, schools, and hospitals could be established for the local community. Barrow's Presbyterian mission and school were founded in 1890 (Jenness, 1962; Blackman, 1989). One curious side effect was the observance of the sabbath as a day of rest, even during the whaling season (Stefansson, 1913: 93).

By 1920, however, the commercial whaling era was over. Spring steel had replaced baleen in manufactured goods, and the whales were too scarce to be worth the effort of catching. Iñupiaq whaling returned to being a subsistence activity, although the whalers were now using the new weapons introduced by the Yankee whalers. The most significant effect of the commercial whaling era, however, was that the Iñupiat had now been brought into regular contact and interaction through trade with American society.

Reindeer herding

Another change brought about during the whaling era was the introduction of reindeer herding. Hughes (1965: 32) notes that very low caribou populations during the last decade of the nineteenth century, combined with the decimation of whales and walrus by the commercial whalers, led to the "introduction of domestic reindeer from Asia to buttress the economies and provide a partial replacement." Jenness (1962: 12) writes that the reindeer prevented widespread starvation among Eskimos in the early twentieth century. Reindeer were first brought to Barrow in 1898 for the relief of stranded whalers (Blackman, 1989: 17), but soon were herded by the Iñupiat.

Although it was "conceptually ideal for Alaskan native life," Spencer writes that "As a problem in applied anthropology, the reindeer emerges as a predictable mistake" (1959: 364, 365). The Iñupiat had no cultural basis for the pastoral patterns of reindeer herding. Some herds and herders did well, and reindeer herding exists today in the Nome region of the Seward Peninsula. In Barrow in the long run other opportunities proved more attractive. Fall whaling took precedence over herding for Barrow residents, which led to huge losses of reindeer due to stampedes during the ensuing roundup. The Depression destroyed much of the market for meat and hides. Arundale and Schneider write:

> Although herding began to improve in 1940, matters started to deteriorate again for the Barrow herd in 1944. The attraction of wage labor in Barrow at the end of World War II made it increasingly difficult to find people who would herd consistently. (1987: 65)

The experiment of reindeer herding ended primarily because other ways of earning a cash income allowed people to participate in subsistence as well. Reindeer herding required a change of lifestyle in some ways greater than the change required by the transition to a wage economy.

The fur trapping era

In the 1920s, following the collapse of the whalebone market, fur trapping, primarily for white fox, became popular across the North Slope. Arundale and Schneider report:

> when commercial whaling ceased, Charles Brower placed the men from his whaling crews and their families in groups of two or three along the coast to trap. Since Brower had 10 to 15 crews of about seven men each, a considerable number of families were involved. (1987: 62)

Trading posts were established at various points, and families moved into areas that had not been inhabited within the historic past (Kevin Waring Associates, 1988: 10). A North Slope Borough study (1980: 3) notes: "the Iñupiat gradually lost their dependence on large villages and dispersed to small, seasonal settlements along the coast." The same study quotes Isaac Akootchook:

> I remember on our trips from Barter Island [Kaktovik] to Utqiagvik [Barrow] in the 1930s spending every night with people at each stop. There were houses along the coast every 20 to 30 miles. (*ibid.*)

The traditional pattern of settlement had changed to pursue a new means of participating in the American market economy.

Jenness describes the consequences of this change in economic base:

> Eskimo economy had in fact changed from one of mere subsistence on the large game animals to a money economy built around the market value of certain furs. . . . The transition had taken place gradually, and, in the main, painlessly, for the trapping of fur-bearing animals is only a specialized form of hunting. . . .

The Iñupiat and subsistence hunting

> Nevertheless, the change carried in its train some far-reaching consequences, both social and economic. Eskimo hunting, whether of whale, walrus, seal, or caribou, had been largely a cooperative enterprise in which the whole community participated; but trapping was a solitary pursuit that could be shared at best by two families only. (1962: 14)

Unlike whaling, which had relied upon a traditional activity, trapping required a significant change in patterns of hunting. It was, however, only a seasonal activity and thus did not require the same commitment of time and effort as reindeer herding.

In the 1930s the Depression led to the collapse of the fur market, as it had with the reindeer market. Conditions in Barrow at this time were poor. Blackman writes:

> Fuel was in short supply and fur prices were at an all-time low, resulting in a subsequent loss of store credit. Many Barrow people are reported to have migrated inland in 1936 to take advantage of the resources there. . . . Were it not for the reindeer herds many people might have starved to death. (1989: 23)

Opportunities for widespread participation in the market economy through the use of animal resources were effectively gone by the end of the 1930s. Use of wildlife was again almost exclusively for subsistence.

Wage employment

Construction formed the base for the next economic boom in northern Alaska. In 1944 the Naval Arctic Research Laboratory was established three miles north of Barrow. Exploration for oil in the newly-created Naval Petroleum Reserve–4 (now the National Petroleum Reserve–Alaska, or NPR–A) also brought many job opportunities to the region in the 1940s and 1950s. Construction of the Distant Early Warning (DEW) line in the mid-1950s created jobs along the coast from the Bering Strait around to the Canadian border in Alaska, and across the North American Arctic to eastern Greenland. For the first time in northern Alaska large numbers of people were employed for wages.

Trapping and herding had dispersed people along the coast; this was now reversed. According to Jenness:

> Numbers of Natives left their reindeer herds, abandoned their trap-lines, and moved with their families to army and air force establishments. . . . the majority settled around the military establishments at Barrow, Kotzebue, and half a dozen villages within the Bering Sea, where they swelled the local Eskimo population, but left the neighboring coastlines denuded of a notable percentage of their inhabitants. (1962: 40)

Blackman (1989: 26) notes that the population of Barrow increased by 300 percent between 1939 and 1950. Not only were Barrow's previous residents returning, but many families from other villages on the North Slope were moving to Barrow.

Wage employment demanded a major change in lifestyle for Iñupiat workers. Whaling, herding, and trapping were extensions or adaptations of traditional activities, requiring considerable knowledge of the land or sea and of animal behavior. Whaling and trapping, the more successful of the three, were also seasonal. Wage employment was a full-time prospect. Spencer (1959: 363) writes that "the Barrow residents . . . employed at the naval installation [NARL] work mostly a 63-hour week." Turnover was high. Blackman (1989: 26) writes that "during the seven years of oil exploration . . . the average length of employment was only two to five-and-a-half months."

Such a figure indicates that, in general, wage employment took some getting used to, at least at the individual level. Because of the strong family ties within the Iñupiaq community, Spencer (1959: 363) notes, "Virtually every family profits either directly or because of the dissemination of cash by wage-earning residents." The difficulty lay in figuring out how to join in the cash economy without giving up one's participation in the subsistence economy. While at first it may have appeared as an either/or proposition, by the 1980s success was often regarded as the ability to do both (Kruse, 1986).

Political power

In addition to profound economic changes, the late 1940s and early 1950s brought political change to Iñupiaq society. To start, village councils were formed in most northern Alaska villages. Authorized under the Indian Reorganization Act of 1934, these councils allowed a measure of self-determination for village residents. Chance writes:

> The opportunity to develop local self-government using local initiative gives the Eskimo of this region an advantage not always found among peoples undergoing rapid modernization. (1966: 69)

The village councils were effective at adapting traditional ways of settling disputes to a western political institution. VanStone describes the Point Hope village council resolving a question of ownership of a dead walrus that had floated and been recovered by someone other than the hunter who shot it. The decision was reached by consensus, based upon the Iñupiaq customs of ownership. VanStone further comments:

> The [village] council is very effective in dealing with immediate problems similar to the one just described [the walrus] but considerably less successful in handling long-range problems. Often good ideas are brought up and discussed at the

> meetings and approved. However, nothing is done about them and they tend to die a natural death. (1962: 105)

In 1960–61 the Point Hope village council became the focus of a major controversy that is often regarded as the beginning of Eskimo political empowerment. The Atomic Energy Commission (AEC) of the U.S., under the leadership of Edward Teller, wanted to test the possibilities of peaceful uses of atomic energy by using nuclear blasts to excavate a harbor in the coast thirty miles from Point Hope. When told of the plans for "Project Chariot," the residents of Point Hope were opposed for reasons of personal health and of environmental damage to important hunting grounds both on land and at sea. However, no one had ever successfully opposed the AEC (O'Neill, 1989; Morgan, 1988).

In a letter to the Secretary of the Interior dated July 25, 1961, the members of the village council wrote:

> Mr. Secretary, it seems to us very appalling that there has never been any serious effort in consultation of the people of Point Hope concerning the transfer of land by the Bureau of Land Management to the Atomic Energy Commission for the Project Chariot. There was, also, a pronounced lack of orientation upon the probable adverse effects of the Project. If this undertaking is allowed to continue to its ultimate conclusions and if any degree of harm to our hunting grounds should result from the nuclear explosion at Cape Thompson, we will and must resort to legal channels to sue for our incalculable heritage and our age-old aboriginal rights to hunt on our land. It is saddening to us that such declarations have to be made but we feel deeply that our way of life in the village of Point Hope is being dangerously threatened. (in Morgan, 1988: 174–5)

National interest groups such as the Committee for Nuclear Information, the Sierra Club, and the Association of American Indian Affairs came together to support the Iñupiat. O'Neill writes:

> By the summer of 1962, the *New York Times* reported: "Project Chariot may well be dead, killed by adverse publicity about its effects on Alaskan Eskimos and their hunting grounds." (1989: 36)

With the help of powerful allies, the villagers of Point Hope had realized their political strength. Protection of subsistence was an issue of paramount importance, and remains a rallying point to the present day.

At the same time, Barrow residents were fighting the new state government on another hunting issue. In the spring of 1961 state wildlife agents made it known that they would be enforcing the closed season on migratory birds established by the 1916 migratory bird treaty with Canada (see Chapter 2, page 28). Sadie Neakok, an Iñupiaq and Barrow's magistrate at the time, recalls:

> The only way we could solve the problem was for every man, woman, and child that had shot a duck, or gotten a waterfowl, to go and stand in front of the game

warden when he made an arrest . . . We did this for our own good, to make the state understand that we meant business. . . .

. . . And that night, the game warden wrote everybody's name down that was standing before him – took their statements, some 148–150 people. . . .

. . . The governor's office called in a special meeting, and they decided our hunting of waterfowl would be made neutral to where our people could hunt ducks for food anytime they wanted. So that was the one area that we resolved on our own. (in Blackman, 1989: 182–183)

Rather than accept the offer of the state agent to look the other way when people hunted ducks, the Iñupiat of Barrow confronted the issue head on, in order to resolve the problem and to demonstrate how important it was to them.

The Alaska Native Claims Settlement Act

In Barrow, Point Hope, and across the whole state, Alaska Natives were beginning to fight for recognition of their rights to maintain an active culture. In the early 1960s, O'Neill writes:

This flurry of activism marked the beginning of a new era of political accomplishment for Alaska natives, which reached its apex in 1971 with the passage of the historic Alaska Native Claims Settlement Act. (1989: 34)

The discovery of oil at Prudhoe Bay in 1967 created the impetus to settle the land claims of Alaska Natives. The Trans-Alaska Pipeline needed to be built soon, and to do so required that the necessary lands be available for the pipeline corridor across the state.

The Alaska Native Claims Settlement Act (ANCSA), passed on December 18, 1971, established 12 regional and dozens of village corporations across the state, which were the recipients of 44 million acres of land – about ten percent of the state – and $962.5 million in cash payments. In exchange, all aboriginal claims by Alaska Natives were extinguished. All persons with one quarter or more Alaska Native blood, and who were born before the passage of the Act, are shareholders in the ANCSA corporations. The corporations are legislated to be run for profit, but also to preserve the cultural, social, and economic interests of the Natives in each region. These conflicting aims have led to some difficulty in the management of the corporations and in interpreting their role in the Native and business communities (Berger, 1985; Langdon, 1986; Robinson *et al.*, 1989a, 1989b).

In selecting village corporation lands Natives were faced with a dilemma. Berger describes the problem:

Should a village corporation select land traditionally used for hunting and fishing or land to be used for economic development? The two types of land are often

> not the same . . . some regional corporations had to choose lands on a checker-board basis because their selections conflicted with state-selected lands. This practice prevented the acquisition of large blocks of holdings and it kept access open to state lands. (1985: 91)

If the lands were selected with subsistence in mind, this in no way ensured protection of subsistence activities. Berger continues:

> Although, as property owners, Natives have the exclusive right to wildlife on their own land, they have no rights as Natives for hunting, trapping, or fishing reserved for them over the ninety percent of Alaska in which their rights were extinguished. Even on Native lands, the state asserts its jurisdiction over fish and wildlife. (*ibid.*: 92)

ANCSA failed to resolve the issue of Native subsistence and its place in the regulatory system. Subsequent legislation, such as the Alaska National Interest Lands Conservation Act of 1980 (ANILCA) (see Chapter 4, pages 58–61), has attempted to rectify this, but with only partial success. After 1991 corporation shares and land can potentially be sold, which could complete the alienation from traditional lands that ANCSA was designed to prevent. In short, ANCSA has failed to provide long-term benefits for Native Alaskans.

Oil wealth and the North Slope Borough

At the same time further political development was underway on the North Slope. The discovery of oil at Prudhoe Bay in 1967 led to the incorporation of the North Slope Borough on July 1, 1972. The bulk of the tax base of the North Slope Borough (NSB) is the oil industry operating at Prudhoe Bay and the surrounding areas. Revenue generated from taxation has allowed the NSB to fund massive capital improvements projects across the region and to become the largest employer of North Slope villagers (Wolfe *et al.*, 1986).

Under Alaska's Constitution, regions can establish themselves as boroughs, which are roughly equivalent to counties in most other states. Boroughs can gain home rule status, allowing the NSB to control law enforcement, municipal services, the school district, zoning, and other local activities. It also has a Department of Wildlife Management (see Chapter 6, page 101–3) which, although lacking in regulatory authority, carries out research projects on issues of local concern.

This influx of cash from oil development through the NSB and into the regional economy has created another boom in the cycle that has characterized the region's economy in this century. In the 1970s this played a role in the increase in the number of whaling crews that were outfitted each year (International Whaling Commission, 1982). It has also played a role in a growing sense of cultural awareness throughout the region. The NSB has sponsored conferences on traditional laws and on Arctic science, and it played a large role in the establishment of the Inuit Circumpolar Conference, an organization of Inuit peoples from Chukotka in the Soviet Union, across Alaska and Canada, to Greenland.

The discovery of oil at Prudhoe Bay has for the first time placed substantial financial resources directly under the governmental control of North Slope Iñupiat. Individuals are enjoying a period of prosperity, as they had during the commercial whaling, fur trapping, and Arctic construction eras. But the wealth of the local government has opened new possibilities to the Iñupiat. So far, these range from constructing a utilidor to provide running water in Barrow to establishing the Iñupiat History, Language and Culture Commission to conduct and sponsor anthropological research.

Nelson (1969) had noted in the 1960s that much of the traditional knowledge and skill of the Iñupiat was being lost in the modern era. The NSB has made a substantial effort to prevent that from occurring. In Blackman's words:

> more than anything else, the borough has given the Iñupiat of the North Slope a sense of self-determination and confidence in their future. (1989: 32)

Current subsistence patterns

Despite all the economic, social, and political changes that have taken place in the past 150 years, the Iñupiat still consider themselves to be hunters. Discussing her daughter, one Iñupiaq woman recently said, "I want her to marry a good hunter." Kruse shows the importance of subsistence as a socially binding force on the North Slope:

> 77 percent of Inupiat households receive subsistence food from other households and 64 percent of Inupiat households gave, sold or traded subsistence foods. Almost half the households gave or lent either money or equipment for subsistence activities. Sharing patterns connect households within villages, connect villages within the North Slope, and connect the region to families and individuals living outside the North Slope. Finally, 81 percent of Inupiat men perceived that their hunting activities provide a chance to get food for their community in addition to meeting their family's needs. (1986: 146)

Subsistence is vital to the self-perception of Native people throughout Alaska, for it is a tangible, communal part of the indigenous culture, which can be shared and passed on (Loon, 1989; Andersen, 1989).

In addition, numerous studies have shown the importance of subsistence hunting to local economies throughout the state (e.g., Moore, 1980;

The Iñupiat and subsistence hunting

Nelson, 1981; Schroeder *et al.*, 1987; Jacobson and Wentworth, 1982; Kruse, 1986; Stephen R. Braund & Associates and Institute of Social and Economic Research, 1988, 1989a, 1989b). In a U.S. Fish and Wildlife Service study of the village of Kaktovik, Jacobson and Wentworth write:

> The essence of the economic importance of the fish and wildlife to Kaktovik people lies not only in their needs and preferences for subsistence foods, but in their ability to provide their own food from the area in which they live. (1982: 28)

Subsistence in rural Alaska is economically efficient and culturally vital. In northern Alaska, Iñupiat hunters continue to make use of all of the resources of the region. A study by Stephen R. Braund & Associates and the Institute for Social and Economic Research describes subsistence production in Wainwright and Barrow over, respectively, two- and three-year periods. A summary of resource use from the first two years of the Barrow study are shown in Table 3.1. While the relative importance of each resource may vary from year to year, depending on weather and ice conditions and on the local abundance of each species that is hunted, the Iñupiat remain heavily dependent upon their harvest of local resources.

Table 3.1 Subsistence production in Barrow, Alaska, between April 1, 1987, and March 31, 1989. Figures given are averages per capita (Stephen R. Braund & Associates and Insitute of Social and Economic Research, 1989a).

Resource category	Year one (lb.)	Year two (lb.)	Average (lb.)
Marine mammals	114.4	109.2	111.8
Terrestrial mammals	72.5	63.1	67.8
Fish	22.9	16.1	19.5
Birds	7.2	7.1	7.2
TOTAL	217.1	195.6	206.3

The Iñupiat also use vast areas for hunting and trapping (Figure 3.2). These lands are far greater in extent than the corporation lands established under ANCSA. They are also extensive and variable enough that precise delineation of hunting territories is impossible. Just as harvests are seasonal depending upon resource availability, hunting grounds vary with the distribution patterns of the animals. Modern transportation – such as snowmachine, motorboat, all-terrain vehicle – is also necessary in order to reach remote areas. In the past, people would travel extensively at certain times of the year, but today, with schools, jobs, and other ties to permanent villages, faster means of travel are required.

Subsistence remains a vital part of life on the North Slope. It is essential

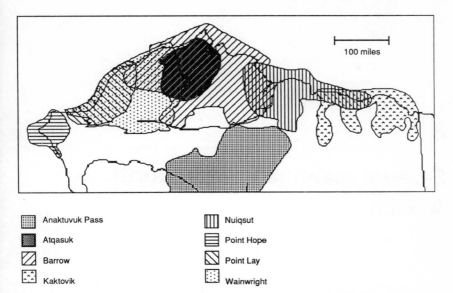

▦ Anaktuvuk Pass		▥ Nuiqsut	
■ Atqasuk		▤ Point Hope	
▨ Barrow		◨ Point Lay	
░ Kaktovik		░ Wainwright	

Figure 3.2 Map of subsistence use areas of North Slope villages for all resources. See Figure 6.1 (page 102) for location of villages (Pedersen, 1979; Stephen R. Braund & Associates and Institute of Social and Economic Research, 1989a, 1989b).

to the identity of the Iñupiat, and plays an important role in the economy of the region. While many of the tools have changed, the basic connection to the land and to local resources remains intact.

4

Federal management in northern Alaska

Huffman and Coggins write that in natural resource regulation,

> the prevailing regulatory mode in the United States is "cooperative federalism," an intricate and delicate system of balancing and allocating governmental powers between state and federal governments. Because that intergovernmental relationship differs, depending on the resource and the statute at issue, the federal role varies widely. (1986: 53)

Although the system may be intricate and delicate, it is not a carefully and thoroughly planned one. Huffman and Coggins continue:

> The federal statutes for environmental protection do not form a seamless web. Each law was enacted individually as a response to one particular problem. The laws do not address all environmental problems, and they are seldom well-coordinated with one another. (*ibid.*: 56)

This is especially true where wildlife resources are concerned. Since hunting regulations and habitat preservation laws are seldom coordinated, the system does not provide the means to ensure adequate, ecologically sound protection of animal resources. This is not to say that such protection does not occur; merely, there is no guarantee that it will continue to happen as pressure increases on both resources and habitat.

In northern Alaska the federal government is responsible for the management and regulation of federal lands and of marine mammals and migratory birds. The federal government also has responsibility for mineral resources on federal lands and on the outer continental shelf. At the present time, the federal government controls subsistence regulation on federal lands, because the State of Alaska's subsistence regulatory policy following the *McDowell* decision is inconsistent with the Alaska National Interest Lands Conservation Act of 1980 (ANILCA) (see Chapter 2, page 30). I will not examine in detail the effects of the *McDowell* decision on subsistence regulation, because it is too early to tell what long-term effects that decision will have.

This chapter examines the roles of international treaties, two federal statutes, and five federal agencies in managing and regulating wildlife and local wildlife use in northern Alaska.

International treaties

Seven international treaties to which the United States is party cover four categories of wildlife used in northern Alaska. Four treaties – with Canada (1916), Mexico (1936), Japan (1972), and the Soviet Union (1976) – concern migratory birds; the International Convention for the Regulation of Whaling of 1946 concerns whales; the International Agreement on the Conservation of Polar Bears and their Habitat, signed in 1973, concerns polar bears; and the 1987 agreement on the conservation of the Porcupine Caribou Herd with Canada concerns caribou. These treaties are designed to promote conservation of the resources they cover and to formalize and unify conservation methods used by different countries. While they have achieved notable overall successes, the difficulty of amending treaties means that in some cases customary uses of animals are illegal, in others that sound management efforts are frustrated by the lack of flexibility in a given treaty, and in still others that political considerations increase with the number of countries that have influence in decisions concerning management and use.

Migratory birds

The preamble to the 1916 Convention for the Protection of Migratory Birds – which was signed by the U.S. and Great Britain, the latter signing on behalf of Canada – states:

> Whereas, Many of these [migratory bird] species are of great value as a source of food or in destroying insects which are injurious to forests and forage plants on the public domain, as well as to agricultural crops, in both the United States and Canada, but are nevertheless in danger of extermination through lack of adequate protection during the nesting season or while on their way to and from their breeding grounds:
>   . . . [the treaty parties] being desirous of saving from indiscriminate slaughter and of insuring the preservation of such migratory birds as are either useful to man or are harmless, have resolved to adopt some uniform system of protection

49

which shall effectively accomplish such objects. (United States and Great Britain, 1916)

Few would object to the goals of the convention, but the means require that "The close season on migratory game birds shall be between March 10 and September 1," forbidding the traditional spring hunt in Alaska and northern Canada, and banning hunting during most of the time birds are in those areas.

There is no doubt that this restriction was intended to apply to Natives from the beginning. Article II of the convention makes specific allowances for Indians and Eskimos to take certain non-game birds for food and clothing at any time. No such exemption is provided for ducks, geese, and other game birds. The Alaska Game Law of 1925, the first to be enacted after the migratory bird treaty, states: "nor shall any . . . regulation contravene any of the provisions of the migratory bird treaty Act" (Alaska Game Commission, 1925: 5). Indians, Eskimos, prospectors, and travellers may take animals and birds when in absolute need of food, but no spring hunting season may be authorized.

Sudden enforcement of the provisions of this treaty led to the Barrow "Duck-In" incident in 1961, described in Chapters 2 and 3 (pages 28 and 42). While the treaty does not permit the establishment of an open season for Native hunting in the spring, a loose interpretation of "absolute need of food" can, in practice, make room for a spring harvest. Uhl and Uhl point out the drawback to such loose interpretation:

> The fact that international treaties are involved and are immutable has been the usual official response to concerned citizens seeking a legal spring open season. Practical subsistence living has therefore brought about a traditional disregard for the law that has over the years penetrated very deeply in the philosophy by which contemporary people live. (1977: 66)

Because it hinders management efforts to gain cooperation and respect of local people in northern Alaska, this treaty is counterproductive in its prohibition of spring subsistence use of migratory birds. Hunting has not ceased, but is done outside the regulatory framework designed to protect bird stocks. The treaty with Canada forbids management agencies in the U.S. the flexibility they need to recognize the importance of the spring hunt and to incorporate it formally into management policies and regulations.

The United States has entered into three more treaties concerning migratory birds, two of which were signed after the Barrow Duck-In and the rise of the Native rights movement in Alaska. In 1936 the U.S. and Mexico signed the Convention for the Protection of Migratory Birds and Game Mammals. While similar to the treaty with Canada, the treaty with Mexico allows a Native subsistence harvest. In 1972 the U.S. and Japan signed a convention for the Protection of Birds and Their Environment. Article III of this treaty states:

> Exceptions to the prohibition on taking may be permitted in accordance with the laws and regulations of the respective Contracting Parties in the following cases:
> . . .
> (e) Taking by Eskimos, Indians, and indigenous peoples of the Trust Territory of the Pacific Islands for their own food and clothing. (United States and Japan, 1972)

Rather than simply permitting unlimited hunting by Native people, the treaty takes the more appropriate management step of allowing such hunting in accordance with applicable laws and regulations. Permitting the legalization of Native harvests allows for sensible management practices determined by the individual nation.

The 1976 convention between the United States and the Soviet Union concerning the Conservation of Migratory Birds and Their Environment contains a more detailed clause allowing each party to provide for Natives of both Alaska and certain regions of the Soviet Union to harvest "for their own nutritional and other essential needs" (United States and Union of Soviet Socialist Republics, 1976). The U.S. Senate report on this treaty comments:

> the subsistence provisions of the three earlier treaties lack the administrative flexibility necessary to deal with the issue in a responsible manner. In contrast to these earlier inadequacies, the USSR convention contains the most modern and workable language on subsistence and avoids the errors of the past. (quoted in *Alaska Fish and Wildlife Federation v. Dunkle*, 1987)

While the treaties with Mexico, Japan and the Soviet Union allow for a spring hunt, that provision cannot be implemented yet because the treaty with Canada is more restrictive. In *Alaska Fish and Wildlife Federation v. Dunkle* (1987), the Ninth Circuit Court ruled that until all the treaties are consistent, hunting regulations must be consistent with the most restrictive treaty, which is the one between the U.S. and Canada. An amendment to the U.S.–Canada treaty permitting authorization of a spring harvest for Natives in Alaska and Canada was signed in 1979, but has not been ratified by either side.

Discussing the management dilemma in Canada over subsistence hunting and the migratory bird treaty, Bromley writes:

> Management authorities recognize that managed subsistence use of waterfowl is desirable and consistent with resource conservation. As a consequence, they also realize that expeditious action must be taken to provide the legal opportunity for spring hunting by subsistence hunters. By doing so, authorities may work with hunters to develop enforceable regulations that will provide for both sustainable subsistence harvest and conservation of waterfowl within a continental framework. (1988: 53)

Federal management in northern Alaska

The outdated provisions of the treaty with Canada are more of an obstacle than a help in managing local use of bird resources in northern areas.

Whaling

In 1946 fifteen nations signed the International Convention for the Regulation of Whaling. This convention established the International Whaling Commission (IWC), which in 1949 issued its first schedule of regulations. Paragraph 2 of the schedule states:

> It is forbidden to take or kill gray whales or right whales [including bowheads], except when the meat and product of such whales are to be used exclusively for local consumption by the aborigines. (IWC, 1950: 15)

Under this exemption Iñupiaq and St. Lawrence Island Yupik whalers in Alaska remained free to continue their subsistence harvest of the bowhead whale, outside the regulations of the IWC. In 1977 the IWC moved to end the aboriginal exemption, at least insofar as it applied to bowheads, and to ban the Alaska harvest in order to protect the stock of bowheads, which was believed at the time to be critically low (IWC, 1978a: 22). In December 1977, in response to pressure from the Eskimo whalers and the United States, the ban was replaced with a quota which still exists (see this chapter, pages 65–7 and Chapter 7, pages 110–15)

As a regulatory regime the IWC fills a valuable role. On the issue of Alaska bowhead whaling, the IWC forced the Natives to control their hunting by limiting their harvest to sustainable levels and by improving their hunting techniques. In the absence of any domestic pressure to try to manage whaling for sustainable yield, the IWC's action was beneficial (Huntington, 1989). As an organization caught in popular sentiment about the fate of the world's whales, however, its concerns have become political. While political considerations affect wildlife management issues within the U.S., the difficulties of promoting ecologically-based management are multiplied when many nations are involved.

Subjecting the management of the use of whales to an international body limits the ability of the U.S. to manage its own resources and their use. This is not to say that the IWC manages whaling poorly, or that a federal agency would necessarily do a better job; rather that, as with the bird treaties, management and regulatory flexibility is enhanced when fewer parties and fewer predetermined limitations are involved. Strictly speaking, the IWC bowhead quota both protects the resource and allows for a harvest to satisfy Native needs, and so meets the requirements of an effective regime. The point of concern, however, is that, with no binding legal requirements, the IWC's future actions may change the quota or the quota system. Barring an official objection by the U.S. government, those actions would not be subject to review. In this light, the whaling convention is not the most appropriate regulatory form for managing Eskimo whaling.

Polar bears

The 1973 International Agreement on the Conservation of Polar Bears and Their Habitat provides for far greater flexibility in the management of polar bear use. Article III states:

> any Contracting Party may allow the taking of polar bears when such taking is carried out:
> . . .
> (d) by local people using traditional methods in the exercise of their traditional rights and in accordance with the laws of that Party; or
> (e) wherever polar bears have or might have been subject to taking by traditional means by its nationals.

The objective of the agreement is to provide the framework for international cooperation in the preservation of polar bears and to allow the parties – Canada, Denmark, Norway, the Soviet Union, and the United States – to coordinate their management efforts. Stirling writes:

> from a biological standpoint . . . the agreement is remarkably sound scientifically; it is not simply a protectionist document contributing solely to the welfare of bears and of little substance to related environmental issues. (1986: 167)

Management practices in the U.S., however, do not follow the recommendations of the treaty and its polar bear specialist group. The Marine Mammal Protection Act limits hunting of polar bears to Alaska Natives, but provides no regulatory mechanism for controlling the harvest or for limiting the take of females (Lentfer, 1976: 55). Conservation initiatives on the part of the North Slope Borough (NSB) may help bring local management practice into compliance with the international agreement (Amstrup and DeMaster, 1988: 50) (see Chapter 7, pp. 130–3).

What, then, is the use of an international treaty which provides for adequate management of polar bears when the U.S. does not manage in accordance with that treaty? The agreement allows for the discretion of each party in establishing hunting regulations and limits, and so incorporates the best provisions of the U.S.–U.S.S.R. bird treaty, yet the U.S. fails to comply with its recommendations. The NSB's initiative to limit the take of females and cubs shows the inherent sensibility of the international recommendations, and the fact that they are not contrary to Native hunting practices. It seems ironic and unfortunate that a treaty which allows for adequate local harvests while conserving the resource should have little effect on management policy.

Caribou

In 1987, the United States and Canada signed an agreement on the Conservation of the Porcupine Caribou Herd (see Chapter 7, pages 133–7). The objectives of the treaty are to conserve the shared herd through international cooperation, while ensuring that hunters may continue to use the caribou in accordance with local laws. Thus, there is no requirement in the treaty to alter local hunting laws. Of primary concern in this treaty, however, is the potential disruption to habitat from development of mineral resources in the region. Whether the provisions protecting habitat will be sufficient to stop or alter development plans for portions of the herd's range remains to be seen. Nonetheless, by creating an international board which includes local users, the treaty is effective at promoting international cooperation without disrupting each nation's individual control over harvest regulation and allocation.

In summary, the most restrictive of the migratory bird treaties is too limiting to provide for adequate management of bird populations in regard to the spring subsistence harvest in Alaska and northern Canada. The whaling convention restricts the autonomy of the U.S. government in its relationship with Alaska Natives, and it allows the member nations of the IWC to control the bowhead quota, which is the most significant part of the management of the bowhead whale. The polar bear agreement provides for adequate harvests within the goal of conservation of the resource, but in the U.S. it is pre-empted by the Marine Mammal Protection Act. The result is non-compliance with the recommendations of the agreement, although polar bear stocks are healthy at present. Local management initiatives may bring U.S. harvests into compliance with the international agreement. The Porcupine Caribou Herd agreement specifically delegates the regulation of hunting to the individual country, state, or territory, while establishing an international board to monitor coordination of conservation policy between the U.S. and Canada.

The influence of these seven international treaties in the management and regulation of wildlife use in northern Alaska is variable both in extent and direction. To the extent that treaties foster cooperation in the conservation of resources, they are beneficial; to the extent that they infringe upon a nation's ability to manage the use of resources in a sound manner, such treaties hinder effective management.

The Marine Mammal Protection Act of 1972

In 1972 the U.S. Congress passed the Marine Mammal Protection Act (MMPA), giving the federal government jurisdiction over all marine mammals. The U.S Fish and Wildlife Service in the Department of the Interior was given authority over walruses, polar bears, sea otters, and manatees, while the National Oceanic and Atmospheric Administration in the Department of Commerce was given authority over all other marine mammals, which include whales, dolphins, seals, and sea lions. The act also mandated, with certain exceptions, a "moratorium on the taking and importation of marine mammals and marine mammal products" (Section 101(a)).

For marine mammal management in Alaska, the most significant exception to the moratorium is its exemption of Alaska Natives, as long as the Native harvest is for subsistence, or for making handicrafts or clothing, and is done in a non-wasteful manner. Unless a species is determined to be depleted, no regulations can be imposed upon Native harvests (e.g., *People of Togiak v. United States*, 1979). One drawback to a Native-only exemption is that not all potential local users of the resource are permitted to hunt. On the other hand, creating too large a class of authorized users might lead to excessive hunting, which in turn could necessitate substantial regulation.

The dilemma that the MMPA attempted to resolve with the Native exemption is summed up in the opinion of the U.S. District Court in *People of Togiak v. United States*:

> Substantively, two major competing policy considerations are here involved – the need for protecting marine mammals from depletion, on the one hand, and the responsibility of the federal government to protect the way of life of Alaskan Natives, including their tradition of hunting marine mammals for their subsistence, on the other. What emerges vividly from an examination of the total statutory scheme is that the Congress carefully considered these competing considerations and deliberately struck a balance which permits continued hunting by the Alaskan Natives as long as this is done in a non-wasteful manner, is restricted to the taking of non-depleted species, and is accomplished for specified, limited purposes. (1979: 426–427)

This section examines the extent to which that deliberate balance has succeeded in protecting both the resource and its use.

The first Congressional act concerning walruses was the Walrus Act of 1941 (see Chapter 7, pages 116–17). That act forbade hunting of walrus, except by Alaska Natives engaged in subsistence. The International Convention for the Regulation of Whaling in 1946 also exempted aboriginal people from the ban on the harvest of gray and right whales (see previous section). In 1956 the Walrus Act was amended to permit non-

Federal management in northern Alaska

Native hunting, partly to help protect the walrus stocks by allowing Natives to gain economic benefit from guiding rather than from ivory hunting (Fay, 1957). In northern Alaska no other acts specifically regulated marine mammals until the MMPA was enacted.

Apart from the Native exemption, no hunting is permitted under the MMPA, and any incidental take must have negligible effect on the population in question. The Native exemption, however, leaves a large hole in management. Unless a species is depleted, federal regulation of Native take is limited to ensuring that the harvest is for subsistence or handicrafts and is non-wasteful. If a species is determined to be depleted, then regulations can be issued. This is a particularly insensitive response to population changes, for the regulatory reaction can only happen after the crisis has occurred.

The idea of a Native exemption is an attractive one, for it avoids the problem of deciding how to formulate and implement regulations for a subsistence hunt. By limiting harvests to a group which has traditionally used the resource and by encouraging non-wasteful hunting, the burden on the resource may be minimized. Case writes:

> the advantage of the MMPA is that it favors little regulation by the State. In fact, it has led to substantial deregulation of Native taking of marine mammals for subsistence purposes. As a result, Native subsistence practices are left theoretically undisturbed, except in those rare instances when regulatory intervention is truly necessary for conservation purposes . . .
>
> . . . In the absence of regulation, individual subsistence users . . . are free to determine for themselves when, where, and how much they will hunt. . . . [This] does reduce the potential for conflict between the state and indigenous systems of wildlife management by reducing the opportunity for regulation by the State. (1989: 1034)

While the absence of governmental regulations may reduce conflict and controversy with Native hunters, complete lack of harvest limits may hinder management in the long run. Several co-management regimes for marine mammals have been created by Alaska Natives. While some are direct responses to governmental actions, others are designed to fill the gap in management left by the MMPA, to prevent species from becoming "depleted" (see Chapter 7, pages 110, 115, 126 and 130).

The State of Alaska has also attempted to fill that gap. In 1972 the state requested the return of management authority for ten species of marine mammals, including walrus, polar bears, sea otters, beluga whales, Steller sea lions, and five species of seals. In 1976 the state regained management control of walrus. The state, however, is prohibited by its constitution from discriminating on grounds of race, and so wasn't able to maintain the Native exemption. Instead, a regulatory system was established that favored residents of those areas where walrus were traditionally harvested.

In 1979 management was returned to the federal government, because the state felt it could not manage walrus effectively with the constraints imposed upon it by the federal government.[1]

In 1987 the state reexamined the issue of state management of marine mammals. Taking the position that "It is the state's goal to facilitate sound conservation and management of marine mammals in a non-divisive manner, regardless of who has actual management authority," an Alaska Department of Fish and Game (ADF&G) report made four proposals regarding the state's role in marine mammal management. Their recommendations would keep regulatory authority with the federal government, but increase the role of the state and major interest groups. The report states:

> This action might require amendments to the MMPA. Under this system management plans would be developed by an Alaska Marine Mammal Council consisting of representatives from federal agencies, the ADF&G, and major interest groups. A Marine Mammal Advisory Committee would be established to provide for public involvement and assist in the development of draft management plans. Management plans would be approved by the Secretary of Interior or Commerce, then implemented through normal federal procedures or cooperative agreements. (Pamplin *et al.*, 1988: 8)

In effect this would formalize and extend the process that has occurred with bowhead whales, beluga whales, and walrus. While the creation of another level of management activity may complicate still further the regulatory regime, a clear system of representation and the development of consistent management practices could substantially improve the ability of the MMPA to provide for the long-term health of marine mammal stocks and for their use by Native people in Alaska.

One area of contention in Alaska at present concerns the use of sea otter skins for handicrafts. The U.S. Fish and Wildlife Service (FWS) has proposed regulations prohibiting the sale of sea otter handicrafts and clothing, on the grounds that none were being made in 1972 when the MMPA was passed, and that therefore they are not traditional handicrafts (U.S. FWS, 1988a). Natives from throughout the range of the sea otter in Alaska have formed the Alaska Sea Otter Commission to fight the FWS proposal. At issue is the interpretation of the Native exemption and the ability of Natives to continue to adapt and develop their use of marine mammal resources. In *Katelnikoff v. U.S. Department of the Interior*, the District Court wrote:

> the purpose of [the Native exemption] was to enable natives to *continue* to produce native arts and crafts; what was to be protected was the right to be left alone and to continue their centuries-old way of life and the chosen trade of their forefathers. (1986: 665) (emphasis in original)

If the MMPA defines a static system of use, it fails to make adequate provision for local use, because patterns of use will change. An effective regulatory or management regime will adapt as well.

A second significant exemption allows for incidental take during the course of other activities. The MMPA defines "take" to mean "to harass, hunt, capture, or kill, or attempt to harass, hunt, capture, or kill any marine mammal" (Section 3(12)). It also allows authorization of unintentional takes if they are incidental to industrial activity and if they will have

> a negligible impact on such species or stock and will not have an unmitigable adverse impact on the availability of such species or stock for taking for subsistence purposes. (Section101(5) (A) (i))

Offshore oil and gas exploration is fast increasing in the Beaufort and Chukchi Seas, carrying with it the possibility of adverse impacts on local marine mammals. A group of oil companies applied in 1988 to the National Oceanic and Atmospheric Administration for authorization for incidental take of whales and seals (Amoco Production Company *et al.*, 1988).

The industry application seeks permission only for harassment in the course of its offshore activities, but with considerable local concern centering on the possibility of a blowout of one of the offshore wells, the issue of incidental take has become a prominent one. Whether the possibility of significant impact is great enough to invoke the MMPA and to halt or control offshore activity is uncertain. The possible impacts of such development are examined below in the section on the Minerals Management Service. The MMPA contains the language and the authorization to control activities which may affect marine mammals; whether that control is warranted in this situation and whether it will materialize have yet to be determined.

The Alaska National Interest Lands Conservation Act of 1980

In 1971 the Alaska Native Claims Settlement Act (ANCSA) required that Congress enact legislation defining the status of federal lands in Alaska. In 1980 this was accomplished by the Alaska National Interest Lands Conservation Act (ANILCA), which protected 104 million acres of land, or 28 percent of the state (Nash, 1982: 272). In addition to creating new or enlarging existing national parks and national wildlife refuges, ANILCA mandated a system of subsistence regulation and management for federal lands, including the establishment of local advisory committees and six regional advisory councils. For each of the seven National Parks, a subsistence resource commission was set up to create regulations for local subsistence use within the park.

The specific subsistence management and regulatory provisions of ANILCA are addressed in the sections of this study that cover the agencies responsible for their implementation: subsistence resource commissions are examined in the section on the National Park Service (pages 68–72, this chapter); local and regional advisory councils in Chapter 5, page 87–9. This section provides an overview of the act and its implications for resource management.

ANILCA, in Nash's words (1982: 272), is "the greatest single act of wilderness preservation in world history." At a stroke the 104 million acres allocated by ANILCA doubled the amount of land in national parks and wildlife refuges across the U.S. (*ibid.*: 301). The numbers are impressive. ANILCA created six new national parks and enlarged an existing one. It created two new national monuments and enlarged two others. It created two new national preserves. It created nine new national wildlife refuges and enlarged seven existing ones. It created one national conservation area and one national recreation area. It enlarged two national forests, creating within them two national monuments under Forest Service administration. It designated 26 national wild and scenic rivers, and it tripled the amount of land in the national wilderness preservation system. In all, the area encompassed by ANILCA is larger than the state of California.

One drawback to these classifications is the obvious fragmentation of lands. Different federal agencies, with different land use mandates and policies, administer neighboring areas. State and Native lands are mixed in as well. Since in remote areas the boundaries of the refuges and parks are seldom marked, hunters may not be aware that they have crossed into the jurisdiction of a different agency. Villages that have similar use patterns, but are situated within or near lands managed by different agencies, may be regulated in different fashions. Such a situation frustrates attempts to provide equally for the state's rural wildlife users.

In addition to preserving lands with "nationally significant natural, scenic, historic, archeological, geological, scientific, wilderness, cultural, recreational, and wildlife values" (Section 101(a)), ANILCA declared:

> It is further the intent and purpose of this Act consistent with management of fish and wildlife in accordance with recognized scientific principles and the purposes for which each conservation system unit is established, designated, or expanded by or pursuant to this Act, to provide the opportunity for rural residents engaged in a subsistence way of life to continue to do so. (Section 101(c))

Title VIII of ANILCA addresses the issues of subsistence uses, left unsettled since the passage of Alaska Native Claims Settlement Act (ANCSA) formally extinguished Native hunting and fishing rights in Alaska. Unlike the MMPA passed eight years earlier, ANILCA defines subsistence users as all residents of rural areas of Alaska, specifically including non-Natives, primarily so that the provisions of ANILCA would not conflict with the state constitution's prohibition on racial discrimination (Case, 1989).

Federal management in northern Alaska

The reason for this was to enable ANILCA to influence state policy regarding the regulation of subsistence use. Case writes:

> Typical of "cooperative" American federalism, Title VIII did not compel the State of Alaska to do anything, but it made the State an offer it couldn't refuse. The law Congress enacted provided "rural Alaska residents" a subsistence preference only on "public lands" – defined elsewhere in ANILCA to be *federal* "lands, waters and interests therein." ANILCA did not *require* the State to adopt a subsistence preference or establish advisory councils and committees for regulation of fish and game on state or even Native lands. But the price of not doing so was that the State would not be able to regulate fish and game on the more than one-half of the land in the state still in federal ownership. (1989: 1017) (emphasis in original)

The state passed a subsistence law that was in compliance with ANILCA, but in 1989 the Alaska Supreme Court decided in *McDowell v. State of Alaska* that the rural preference was in violation of the state constitution (see Chapter 2, page 30). The State of Alaska did not act to return to compliance with ANILCA, and so on July 1, 1990, the federal government took over the regulation of subsistence uses on federal lands. Whether and how the state will attempt to regain management authority is uncertain.

In any case, ANILCA attempts to protect both natural resources and the rural Alaska way of life. The chief difficulty arises in defining that way of life. Section 803 states:

> As used in this Act, "subsistence uses" means the customary and traditional uses by rural Alaska residents of wild, renewable resources for direct personal or family consumption as food, shelter, fuel, clothing, tools, or transportation; for the making and selling of handicraft articles out of nonedible by-products of fish and wildlife resources taken for personal or family consumption; for barter, or sharing for personal or family consumption; and for customary trade.

Langdon writes:

> Definition and application of the term "traditional" has become a significant stumbling block in certain cases for present subsistence activities. Several parks allow airplane usage for subsistence practices while several others do not. (1984: 30)

As with the Marine Mammal Protection Act, the question of modification of use practices is difficult to resolve. If the regulatory regime is too permissive, the resource may suffer. If the regime is too strict, the users may be confined to a static way of life and be unable to benefit from new innovations.

The state also faces individual challenges to specific regulatory issues, such as the state's definition of "rural." Case notes:

> that it has taken seven years to litigate ANILCA's implementation does not bode well for the immediate future. Rather than reducing the level of regulation or

enhancing the likelihood that regulation will be consistent with Native culture and values, the ANILCA/state scheme thus far has had the effect of taking the regulation of subsistence out of Native communities and further complicating it with centralized rulemaking and litigation. (1989: 1021)

The system of advisory committees and councils, designed to decentralize the regulatory system by providing input from each region separately, has also failed to live up to expectations. Chronic lack of funding and staff is a major problem (U.S. Fish and Wildlife Service, 1988b). Schaeffer *et al.* write:

> The situation is just as if the State of Alaska had invited the Native Alaskan hunter to the meeting, then asked him to please sit in the back and remain quiet.
> The tools contained in Title VIII of ANILCA may provide a remedy for this situation. (1986: 25–26)

The promise of ANILCA in resolving and simplifying the regulation of subsistence has been delayed by the difficulties of its implementation. The *McDowell* decision merely complicates the issue further, leaving in doubt the direction of future changes to the structure of subsistence management and regulation in northern Alaska.

The U.S. Fish and Wildlife Service

A branch of the Department of the Interior, the U.S. Fish and Wildlife Service (FWS) is responsible for migratory birds, other migratory animals, some marine mammals, and the national wildlife refuge system. In Alaska the FWS manages migratory birds, polar bears, walrus, and sea otters, sixteen national wildlife refuges, and, as of July 1, 1990, all game on federal lands. Earlier sections in this chapter cover international treaties regarding migratory birds and polar bears, and the Marine Mammal Protection Act of 1972. Pages 115–26 and 130–33 in Chapter 7 examine co-management of walrus, migratory birds, and polar bears. In this section, I examine FWS's role and policies regarding migratory birds, marine mammals, and land management. Since it follows the *McDowell* decision, the final status of which is uncertain, I do not examine FWS's role in subsistence management on federal lands.

Migratory birds

The FWS is responsible for managing migratory birds in accordance with the four international treaties to which the U.S. is party. Under the Migratory Bird Treaty Act of 1918, the FWS issues regulations on hunting seasons and limits and sells federal duck stamps, which provide revenue for fish and wildlife enhancement. Individual states may issue their own regulations, provided they are not less restrictive than the federal ones. In Alaska the primary issue is the regulation of the spring subsistence hunt. Legally, the hunt is forbidden by the migratory bird treaties with Canada and Mexico. In practice, the spring hunt is very important, since it provides the first fresh meat after the winter. As the Barrow Duck-In protest showed in 1961, the hunt could not be easily stopped (see Chapter 2, page 28 and Chapter 3, page 42).

The dilemma the FWS faces, however, is that several species of migratory birds were or are in population declines, and the spring hunt is a factor in population dynamics and in management efforts. Because of the treaties, the FWS is not able to address the issue directly, for regulation of an illegal harvest is not permissible. However, by issuing explicit enforcement priorities that make it clear that the FWS will not prosecute non-wasteful subsistence hunters (U.S. Fish and Wildlife Service, 1988c), the agency is able to control the hunt and to engender some degree of cooperation from the hunters. The Yukon-Kuskokwim Delta Goose Management Plan (see Chapter 7, pp. 120–26) is the chief success of this approach, allowing the spring hunt to continue so long as the bird populations are above certain levels. The goose plan also fosters cooperation among the users, all of whom share an interest in the long-term health of goose stocks.

So far FWS policy has been reasonably successful in allowing subsistence uses to continue, although the situation is not a good one over the long term. By tolerating illegal uses of wildlife the FWS may be choosing the lesser of two evil paths, but as Uhl and Uhl point out (1977: 66), this has engendered a "traditional disregard for the law" among contemporary subsistence users. It is beyond the authority of the FWS to change the treaties, although it has been pushing for ratification of the amendments signed with Canada in 1979 that would permit Native spring subsistence harvests.[2] Until the treaties are amended, the pragmatic approach taken by the FWS has at least allowed for the needs of local people while protecting the resources that are most at risk.

Marine mammals

Under the Marine Mammal Protection Act of 1972 (MMPA), the FWS has authority over two species of marine mammals in northern Alaska, polar bears and walrus. Only Alaska Natives are permitted to hunt these animals, and the FWS may not regulate the harvest unless the species in question is determined to be "depleted." At present, the stocks of neither polar bears nor walrus are depleted, although there is some concern over possible declines of walrus (e.g., Fay *et al.*, 1989). The FWS also has authority over such management considerations as incidental take and population monitoring. In 1988, in an effort to monitor the harvest, the FWS issued a policy requiring all polar bears and walruses to be tagged when caught. In addition the FWS has signed a memorandum of agreement with the Eskimo Walrus Commission concerning research and management priorities and coordination (see Chapter 7, pages 119–20).

The marking, tagging, and reporting program is at the local level the most visible of FWS's activities. Local residents have been commissioned as taggers in most coastal villages so that there is neither a problem of access to tags nor a need for permanent FWS personnel to travel to all villages regularly. The program involves recording the sex and size of the harvested animals and attaching metal tags to the skull and hide of the polar bear and the tusks of the walrus. In addition to allowing the harvest to be monitored the program is aimed at curtailing illegal trade in marine mammal parts by recording and marking each tusk, skull, and hide. According to Wells Stephensen (pers. comm., 1989), the FWS agent in charge of the program, many walrus hunters like the tagging and marking process because it makes stolen tusks easy to identify.

The FWS has made an effort to make the program as easy as possible for the hunters. Hunters are allowed 30 days in which to have the parts tagged. While the rule applies to all raw parts caught after the passage of the MMPA in December 1972, an FWS bulletin posted in the villages states:

> Because of the difficulty in informing all coastal Native villages and people of this rule, the U.S. Fish and Wildlife Service provided 180 days to allow individuals to tag all specified marine mammal parts in their possession. The Service does not want to prosecute anyone; however, the deadline to get these items tagged ended in May 1989. All taggers are instructed to continue to tag these parts in all villages and hunters who possess raw unaltered parts should have them tagged immediately.

The priority is the management program, not enforcement of small violations, and so the FWS is taking a low-key approach to encourage cooperation. Since the taggers are local people they often know when someone has caught an animal, and so can go straight to the hunter to complete the reporting and tagging process. While full cooperation may take a while to achieve, the program has worked fairly well so far.

One shortcoming of the FWS approach is the lack of management information that is given back to the hunters and the communities. This problem is shared by many agencies involved with management of local use of wildlife resources. The collection of data is too often a one-way street, with little explanation of how the data will be used, and what results have been obtained thus far. Whether this is a product of wildlife managers' having too little time to report to the people they study, or whether it is because of an assumption that the people are not interested in the formal results of the studies, it is a link that is too often missing in the interaction of managers and hunters. The FWS's implementation of the reporting and tagging rule has been sound, but more attention could be paid in the future to this side of management.

Land management

The most controversial lands issue on the North Slope at present stems from Section 1002 of ANILCA, which states:

> The purpose of this section is to provide for a comprehensive and continuing inventory and assessment of the fish and wildlife resources of the coastal plain of the Arctic National Wildlife Refuge [ANWR]; an analysis of the impacts of oil and gas exploration, development, and production, and to authorize exploratory activity within the coastal plain in a manner that avoids significant adverse effects on the fish and wildlife and other resources.

Significant reserves of oil and gas may underlie the coastal plain, which could make up for the projected decline in productivity from the Prudhoe Bay complex. On the other hand the area is often the calving ground for the Porcupine Caribou Herd, which is important for subsistence in Kaktovik, and crucial for the villages of Arctic Village and Venetie in Alaska and Old Crow in the Yukon Territory (see Figure 7.10, page 134). Industrial activity may have an impact on the distribution and movements of the herd (see Chapter 7, pages 133–6), as well as on other resources used for subsistence.

Determining the extent and significance of possible impacts is difficult. The FWS has prepared for ANWR, and for the other national wildlife refuges, a document containing the following: comprehensive conservation plan, environmental impact statement, wilderness review, and wild river plans (U.S. Fish and Wildlife Service, 1988d). The purpose is to assess alternative ways to manage the refuge, and to recommend one of the alternatives to the Secretary of the Interior. The current plan's preferred option would maintain current management practices, permitting oil and gas studies where compatible with the goals of refuge management. The final decision whether to open the coastal plain to oil and gas activity, however, lies with Congress, which has not acted on several bills that would either allow various degrees of industrial activity or designate the whole area as "wilderness," prohibiting any industrial activity at all.

In managing the refuges the FWS has authority over the activities that occur within the refuge and also has authority to enforce both federal laws and state hunting regulations within the refuge. (The relevance of the latter may change after the *McDowell* decision.) In carrying out the mandate of ANILCA with regard to the subsistence priority, the FWS in ANWR classifies all local uses of wildlife as "subsistence" (*ibid.*: 142). The plans for both ANWR and the Selawik National Wildlife Refuge in northwest Alaska contain, as part of a description of the human environment of the refuge, overviews of subsistence use patterns by village residents (*ibid.*; U.S. Fish and Wildlife Service, 1987). According to Jerald Stroebele (pers. comm., 1990), the refuge manager for Selawik NWR, public use in 1988 totalled 43,000 visitor-days, of which only 240 were by hunters from outside the region. Local hunting of wildlife within the refuges is the most significant consumptive use.

One problem with refuge management has been enforcement of hunting regulations on refuge lands. Since the conditions in northern Alaska are so different from those in other parts of the national wildlife refuge system, managers new to the area may have trouble adapting. Pete Schaeffer, an Iñupiaq and member of the Kotzebue Advisory Committee and the Arctic Regional Council, put it this way:

> Just when the FWS people get used to our area, they are transferred somewhere else. There is no consistency. (pers. comm. 1990)

Stroebele, the refuge manager, sees it from a different perspective:

> The laws are so liberal it's impossible to break them unless you do it on purpose – yet they're broken every day. (pers. comm., 1990)

From his perspective the FWS is following a hands-off policy, trying to introduce enforcement practices slowly. Native hunters, however, see the FWS as over-regulating their activities.

Whether the hunters and the FWS can reach agreement on what sort of management is needed will determine whether an antagonistic relationship can be changed for the better. The precedent of the Yukon-Kuskokwim Delta Goose Management Plan shows that such agreement and cooperation is possible. Such a flexible approach should be extended to other areas of FWS involvement in subsistence regulation and management. The FWS must take a sufficiently long-term view of its management priorities to ensure that the local community has time to get used to FWS initiatives and that the FWS has time to adapt to the local situation. Unfortunately, poor experiences in the past remain in people's memories for a long time, creating additional obstacles for new managers to overcome.

The National Marine Fisheries Service

The National Marine Fisheries Service (NMFS) is a branch of the National Oceanic and Atmospheric Administration (NOAA) within the U.S. Department of Commerce. Under the Marine Mammal Protection Act of 1972 (MMPA), NMFS has management authority over whales, seals, and sea lions. South of the Bering Strait a decline in the Steller sea lion population is causing great concern, and the northern fur seal harvest on the Pribilof Islands is intensively monitored and managed. In northern Alaska, NMFS's active management consists only of monitoring the management work of the Alaska Eskimo Whaling Commission and participating in the Alaska and Inuvialuit Beluga Whale Committee (see Chapter 7, pages 110–15 and 126–30). Although biological research is being conducted, there are no current management efforts regarding seals in northern Alaska.

NMFS's role in the management of the bowhead whale is unusual for a government agency. Following the establishment of a quota for the Alaska Eskimo harvest of bowhead whales, NMFS monitored the harvest to ensure that the number of struck whales did not exceed the limit established by the International Whaling Commission. NMFS was also responsible for enforcing the limit and for prosecuting violations. In 1980 uncertainty over the number of strikes that had already been made led to a strike over the quota limit. NMFS began a grand jury investigation of the incident which proved highly controversial. The Eskimo whalers, supported by Senator Ted Stevens, accused NMFS of conducting a "witch hunt" (Abbott, 1980).

From this position of antagonism between NMFS and the Alaska Eskimo Whaling Commission (AEWC), negotiators from the two parties made a significant breakthrough in management strategy (Langdon, 1984; Huntington, 1989). On March 26, 1981, the AEWC and NOAA signed a cooperative agreement delegating management authority to the AEWC (NOAA and AEWC, 1981). At the end of each whaling season the AEWC files a report with NOAA, giving details of all struck and all landed whales, and of other activities that affect whaling and AEWC management. As long as the whalers remain in compliance with the quota, NOAA takes no further action. Since the whalers are essentially governing themselves, except for setting the actual quota, there is not the problem of management coming from the "outside."

The agreement is remarkable not only for its success and for the number of imitators it has, but because a government agency turned management authority over to the group that uses the resource. NMFS continues to conduct research on the bowhead whale and to help fund the AEWC, but hunting regulations are the sole province of the AEWC. With the exception of the means of establishing the quota (see pp. 52–3, this chapter), the management that is provided under this system is effective because it gives authority to the hunters, allowing them to implement appropriate regulations and to take appropriate enforcement actions (see page 52). NMFS can provide some of the resources necessary to make informed decisions, and together NMFS and the AEWC can protect the bowhead whale population from over-hunting while allowing an adequate harvest.

NMFS also participates in the meetings of the Alaska and Inuvialuit Beluga Whale Committee (AIBWC) (see Chapter 7, pages 126–30). Since the impetus for the AIBWC has come from the Canadian hunters and the Department of Fisheries and Oceans Canada, NMFS's role has been limited. The population of beluga whales appears healthy, and so there is little incentive for NMFS to expend the money or effort to duplicate what is being done by the AIBWC, which is funded by the North Slope Borough and the Bureau of Indian Affairs. The Alaska Department of Fish and Game conducts population surveys of beluga whales, relieving NMFS of that responsibility as well.

NMFS has management authority for the four species of seals commonly found north of the Bering Strait: ringed seal, bearded seal, ribbon seal, and spotted seal. NMFS/NOAA is conducting research into contaminant levels in marine mammal tissues, and the Alaska Department of Fish and Game is studying population levels of these species. However, according to Dr. Steve Zimmerman of NMFS in Juneau (pers. comm., 1990), NMFS has neither the money nor the staff to pursue active management of seals. If a population crisis occurred, NMFS would respond; without that incentive, there are too many other demands on available money and personnel. In the meantime NMFS encourages hunters to avoid waste so that the seals will continue to thrive and government action will continue to be unnecessary.

Because few baseline data are available and little is known about the population dynamics of these species, detailed scientific management plans are not possible (H. Braham, pers. comm., 1990; Kelly, 1988a, 1988b, 1988c; Quakenbush, 1988). Unlike for bowheads and belugas, no other agencies or groups exist to help manage the seal harvest. This is not a problem as long as the populations remain healthy. If any become depleted, belated management efforts will be difficult. But without a crisis to galvanize either government agencies or hunter groups into action, active management of seals is unlikely.

Like the Marine Mammal Protection Act (pages 55–8, this chapter), the lack of sensitivity to changes in population or habitat increases the potential for reaching a crisis situation before anyone is aware that there is a problem. While the delegation of authority to the AEWC is a major step forward in promoting effective management of a resource, NMFS's management efforts for northern Alaska seals cannot be effective because they do not exist. The Alaska Department of Fish and Game has attempted to fill at least part of the gap, but only NMFS has the statutory authority to manage seals. The cooperative agreement for bowhead whales is a model of effective management; the lack of management of seals is a potential disaster.

Federal management in northern Alaska

National Park Service

The National Park Service (NPS), part of the U.S. Department of the Interior, has responsibility in Alaska for seven parks, two national preserves, and four national monuments. Four of these areas are in northern Alaska: Gates of the Arctic National Park and Preserve, Kobuk Valley National Park and Preserve, Noatak National Preserve, and Cape Krusenstern National Monument. All four were established under the Alaska National Interest Lands Conservation Act of 1980 (ANILCA) and under this act must allow subsistence harvests. The National Park system affects local subsistence uses of wildlife through land management and through subsistence resource commissions. This section will examine NPS's effectiveness in each of these roles.

Land management

The duty of the National Park Service is to protect and preserve the lands under its jurisdiction while keeping them available for public use and enjoyment (National Park Service, 1986a; 1986b; 1986c; 1986d). In the areas established under ANILCA, public use includes subsistence hunting. In terms of land management, subsistence hunting touches three areas of concern: where the hunting takes place, what means of transportation are used, and how hunting regulations are enforced. One example of each will illustrate the difficulty NPS has in balancing its responsibilities.

Following the creation of the new national parks, preserves, and monuments, NPS began trying to identify subsistence uses within its new lands. Caulfield writes:

> The Park Service interpreted ANILCA's allowance of subsistence uses only "where those uses are traditional" to mean that traditional use areas should be mapped and incorporated into regulation. (1988: 59)

This met with considerable resistance from local residents who "argued that park managers would use the maps as a means of placing further restrictions on their way of life" (*ibid.*). NPS's desire to define traditional use areas conflicted with the open access and adaptability necessary to subsistence harvesters. The idea was eventually dropped.

A second problem involves the use of all-terrain vehicles (ATVs) by residents of Anaktuvuk Pass, a Nunamiut (inland Iñupiaq) village surrounded by Gates of the Arctic National Park and Preserve. Section 811(b) of ANILCA states:

> the Secretary shall permit on the public lands appropriate use for subsistence purposes of snowmobiles, motorboats, and other means of surface transpor-

tation traditionally employed for such purposes by local residents, subject to reasonable regulation.

The status of ATVs under this section is unclear. In addition, Caulfield writes:

> the Park Service had a mandate from Congress to protect "wilderness" values, and was concerned about resource damage which might occur from ATV use. (1988: 60)

Further complicating the issue, the residents of Anaktuvuk Pass have used ATVs on Native corporation lands north of the village. These lands were traded by Arctic Slope Regional Corporation for lands on the Arctic Coastal Plain, making formerly private lands part of Gates of the Arctic National Park and Preserve.

Summer access to hunting grounds for residents of Anaktuvuk Pass relies upon the use of ATVs. A North Slope Borough representative to these negotiations wrote:

> The subsistence access issue in Anaktuvuk Pass may be the most important issue to confront the Nunamiut people. Both the City Council and the Nunamiut Corporation support the eventual open access area of approximately a 36 mile radius of the village for ATV use. . . .
>
> The difficulty I see in the negotiations is that the Nunamiut Corporation and the people of Anaktuvuk Pass speak in terms of broad access areas and broad areas of land, recognizing the natural movement of animals beyond a narrow easement strip. But, more than that the Nunamiut speak of the land in broad areas because that is how they have used it and have grown with it over the years. The Park Service on the other hand, views access in the narrowest terms possible because for them it is not an issue of travel, but of regulation.[3]

As with the concern over codifying resource use areas, different views of the land are part of the cause of the ATV conflict. ANILCA's ambiguity on the question of the use of new technology also hinders responsive, flexible management by NPS and other agencies faced with similar issues.

Because of the constraints on NPS imposed by ANILCA and other federal laws, resolution of the issue will not be easy. Caulfield writes:

> The controversy over the use of ATVs is not yet resolved. Recently, the National Park Service initiated a cooperative research project with residents of Anaktuvuk Pass to determine the vehicular impact on local vegetation and other resources. In addition, negotiations are underway between the Park Service, Nunamiut Corporation, and Arctic Slope Regional Corporation to exchange land and access rights as a means to both protect park values and Anaktuvuk Pass subsistence uses. (1988: 60)

At the moment a short-term agreement between NPS and the Nunamiut is in effect until the land and access rights trade agreement is made final (NPS, 1991), although it is by no means certain that the agreement will receive the necessary approval from Congress. The agreement would create a roster of eligible ATV users, preventing new residents of the village from using ATVs inside the Park. This might place a strain on relationships within the town, especially if it prevents friends from hunting together. Furthermore, there are already some indications that the terms of the agreement are too restrictive for the Nunamiut, who follow caribou beyond the lands being opened to ATVs (author's observations, 1991).

Under the circumstances NPS has done a reasonable job of balancing different interests in the short term, but the long-term picture remains uncertain. Some Nunamiut hunters believe that they are in "ninety per-cent" agreement with NPS over the issues of access and hunting (Paul Hugo, Raymond Paneak, pers. comm., 1991). However, some residents of Anaktuvuk Pass still harbor a great deal of resentment towards NPS and the attitudes of some of its personnel. Complex agreements such as the current land exchange proposal will do little to instill faith in NPS and its motives, for it avoids the central issue that the Nunamiut would like to be left alone to do what they have always done – travel the land to follow the game. From the local perspective, greater clarity in ANILCA might have prevented the issue from arising at all.

The third issue of land stewardship is that of enforcing regulations. Until the *McDowell* decision led to the federal takeover of hunting regulation on federal land on July 1, 1990, NPS had responsibility for enforcing state game laws on NPS land. In the Noatak National Preserve this led to an incident between NPS and the local Native community. According to Kate Rooney of the NPS office in Kotzebue, local residents had asked for increased enforcement of game laws against sport hunters in the preserve (pers. comm., 1990). NPS, however, cannot be selective in its enforcement and ended up inspecting the hunting camp of a Kotzebue elder. The man was cited for a misdemeanor for hunting Dall sheep without a permit.

This event made a poor impression on the local Native community. Schaeffer *et al.* write:

> The National Park Service has very poor lines of communication with the residents of northwest Alaska. . . . The Park Service has made no attempt to work with local communities and hunters. As a result, . . . increasingly poor relationships [are] being built up between the federal agencies and local hunters. (1986: 7)

Brewster notes:

> The Iñupiat believe the NPS is restricting, rather than protecting and allowing for, subsistence. (1987: 40)

Rooney points out that no such enforcement incidents have occurred since then, but clearly the credibility of NPS in the eyes of local residents has been badly damaged.

Differing standards of enforcement and response to the local situation add to the complexity of having several state and federal agencies operating side by side in northern Alaska. NPS has so far been insensitive to local conditions until a crisis occurs. The promise of the National Park lands in northern Alaska has not yet been realized for local residents.

Subsistence Resource Commissions

When ANILCA created Alaska's new national parks, preserves, and monuments, it required the creation of a subsistence resource commission for each area. Each commission has nine members, three appointed by the Secretary of the Interior, three by the Governor of Alaska, and three by the regional advisory council also established by ANILCA. Section 808 of ANILCA states:

> each commission shall devise and recommend to the Secretary and the Governor a program for subsistence hunting within the park or park monument. . . . Every year thereafter, the commission . . . shall make recommendations to the Secretary and the Governor for any changes in the program or its implementation which the commission deems necessary.

The powers of the commissions are not just advisory. Section 808 continues:

> The Secretary shall promptly implement the program recommendations submitted to him by each commission unless he finds in writing that such program or recommendations violates recognized principles of wildlife conservation, threatens the conservation of healthy populations of wildlife in the park or park monument, is contrary to the purposes for which the park or park monument is established, or would be detrimental to the satisfaction of subsistence needs of local residents.

While there is room for interpretation of what constitutes an inappropriate recommendation, the commissions are designed to play the lead role in regulating subsistence activities within the parks, preserves, and monuments.

The recommendations of the subsistence resource commission for Gates of the Arctic National Park and Preserve covered seven issues:

1. Communication between park managers and local rural residents.
2. Eligibility and resident zones for subsistence hunting.
3. Access to the park and the resources.
4. Designation of traditional use areas.
5. Regulation of subsistence uses of wildlife and fisheries.

6. The subsistence permit system.
7. Research needs and monitoring.
(Subsistence Resource Commission for Gates of the Arctic National Park, 1987)

Together these comprise a thorough program for subsistence management in the park and preserve. The response from the Department of the Interior, however, stated that recommendations 1 and 6 were outside the authority of the commission and that the other recommendations were either too broad or were inappropriate and could not be implemented.[4]

Caulfield writes that the subsistence resource commissions are at a crossroads:

> some fear that the subsistence resource commissions will not be taken seriously; that managers will treat them as simply one more way to gather public input from special interest groups. Fears have been expressed that the "national interest" in protecting park values will override Native subsistence needs, and that the professional culture of the National Park Service, with its strong tradition of prohibiting consumptive uses of park resources, will bring continued pressure to limit or restrict subsistence. (1988: 62)

Caulfield continues, however, by noting that this attitude may be changing in the minds of some resource managers:

> Other parks in the United States, including Hawaii Volcanoes National Park and Big Cypress National Park, have found ways to accommodate limited consumptive uses of park resources by indigenous people. . . . In Alaska, this accommodation must occur on a significantly larger scale and, in the long term will require meaningful incorporation of the traditional and contemporary knowledge of Native people. With proper support, the subsistence resource commissions can play an important role in this process. (ibid.: 63)

Like the promise of national parks in general in northern Alaska, the promise of the subsistence resource commissions has yet to be realized fully. According to Raymond Paneak of Anaktuvuk Pass, the current chairman of the subsistence resource commission for Gates of the Arctic National Park, NPS is increasingly willing to listen to the commission and to accommodate the interests of local people (pers. comm., 1990). By placing local residents in the lead role of the regulatory process ANILCA laid the groundwork for effective management of subsistence hunting on park lands. It is up to the subsistence resource commissions and NPS to work together to ensure that effective management is actually provided.

The Bureau of Land Management

The Bureau of Land Management (BLM), a branch of the U.S. Department of the Interior, has authority for two large tracts of land in northern Alaska: the Utility Corridor surrounding the Dalton Highway leading to Prudhoe Bay, and the National Petroleum Reserve–Alaska (NPR–A) in the western central North Slope. According to Section 302 of the Federal Land Policy and Management Act of 1976, the BLM "shall manage the public lands under principles of multiple use and sustained yield." The resources managed under these principles include "recreation, range, timber, minerals, watershed, fish and wildlife, wilderness, and scenic, scientific, and cultural values" (BLM and Defenders of Wildlife, 1990). This section examines two prominent BLM projects in northern Alaska: promotion of recreational use of BLM lands and the reintroduction of muskoxen.

Recreational use of BLM lands

In a planning report entitled *Recreation 2000: Alaska*, the BLM states:

> BLM-Alaska provides recreation opportunities that are generally not available on other publicly managed lands in Alaska. . . . BLM tends to manage the accessible primitive areas of Alaska . . . . In many areas of the state, we manage "true wilderness" that provides primitive opportunities without the restrictions of wilderness designation. It is this particular niche which we intend to provide. (BLM, 1989a: 22)

Little of Alaska is accessible by road, and the only road to north of the Brooks Range is currently closed to the public. BLM, which manages the Utility Corridor through which the road runs, is promoting opening the road. The proposed management plan states:

> The Utility Corridor would be managed with an emphasis on recreation. Recreational facilities in the Dalton Highway Recreation Management Area (i.e., roughly the lands visible from the Dalton Highway) would be expanded. New waysides, campsites, trailheads and cabin sites would be identified and developed after completion of a Recreational Area Management Plan. This alternative would seek a mix of private investment in recreational facilities . . . and federal government supported facilities. (BLM, 1989b: ix)

Such a project would attract large numbers of people to the area, which would probably strain the capacity of the facilities. *Recreation 2000: Alaska* describes the drawbacks to road access:

> Since the state highway system is extremely limited in Alaska, any developed recreation facility along the road system receives concentrated use since recreation facilities are generally few and far between in Alaska. This leads to rapid deterioration of the recreation sites because they exceed capacity during peak use season. (BLM, 1989a: 21)

This prospect has led to considerable local opposition to the plan.

Federal management in northern Alaska

In a letter to the Director of the BLM, North Slope Borough Mayor George Ahmaogak expressed concerns over safety, sanitation, road surface quality, and the cost to the North Slope Borough of providing necessary services along the road. In addition, Ahmaogak wrote:

> We have the following concerns related to the issue of Subsistence, and feel that its importance is understated in the current document [the proposed plan]:
>
> 1. In the Final Environmental Impact Statement for the Utility Corridor and the Final Environmental Impact Statement for the Central Arctic Management Area (CAMA) 1988, your agency minimizes past and current subsistence use in the Utility Corridor and CAMA by all NSB villages while stressing recreational opportunities.
> 2. Traditional and historical subsistence use patterns have changed within the Utility Corridor because industrial traffic is given priority over subsistence use within the Corridor so long as access to subsistence areas is not significantly impeded and can be achieved without increasing the safety hazards associated with the transportation activities within the Utility Corridor. The assumption has been made that subsistence use, especially hunting, in close proximity to oil and gas activities is not prudent or safe.
> 3. We feel that recreational activities are equally imprudent, and increase health and safety concerns expressed above.[5]

If subsistence interests have been understated in the plan, there is clearly room for concern that if the plan is implemented, subsistence hunting will suffer from increased recreational use of the area.

According to Mary Leykom (pers. comm., 1990), a BLM field officer in Kotzebue, the BLM, unlike the National Park Service or the U.S. Fish and Wildlife Service, has so far not been unpopular with local residents. This could change, however, if the BLM continues to promote increased recreational use of its lands. While there is a legitimate interest in allowing public use and access on public lands, the effects on local subsistence must be taken into full account. Leykom further commented that although the BLM must file impact statements noting the effects on subsistence, the process often amounts to rubber stamp approval of BLM proposals.

Land management activities can have a large impact on local hunting patterns and practices. While direct competition for subsistence resources may be small, particularly since the area within five miles on either side of the Dalton Highway is closed to all but bow-and-arrow hunting (Alaska Department of Fish and Game, 1990: 20), the increase in people and road traffic may disrupt animal movements and interfere with the hunters. This increase in visitors is unlikely to benefit local residents and may hinder their subsistence activities. The BLM's proposal does not promote effective management of local use of the resources because it does not give priority to those uses, potentially preventing local residents from harvesting what they need.

74

Reintroduction of muskoxen

Muskoxen once ranged across the tundra in northern and western Alaska; in the late nineteenth century they were exterminated in Alaska. In 1935 and 1936, 31 muskoxen were brought from Greenland and released on Nunivak Island in the Bering Sea. This stock thrived and provided a core stock for reintroductions to the mainland. Herds have been brought to both the east and west ends of the North Slope and to the Seward Peninsula near Nome and the BLM plans another transplant, to the area near Ivotuk Creek in the north central Brooks Range (see Figure 4.1).

The BLM's interest is in helping to reintroduce the species to its former range (BLM, 1989b: 2–32, 1989c). The herd near Kaktovik in the Arctic National Wildlife Refuge is growing rapidly but will take time to spread across the North Slope. In addition to the esthetic value of having muskoxen in the region, they would again be a viable subsistence resource for local residents. (See Chapter 5, page 85–7, for a discussion of the status of the muskox as a subsistence resource.) However, since the number of animals involved in the initial transplant is low, no hunting would be permitted for several years.

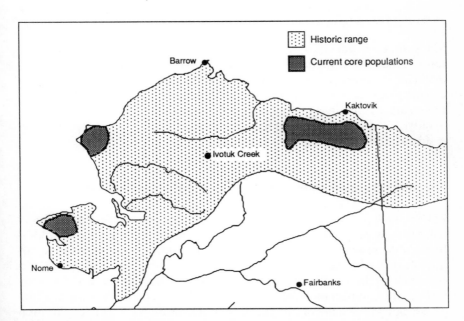

Figure 4.1 Historic and current range of muskoxen, *Ovibos moschatus*, in northern Alaska, with BLM's proposed reintroduction site (BLM, 1989c).

Federal management in northern Alaska

The BLM's environmental assessment of the muskox transplant recognizes the necessity of local support for the project. Some difficulties with the reintroduction near Kaktovik have made local residents wary of the results of the transplant (see Chapter 5, page 86). The BLM has held public meetings at the villages of Barrow, Atqasuk, and Anaktuvuk Pass, and has made presentations to the North Slope Borough Fish and Game Management Committee. At the January 24, 1990, meeting of the latter, members of the committee expressed concerns over hunting of the animals and whether new regulations would have to be imposed for the muskoxen. Roy Massinton of the BLM pointed out that hunting regulations are the province of the state, but that Kaktovik's subsistence use of muskoxen had been affirmed by the Alaska Board of Game in November 1989, and so it was likely that other villages on the North Slope would also have subsistence priority for muskox.

While the BLM is clearly interested in the reintroduction, it has been working hard to get local support before it takes place. The environmental assessment states:

> For this project to succeed, the cooperation of the rural residents surrounding the release site is essential. Initially, the reintroduced muskoxen will not be available to any type of harvest activity. Because muskoxen are so vulnerable to modern hunting techniques, the cooperation of the rural residents must be obtained before the project progresses further. If this cooperation can not be obtained the project will not be attempted. (BLM, 1989c: 28)

Since the reintroduction of muskoxen would provide an additional subsistence resource without any long-term adverse environmental consequences, it has great potential benefit to local residents. The BLM's efforts to gain local support are important and necessary and should ensure that the misunderstandings surrounding the muskox harvest near Kaktovik are avoided. The BLM is promoting this plan effectively in regard to local residents and local use of subsistence resources.

The Minerals Management Service and industrial development

For the most part the regulatory and management structure for wildlife and wildlife use in northern Alaska has concentrated on controlling local hunters to ensure that the resources remain healthy. With the exception of migratory birds, most species are hunted primarily by local people, so there is little direct competition for the animals. Onshore industrial activity has had little impact on local subsistence, largely because the Prudhoe Bay area is not within a major hunting ground. Offshore oil and gas exploration changes the picture.

The Minerals Management Service (MMS), a branch of the U.S.

Department of the Interior, has authority over the mineral exploration and development of the Outer Continental Shelf (OCS) of the U.S. In northern Alaska MMS has sold leases for oil and gas exploration in the Beaufort and Chukchi Seas, and several companies have begun conducting seismic surveys and drilling exploratory wells. For the first time since the commercial whaling era, local hunters are facing competition offshore for use of resources and habitat. Although a detailed examination of industrial development is beyond the scope of this paper, a look at the work of MMS illustrates the potential conflict between industrial development and subsistence hunting.

To be effective in terms of protecting local hunting, the regulation and management of wildlife and wildlife use must minimize the effects that other activities have on animals and on the hunting practices of local people. On land, preliminary exploration, by seismic testing and exploratory wells, can be done in winter when far fewer animals are on the northern tundra than in summer. Offshore, the pack ice means drilling from mobile platforms is risky in winter, making late summer and fall the best times for exploratory work. This coincides with both the fall migration of whales and the time when walrus use the northern part of their range. Also, since marine species migrate along the coast, effects on the animals may be felt in many villages along the coast.

MMS's role in wildlife management in northern Alaska is indirect and different from the roles of the other federal agencies examined in this chapter. It is, however, no less significant in the long run. While other regulatory efforts have aimed to quantify local harvest levels in order to determine the sustainable yield of the resources and to avoid exceeding that limit in the future, industrial activity can change the existing balance. Commercial whaling changed the populations of whales and walrus, altering the structure and distribution of villages across northern Alaska. Unless properly controlled, industrial development could potentially have a similarly disruptive effect. From the local perspective, hunting and wildlife resources must be the primary considerations in deciding what activities will be permitted on the Outer Continental Shelf.

MMS has sponsored and continues to sponsor a great number of environmental studies both to assess the Outer Continental Shelf environment and to determine the effects development has or may have on marine animals and habitat (see MMS, 1989). In addition, specific actions such as lease sales must be accompanied by an Environmental Impact Statement (EIS) identifying and evaluating potential impacts from both normal operating activities and from catastrophic occurrences such as oil spills (e.g., MMS, 1987; 1988; 1990). These recommendations are sent to the Secretary of the Interior, who decides which proposed alternative will be taken.

To ensure that it addresses local concerns, the final EIS must include and respond to public testimony. For example, the final EIS for Chukchi Sea lease sale 109 contains written comments from ten federal agencies, the State of Alaska, the North Slope Borough, the City of Wainwright, five oil companies, three concerned groups and one individual. Public hearings were held in Barrow, Point Hope, Point Lay, Wainwright, and Anchorage, gathering testimony from 35 individuals (MMS, 1987). Such testimony is incorporated into the record and the draft EIS is often amended as a result of issues that are raised.

The hearings process, while securing a degree of public participation, does not create a suitable forum for discussing what is to local hunters the central issue: should development occur at all? The EIS hearings are held for the purpose of gathering specific comments on how to improve the EIS. While some who testify at the hearings make specific suggestions, most of the hunters question the need for and the safety of development, speaking from their own experience in the fickle environment of the pack ice. Since they do not address the EIS specifically, these comments require no response and the process does not provide for further discussion of their concerns. The public hearings do not constitute a means for local people to express their concerns in a relevant forum.

After the lease sale, further development requires further administrative steps. According to the National Environmental Policy Act of 1969, before development can proceed a "Finding of No Significant Impact" must be published, including descriptions of any mitigation measures necessary to eliminate significant impacts. The crux is the definition of "significant." Most of the environmental data available are of insufficient resolution to determine the impacts on many species. Significant impacts are hard to prove or to disprove, and the absence of proof that significant impacts will occur is often sufficient for a Finding of No Significant Impact. For example MMS mitigation plans include descriptions of oil-spill clean-up methods which are untested in extreme conditions (MMS, 1990: IV-A). The Alaska Oil Spill Commission (1990) found that the chances of controlling a remote oil spill were "bleak," and recommended awaiting better methods of transportation before proceeding with development. MMS, however, has not delayed any activities on the Outer Continental Shelf.

Many of the potential impacts are extremely unlikely to occur during the exploratory phase of oil and gas activity. Before any further steps are taken the active companies must submit to more permitting procedures and file additional plans and assessments of risk. However, the exploratory phase is not without impacts itself. The presence of ship traffic and drilling rigs adds a substantial amount of noise to the offshore environment. MMS-sponsored studies of the effects of this noise on migrating bowhead and beluga whales are inconclusive so far. The Eskimo whalers, who are opposed to offshore drilling, report that the bowhead whales have been behaving differently on their fall migration since drilling activities began (Edward Hopson, pers. comm., 1989). While there seems to have been little effect on the number of whales taken in the fall harvest, the Eskimo hunters are very wary of the potential for changes in animal distribution and behavior as a result of offshore industrial activity.

While legal constraints on permissible impacts appear to give strong protection to the environment, a closer look at the predicted impacts from oil and gas development in the Chukchi and Beaufort Seas shows the Eskimos' concerns are well founded. According to the draft EIS for Beaufort Sea lease sale 124 (MMS, 1990: IV-N-1), there is a 99 percent chance that oil and gas development in the Chukchi and Beaufort Seas will produce an oil spill in excess of 1000 barrels, and there will most likely be eight such spills. In all Outer Continental Shelf operations in the U.S. since 1964, only 20 spills of greater than 1000 barrels have occurred. In other words, the number of large spills expected in Arctic waters equals 40 percent of the number of spills that have occurred to date in the entire Outer Continetal Shelf. The timing and position of these spills may maximize or minimize their impact, but the risk to subsistence resources and subsistence hunting exists. From the local hunters' perspective, this system does not provide adequate protection of subsistence resources in the long run and so is not an effective means of managing subsistence resources and the potential impacts on those resources.

Conclusions

Federal management of wildlife resources in northern Alaska is piecemeal at best. Between the Bureau of Land Management, the Fish and Wildlife Service, and the National Park Service, federal agencies manage the majority of North Slope lands. Offshore, the Minerals Management Service is responsible for the Outer Continental Shelf. Marine mammals are under the authority of the National Marine Fisheries Service and the Fish and Wildlife Service, and the latter also has authority for migratory birds. Federal legislation and international treaties limit the actions of hunters and regulatory agencies alike. It is impossible to comment on the overall state of federal management, since its parts are so varied. This variety itself, however, gives considerable insight into what works and what doesn't in the context of regulating local hunting in northern Alaska.

To determine an optimal management system, five points can be drawn from the examples of federal management:

1. *The system must be flexible.* Rigid international treaties and static views of subsistence hunting make management difficult because they do not allow for simple changes to the regulatory structure that would ease both the work of the managers and the life of the hunters. The worst examples are the migratory bird treaties, which forbid the spring hunt

altogether. Since those hunts will continue anyway, it makes management difficult, and breeds a contempt for regulation which can carry over to other regimes. The best example is the National Marine Fisheries Service's delegation of management authority to the Alaska Eskimo Whaling Commission. Placing the interests of sound management first, NMFS allows the Eskimo whalers themselves to regulate and administer the harvest quota. This response has led to one of the most effective management regimes in northern Alaska (see Chapter 7, pages 110–15).

2. *The system must be responsive to local conditions and concerns.* Although many regimes are designed for responsiveness, in practice they seldom achieve it. The subsistence resource commissions of the National Park Service are the mechanism for ensuring that local concerns are taken into full account, but so far they have not lived up to that promise. The Alaska National Interest Lands Conservation Act created both the subsistence resource commissions and the regional advisory councils. Because of budget constraints, administrative problems, and the difficulty of breaking into an existing system, these have not given local people the clout to affect the regulatory system. The Minerals Management Service does not give local people the proper forum to discuss whether development should occur, but limits discussion to specific parts of the process. On the positive side, in its muskox reintroduction plan, the Bureau of Land Management has shown sensitivity to local concerns by promising that the project will not begin unless it receives local support.

3. *Effective management must take into account a broad range of factors that affect resources and resource use.* Too often, the mandate of local commissions or public hearings is narrowly limited. The subsistence resource commissions of the National Parks are given authority over a narrow sector of management. Their recommendations on issues outside that sector, such as promoting recreational use of the park, are not implemented because, although they are valid management concerns, the recommendations exceed the authority of the commission. The Minerals Management Service's hearings address only the specifics of an administrative step to leasing, not the broad issues of development.

4. *The management system must respond before a crisis occurs.* The Marine Mammal Protection Act does not allow limits on Native harvests unless a species is depleted – in other words, until a crisis has already happened. Harvest limits may not be the only or the best way to manage a species, but the idea that nothing need be done while animal stocks are healthy is potentially disastrous. The National Marine Fisheries Service has done little with seals, so little baseline data are available should a crisis develop. The viruses that have affected seals in such places as the North Sea in Europe could wreak similar destruction on Arctic seals,

but the extent of the damage would be hard to assess since little is known about the population dynamics of the seals.

5. *Local cooperation and support are vital to an effective regime.* The Fish and Wildlife Service's tagging and marking program for walrus and polar bears depends upon the cooperation of the hunters and the local communities. A greater effort could be made to tell hunters why the program is necessary and to inform them of the results of the research. Disagreements on the role of federal agencies in land management have created antagonism between managers and local hunters, hindering effective management. The perspectives of the two groups may be different, but shared concerns can be the basis for cooperation. This can be seen in the cooperative plans between hunters and managers for bowhead whales, walrus, and geese (see also Chapter 7).

For the most part, the mechanisms exist within federal agencies to provide effective management. What is lacking is the will to make full use of them to serve the interests of local hunters. While in some circumstances other interests may be regarded as more significant from the national perspective, managers have still not made full use of the opportunity to provide effective local management wherever possible in northern Alaska. Until this begins, encouraging greater coordination and cooperation between agencies will be of little help in providing effective management of local resource use.

Notes

1. Letter from Ronald O. Skoog, Commissioner, ADF&G, to Lynn A. Greenwalt, FWS, June 22, 1979.
2. Bob Leedy of the FWS, speaking to the North Slope Borough Fish and Game Management Committee, Anchorage, Alaska, April 4, 1990.
3. Memorandum from John W. Carnahan, Deputy Director, Planning and Community Services Department, to George N. Ahmaogak, Sr., Mayor, North Slope Borough, January 20, 1986.
4. Letter from Susan Recce, Acting Assistant Secretary for Fish and Wildlife and Parks, U.S. Department of the Interior, to Benjamin Nageak, Chairman, Subsistence Resource Commission, Gates of the Arctic National Park, May 18, 1988.
5. Letter from George N. Ahmaogak, Sr., Mayor, North Slope Borough, to Cy Jamison, Director, Bureau of Land Management, December 22, 1989.

5

State management in northern Alaska

The State of Alaska, through the Boards of Fisheries and Game and the Alaska Department of Fish and Game (ADF&G), manages fish and land animals within the state. ADF&G is organized in eight divisions, three of which are examined in this chapter. The divisions of Boards, Subsistence, and Wildlife Conservation are most active in northern Alaska, although the Divisions of Commercial Fisheries and Sport Fish work in the Kotzebue area. These divisions make recommendations concerning hunting seasons and limits, conduct research on subsistence and on wildlife populations, monitor harvests, and gather public input on how to manage Alaska's wildlife (see Figure 5.1). Prior to implementation of the decision in *McDowell v. State of Alaska* (1989) (see page 30), ADF&G had sole authority to regulate all hunting throughout the state. Now, the federal

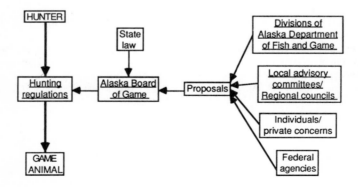

Figure 5.1 Schematic diagram of the regulatory process of the Alaska Department of Fish and Game. Underlined bodies are examined in this chapter.

government also regulates subsistence hunting on federal land, about 65 percent of the state. The means of resolving potential conflicts between federal and state regulations have not been established. In any case, ADF&G plays the major role in the management of land animals in Alaska. This chapter examines ADF&G's activities in northern Alaska and the way in which it balances statewide interests with local ones.

In 1978 the state enacted a subsistence law (see Chapter 2, page 29) to guide the actions of the management agency in regard to subsistence use. This law was amended in 1986 to give subsistence priority to rural residents. This distinction between urban and rural residents was declared invalid by the Alaska Supreme Court in the *McDowell* case on the grounds that it discriminated against urban subsistence users. To date, the Alaska Legislature has not acted to amend the law. Some proposed replacements have suggested classifying individual users on the basis of such criteria as need and past use of the resource. Since the problem is not fully resolved, a discussion here would be speculative rather than substantive, and so I do not examine the effects of the *McDowell* case.

The Alaska Board of Game and the Division of Boards

The Division of Boards provides support for the Boards of Fisheries and Game, which establish hunting and fishing regulations for the state. The division also supports local advisory committees and regional councils, the latter created by the Alaska National Interest Lands Conservation Act of 1980 (ANILCA). Both are citizens' groups which advise the Boards of Fisheries and Game. The entire system is designed to gather public input and to incorporate it into appropriate hunting regulations. This section looks first at the Board of Game and then at the advisory structure supporting it. Since fisheries management is barely active in northern Alaska, I do not examine the Board of Fisheries.

The Board of Game

The Alaska Board of Game establishes hunting regulations for terrestrial mammals and for birds within Alaska. Prior to the McDowell decision, the Board of Game set all hunting seasons and limits in the state. Currently, the U.S. Fish and Wildlife Service also regulates subsistence hunting on federal lands. The Alaska Board of Game has seven members from around the state, chosen by the Governor of Alaska and confirmed by the state legislature. The Board normally meets twice yearly to consider proposals from members of the public, government agencies (including ADF&G), advisory committees and regional councils, and other interested groups.

State management in northern Alaska

As Langdon (1984: 21) puts it, "The state system of fish and game management was developed out of a populist distaste for management by administrative prerogative."

While the legislature and the courts can direct – and on occasion override – the Board of Game, primary state regulatory authority rests with the seven members of the Board. Clearly the composition of the Board has a great influence on the regulations that it issues. Sport hunters often complain that the Board is biased towards subsistence hunters, who in turn claim that the system favors sport hunters. Henry Springer, then chairman of the Board of Game, wryly noted that at least the Board must be fair, since everyone was mad at their decisions.[1]

One frustration felt by many who propose regulations to the Board is the limitation of the Board's statutory authority. At a given meeting of the Board, testimony can be taken on any regulation. However, the Board can change only those regulations for which a legal notice is issued prior to the meeting. The Board's authority is further limited to regulations regarding conservation, development, and utilization of animal resources (Larry Jones, pers. comm. 1990). For example, a proposal by the Arctic Regional Council to allow villages to be exempted from general hunting regulations was beyond the authority of the Board (Magdanz, 1988). Similarly, the Board could not implement a proposal that dealt with wearing orange for safety during the hunting season.

The Boards of Fisheries and Game were also responsible for implementing the state subsistence law. That law had given subsistence uses preference in allocating fish and game harvests, but left to the Boards the task of determining whether subsistence uses exist in each specific harvest. In 1980 the Board of Fisheries adopted ten criteria for establishing subsistence use. In 1981 both boards jointly adopted eight criteria for this purpose. Langdon summarizes the criteria as follows:

1. long-term, consistent pattern of use, excluding interruption by circumstances beyond the user's control such as regulatory prohibitions;
2. a use pattern recurring in a specific season(s) of each year;
3. a use pattern consisting of means and methods of harvest which are characterized by efficiency and economy of effort and cost, and conditioned by local circumstances;
4. the consistent harvest and use of fish or game which is near, or reasonably accessible from, the user's residence;
5. means of handling, preparing, preserving and storing has been traditionally used by past generations, but not excluding recent technological advances where appropriate;
6. a use pattern which includes the handing down of knowledge of fishing or hunting skills, values and lore from generation to generation;
7. a use pattern in which the hunting or fishing effort or the products of that

effort are distributed or shared among others within a definable community of persons, . . .;

8. use pattern which includes reliance for subsistence purposes upon a wide diversity of the fish and game resources of an area, and in which that pattern of subsistence uses provides substantial economic, cultural, social, and nutritional elements of the subsistence user's life. (1984: 26)

The Board, when considering subsistence uses, must make a finding of "customary and traditional use" (ANILCA, Section 803), basing that finding upon the ideas expressed in the eight-point list of criteria.

While subsistence use has priority over other uses of game when there is not enough harvestable surplus to accommodate all uses, the Board of Game does not necessarily apply it over other non-consumptive interests in animal stocks, such as conservation and enhancement. In 1990 the Council of the Native Village of Kwethluk, in southwestern Alaska near Bethel, filed suit in the U.S. District Court against the State of Alaska to allow an emergency harvest of 50 to 70 caribou, since the residents of the village were facing a shortage of meat. The Board of Game had earlier denied the request on the grounds that, although the harvest would not damage the herd, it was contrary to the long-term goal of increasing its numbers. However, federal Judge H. Russell Holland granted a preliminary injunction, finding that:

> the public interest strongly favors the continuation of subsistence hunting when, as in this instance, there is not compelling evidence that the hunt herein authorized will adversely affect the [caribou] herd. (*Kwethluk IRA Council v. State of Alaska*, 1990: 4–5)

Thus, the Board of Game may not always act to protect the short-term interests of local people dependent upon game, especially when faced with conflicting interests for a given stock of animals.

A specific case illustrates the way the Board of Game approaches the subsistence priority in the context of other hunting interests. In its November 1989 meeting held in Fairbanks, the Board considered proposals to change the permit system for muskox hunts in Game Management Unit 26(C), the northeast part of the state, near the village of Kaktovik. Having been extirpated in the second half of the nineteenth century, muskoxen were reintroduced here in 1969 and 1970 and had increased sufficiently by 1983 to allow for a small harvest. Bull muskox hunts on Nunivak Island, where the original transplants from Greenland in the 1930s were placed, were conducted by drawing permit. This entails a lottery for the limited number of permits and a minimum fee of $500 for purchasing the permit. For the hunt near Kaktovik, the hunt was for bulls only, by registration permit. These are issued on a first-come, first-served basis and cost only $25.

The first year the hunt was relatively unknown, and so the permits were issued in Kaktovik to Kaktovik residents. Afterwards, word spread about the hunt and the availability of the permits. Some hunters from outside the area arrived in Kaktovik to camp out in line in front of the ADF&G office in order to get a permit, which upset local residents who felt that this was an inappropriate way to allocate a harvest. Jane Thompson, representing the City of Kaktovik, stated: "Standing in line for a piece of paper to hunt is demeaning, it's not our way." In an extreme example, one individual flew from the lower 48 to Fairbanks, where permits were also being issued that year, to find too many people in line already. He then flew on to Kaktovik to see how long the line there was.

In 1986 the Board of Game considered the Kaktovik muskox hunt and found that the local residents did not have customary and traditional use, primarily because there was no recent long-term use. At the 1989 meeting the question was reconsidered. Again, discussion centered upon the question of long-term use, with new evidence provided by the Division of Subsistence concerning past uses of muskoxen and their prominence in the oral tradition. Board member Jack Lentfer commented that disappearance of game was a circumstance beyond the hunters' control and so should not affect the finding of long-term use as defined by the first of the eight criteria. Since the species had been present in the Kaktovik area and had been used extensively, the Board found that the 100 years interruption in subsistence hunts was not too long to preclude customary and traditional use and found also that Kaktovik residents have customary and traditional use of muskoxen.

Having made that determination the Board also had to decide how to allocate the muskoxen that could be harvested from the stock. The Division of Wildlife Conservation determined that 15 muskoxen could be taken. According to the state subsistence law, if hunting is restricted, subsistence use must receive priority. There was little information, however, on the level of Kaktovik's subsistence need. One suggestion was to give half the animals to Kaktovik and half to other hunters. The difficulty is that subsistence need must be an absolute number, not "half of the available surplus." In other words, if the harvest is increased to 20 animals, Kaktovik's share cannot be increased also, unless the subsistence need is found to be higher than previously determined. In the end the Board decided to allocate seven muskoxen to Kaktovik subsistence hunters and seven to other hunters. In making this decision the Board suggested that when the harvest is increased, another determination could find that Kaktovik's subsistence need is higher than seven animals, leaving open the possibility of an increase in the subsistence allocation.

The "customary and traditional" finding led to some frustration for members of the Board because it seemed logical at the time to extend that finding across the whole of the former range of the muskox. Since they have been reintroduced on the Seward Peninsula and on the western North

Slope as well as near Kaktovik, the issue will soon arise again. However, the legal notice of the meeting mentioned only two game management units and so the Board could not find customary and traditional uses in other areas.

This case illustrates the strength of the Board system in its ability to find an appropriate compromise solution to the issue, by taking testimony from a variety of sources and by responding to the needs of different interests. It also illustrates the weaknesses of the system. First, the Board is constrained within certain legal bounds and cannot act on all factors affecting hunting. Second, the meetings are usually held in Anchorage and Fairbanks and are conducted with a formal, written structure. Both of these frustrate participation of rural residents, something the creation of local advisory committees and regional councils was intended to rectify.

The role of local advisory committees and regional councils

Section 805 of ANILCA required the creation of a system of regional advisory councils made up of residents of the regions and having the following authority:

(A) the review and evaluation of proposals for regulations, policies, management plans, and other matters relating to subsistence uses of fish and wildlife within the region;

(B) the provision of a forum for the expression of opinions and recommendations by persons interested in any matter related to the subsistence uses of fish and wildlife within the region;

(C) the encouragement of local and regional participation pursuant to the provisions of this title in the decision making process affecting the taking of fish and wildlife on the public lands within the region for subsistence uses;

(D) the preparation of an annual report to the Secretary [of the Interior] . . .

This section also provided that the Secretary would not have to implement this section if the State of Alaska enacted laws creating a system of regional advisory councils consistent with the purposes mandated here (see Chapter 4, page 58). Alaska did so, creating the six regional councils called for in ANILCA, based in Juneau, Anchorage, Fairbanks, Dillingham, Bethel and Kotzebue. The state had earlier established many local advisory committees in each region, which have a mandate that includes other hunting as well as subsistence. The councils make recommendations to the Boards of Fisheries and Game. Section 805 states that the Boards

> may choose not to follow any recommendation which it determines is not supported by substantial evidence presented during the course of its administrative proceedings, violates recognized principles of fish and wildlife conservation or would be detrimental to the satisfaction of rural subsistence needs. [see

Chapter 4, page 71, concerning similar provisions for subsistence resource commissions and the National Park Service]

This section examines the Arctic Regional Council, based in Kotzebue, and the ten local advisory committees within the region and their role in providing effective and appropriate regulation of local subsistence hunting in northern Alaska.

The advisory system is a means of ensuring a high level of public participation in the process of creating hunting regulations. It does not automatically favor rural or subsistence hunters. (The stipulation that recommendations may not be detrimental to rural subsistence interests is nothing more than an expression of the intent of ANILCA's general subsistence policy.) The composition of individual committees is the critical factor. A study of the advisory system conducted by the Rural Alaska Community Action Program (RurAl CAP)(1989) found that in three of the six regions sports or commercial users were better represented than subsistence users. In another region, sports and commercial users combined outnumbered subsistence users. Only in the Arctic and Western regions, centered in Kotzebue and Bethel, were subsistence hunters in the majority.

Representation in northern Alaska is heavily weighted toward subsistence uses. Out of 26 respondents to the RurAl CAP study, 24 indicated at least partial subsistence use of resources. On the whole, respondents from the Arctic region indicated that the system was "somewhat" effective, and that the state's implementation of recommendations was fair, though some called it excellent while others called it very poor. Regarding the system of game regulations as a whole, Arctic respondents felt that it did not reflect local conditions and uses. To a greater extent than respondents from other regions, they supported such changes to the regulatory system as "finding alternatives to hunting licenses" and "extending or eliminating hunting seasons" (*ibid.*).

In discussing its own limitations the study points out a difficulty of the advisory system generally in northern Alaska:

Relatively few responses were received from the Arctic or Western regions . . . There is a related cultural dimension: questionnaires are a very western concept, which may make those who are uncomfortable with western culture (or the English language) less likely to fill them out. This is no doubt a particular problem in the Western and Arctic regions. (*ibid.*: 11)

Pete Schaeffer of the Kotzebue Sound Advisory Committee and the Arctic Regional Council points out the problems encountered by Native villagers when confronted with a formal, written system in which they have to make their case (pers. comm., 1990). Recommendations of the advisory committees and councils must still be forwarded to the Board of Game and its legal advisors. Without the experience to argue effectively within the formal system of the Board of Game's authority, many villagers feel their participation in the process is meaningless.

For the advisory committees this has led to frustration with the system and the role of the committees within that system. The lack of authority of the Board of Game to change the regulatory system (for example, to exempt individual villages from state regulations) has led members to question whether the committees are capable of bringing about the significant changes needed to resolve some of the major problems that local residents have with the current system.[2] Although the advisory system is capable of bringing local opinions to the attention of the Board of Game, there is little guarantee that the concerns of the committees and councils will be implemented by the Board.

Some recommendations have brought about changes reflecting local practices, such as allowing the hunting of swimming caribou (Doug Larsen, pers. comm., 1990). Other recommendations call for fundamental changes in the way wildlife regulations are perceived and developed. To implement these types of changes requires an overhaul of the current system and thinking about game management and regulation. The power of the advisory system is limited because it can effect no greater changes than the Board of Game has authority to make, and so it is constrained to making the most out of the existing regulatory structure.

In addition to structural problems, the advisory committees and councils have been understaffed and underfunded (Magdanz, 1988), meaning that several local committees have not had meetings for a few years. Efforts are being made to resurrect some of the committees that have been dormant, but with limited funding to pay for meetings, and lack of enthusiasm due to poor past experiences with the system, it will be hard to get the committees functioning as they were intended. The confusion over the role of the councils and committees after the *McDowell* decision will make this even more difficult.

The Alaska Board of Game, supported by the Division of Boards, has authority to set hunting regulations in the State of Alaska. The extent of public participation sought in the process of creating the regulations is far greater than in any other state (Larry Jones, pers. comm., 1990). The system of regional advisory councils supported by local advisory committees exists to enhance the degree of public participation and to ensure that local and regional interests are properly represented at the Board of Game's deliberations. While it may not be the most appropriate for northern Alaska, this system is capable of providing for most local needs within the structure of formal regulations.

Because of competing interests, or the biases of the Board toward or away from subsistence uses, the regulatory process does not always do so, despite legal provisions in ANILCA and related state law. Public participation, while necessary, does not guarantee effective management from the local perspective. The limitations on the power of the Board of Game affect the responsiveness of the system to the broad concerns of residents of northern Alaska. Such responsiveness is vital to effective management of local use of wildlife. An inappropriate system, no matter how well intended, cannot provide effective long-term management of subsistence resources.

The Division of Wildlife Conservation

The Division of Wildlife Conservation, formerly the Division of Game, is responsible for collecting data and monitoring animal populations through-out the state. In addition to determining population levels and trends, the division advises the Board of Game about acceptable harvests for given stocks and about appropriate management practices for Alaska's wildlife. The Division of Wildlife Conservation maintains a presence throughout the state: ADF&G's only employee in Barrow is the division's area biol-ogist for Game Management Unit 26(A). Since the area biologist is responsible for working with local residents to address their concerns, the division plays a prominent role in wildlife management in northern Alaska. This section examines the relationship between the division's biologists and local hunters.

A recurring theme of wildlife management in northern Alaska is the lasting distrust caused by introducing hunting regulations with little appar-ent concern for local feelings or practices. McCandless describes one problem in the Yukon Territory – issuing hunting licenses to construction crews on the Alaska Highway, which may have led to an excessive moose harvest – as "a political blunder which echoed down thirty-five years" (1985: 81). In 1961 in Barrow, sudden enforcement of the closed season for hunting migratory birds led to the Barrow Duck-In and continued wariness of outside attempts to control harvests (see Chapter 2, page 28; Chapter 3, page 42). One lesson from this episode is that such wariness extends to all management agencies, regardless of whether they are state, federal, or even local. Rural residents often do not distinguish between the various agencies, and a mistake by one may damage the credibility of all agencies in the area.

Overcoming this distrust takes time and effort as well as understanding on the part of the biologists working in the region. Doug Larsen, an area biologist based in Kotzebue at the time of this study, commented that there is increased willingness among local residents for cooperation on game management work (pers. comm., 1990). As people see that the regulatory system can respond to their needs, they are more willing to accept it and try to work within it. The difficulty is that the meetings and proposals of the Division of Boards are not always the best or the only way to involve local residents. Larsen and others have found that individual meetings with hunters and trappers are the best way to find out what people want and to establish a cooperative relationship between the hunters and the managers. Larsen's annual questionnaires to trappers now include comments about animal movements, trends, and other information. Sharing information between managers and hunters has gone a long way to replacing distrust with cooperation.

A specific example of a situation that went badly wrong illustrates the difficulties experienced by game biologists and local hunters. In 1970 the population of the Western Arctic caribou herd was estimated at 242,000 animals. According to Jim Davis of ADF&G, the Department made a "big blunder" at this point in telling northwest Alaska residents that the Western Arctic herd was over-abundant (pers. comm., 1990). Six years later the herd was estimated to have 75,000 animals or fewer, and the hunting season was closed in 1977. Ironically, many villages had continued local abundances of caribou at the time the decline was announced, giving the appearance that the herd was healthy. The credibility of ADF&G and its biologists was low. Local people claimed that the animals had merely gone elsewhere and that the population census had missed them. Some people today refer to the "apparent" crash of the western herd in the 1970s.

The Western Arctic caribou herd today has close to 400,000 animals (Geoff Carroll, pers. comm., 1990), and the hunting limit is five caribou per day. According to Davis, current understanding of the herd and better monitoring of the population make it unlikely that another crash could come as such a surprise. However, the problems that occurred as a result of the 1970s crisis have caused a political backlash that has put the management agencies in a position subservient to the legislature and to public opinion. Davis sees ADF&G struggling to find a mission, unsure of its role in the direction of future management.

From the local perspective, the main issue is the appropriateness of management to local concerns. The Division of Wildlife Conservation does not set hunting regulations, but its biologists are actively involved in the monitoring and research that calculates acceptable harvest levels. More importantly, the area biologists are the ones with whom local hunters are likely to have most contact. If a working relationship can be established between biologists and local residents, the concept of wildlife management will be better received, since both sides can benefit from cooperation. Managers can learn from the observations of hunters who spend a great deal of time in the field, watching animals closely and carefully, and hunters can ensure that the management system is more responsive to their needs if those needs are better understood by the managers.

The institutional commitment to providing for the needs of local hunters is often lacking. Individual managers may work closely with local people, but the management system does not readily accommodate participation by and cooperation with local residents. Part of the problem is that the system is a professional, written one, while Native cultures are oral and personal. If a manager produces a written report on a given animal stock, there is little time or institutional incentive to put that report in a medium designed to inform villagers. John Trent, formerly the area biologist in Barrow, had a monthly radio program entitled "Arctic Journal," which gave news of different issues concerning wildlife and local hunting. He refers to the program as "one of the more effective things I did in Barrow" (pers. comm., 1991). The program was developed out of personal initiative, however, and not as part of ADF&G policy to inform people of its activities.

The Division of Wildlife Conservation plays the leading scientific role in managing Alaska's wildlife. In northern Alaska its biologists often have the most contact with local residents but, as with many of the management regimes in northern Alaska, some past problems continue to cause distrust between managers and hunters. Individual efforts by managers to work more closely with local hunters have improved the situation in many cases; the overall institutional commitment to local involvement, however, has remained low. Better monitoring and understanding of animal stocks has reduced the likelihood of such surprises as the Western Arctic caribou crash of the 1970s, but much remains to be done to produce a management system that holds tangible benefits for local hunters.

The Division of Subsistence

Alaska's first subsistence law, passed in 1978, created a new Subsistence Section within the Alaska Department of Fish and Game (ADF&G). This section was to conduct research and provide information on the role of subsistence in the state and to help define subsistence and incorporate subsistence needs in the regulation and management of fish and game. In other words, the Subsistence Section was the institutional bridge between subsistence users and ADF&G's regulatory system, giving a voice to subsistence and subsistence users throughout Alaska. In 1981 the section was raised to division status, placing it alongside the Divisions of Sport Fish, Commercial Fish, Wildlife Conservation, Habitat, and other branches of ADF&G. Kelso (1981: 25) comments, "This change recognized the importance of the subsistence program to the Department's mission."

Prior to the creation of the Subsistence Section, little data existed on subsistence uses and patterns in rural Alaska. Langdon (1984: 21–22) describes the informal practice of giving subsistence uses preference and allowing enforcement efforts the discretion to favor traditional uses. The level of subsistence harvests, the areas of subsistence use by villagers, the cultural role of traditional foods, the importance of sharing within and between families and communities – all were unknown to the biologically-oriented ADF&G. Kelso quotes a 1981 report of the Alaska House of Representatives Special Committee on Subsistence describing the work of the subsistence section:

> Because the Department [of Fish and Game] had never conducted social research, an immense gap existed between programs for biological studies and programs needed for socio-economic research on subsistence. Indeed, the Department was in no position to provide the extensive data needed by the Boards to make reasonable decisions affecting subsistence. By contrast to the other divisions of the Department, the duties specified by [the subsistence law] for the Subsistence Section give heavy emphasis to socio-economic research with none of the management and enforcement functions normally associated with the Department. . . .
>
> The Section's highly productive research program has provided essential data for decision making by the Boards and has established fundamental baseline data for many areas. Such studies often are the only work ever addressed to these problems; and the Section's groundbreaking applied research has moved the Department of Fish and Game into a potentially productive era of using both biological and socio-economic research tools. (Kelso, 1981: 10–11)

This section examines how well the Division of Subsistence has helped ADF&G live up to this potential.

The volume of data obtained by the Division of Subsistence is impressive. As of April 1989, the division had produced 177 Technical Reports, ranging from brief overviews of a few pages to detailed analyses several hundred pages long. A compilation of the abstracts of these papers describes their importance:

> The heart of the division's work is published in the Technical Paper Series. This series is the most complete collection of current information about subsistence in Alaska. The papers cover all regions of the state. Some papers were written in response to specific fish and game management issues. Others provide detailed basic information on the subsistence uses of particular communities which pertain to a large number of scientific and policy questions. (ADF&G, 1989: i)

In specific cases before the Board of Game, such as the muskox hunt in Kaktovik described above (pages 85–7), the Division of Subsistence provides much of the information needed to determine whether customary and traditional use exists and what level of harvest is needed to satisfy subsistence needs. Its research allows the division to be the best informed advocate for subsistence uses.

Being informed is not the same as being effective. As with most management regimes, the effectiveness of the division depends upon the strength of its link to the individuals and communities whose interests it tries to represent. Here the division encounters two obstacles. First, its employees work for ADF&G, which means that they still carry the burden of the distrust discussed in the previous section. Hannah Loon (pers. comm., 1990), an Iñupiaq who works for the Division of Subsistence in Kotzebue, commented that over-regulation in the early days has left a bad taste in people's mouths. Villagers often do not wish to talk about hunting issues because they are "suspicious and fearful," even when the interviewer is also Native. Individual relationships may go a long way to overcoming this, but, as with the Division of Wildlife Conservation, the institutional problem remains.

The second obstacle is the professional orientation of the division. Technical reports are significant items in the professional culture of an organization like ADF&G. They are not significant items in village culture in rural Alaska. Jim Magdanz, of the Division of Subsistence in Kotzebue, pointed out that ADF&G loses credibility by not consistently sharing information with its constituents (pers. comm., 1990). This is equally true of population estimates and of subsistence harvest reports. A great deal of information is collected from villagers concerning subsistence, but little is returned in a meaningful form. Individual researchers may take the trouble to send their results to the villagers who were studied, but there is often too little time to do so while fulfilling the professional demands of ADF&G.

These limitations, however, do not prevent the division from doing an effective job within ADF&G of representing subsistence interests. None of the federal agencies has a branch dedicated solely to understanding and protecting subsistence uses of Alaska's wildlife. Like the advisory system in the Division of Boards, however, the presence of a means of representation for local subsistence users does not necessarily mean that local interests will be accommodated within the regulatory system. From the standpoint of state-wide public policy, equal status and representation for subsistence may help provide equitable management; from the local perspective, it merely means participation in an opaque and alien system (Jim Magdanz, pers. comm., 1990) when local residents would rather be left alone (Pete Schaeffer, pers. comm., 1990). In other words, the Division of Subsistence does a reasonable job within a regulatory system that struggles to adapt to local subsistence in northern Alaska.

Alaska's hunting regulations

While the research conducted by the various divisions of ADF&G may bring hunters and managers into contact, the final product is the set of hunting regulations containing seasons, bag limits, and restrictions on methods and means of hunting and on possession and use of game. For local residents, these regulations are the most tangible part of wildlife management, for they control, or attempt to control, the actions of the hunter. The regulations provoke distrust when they are seen to be inappropriate; they provoke outrage when they are seen to be too restrictive; they provoke lawsuits when they are seen to be unfair. This section examines how well Alaska's hunting regulations reflect local practices and concerns in northern Alaska.

A 1986 regulation review conducted by the Kotzebue Advisory Committee found that in general "the package of game regulations which affect northwest Alaska . . . has . . . many fundamental problems" (Schaeffer *et al.*, 1986: 25). Many of these problems concern restrictions affecting customary practices of the Iñupiat and therefore are relevant in northern Alaska as well as northwest Alaska. The root of the problem is that the system of hunting regulations – based on individual limits, defined hunting seasons, and limitations on uses and methods – is designed for hunting as a recreational pursuit, not the economic basis of a way of life (see Chapter 2). Efforts to overcome this inherent bias have had limited success. No matter how liberal, Alaska's hunting regulations are an alien system when applied to subsistence use of wildlife.

Subsistence in northern Alaska involves the whole community. Many people may be at least partly dependent upon the catch of one hunter. By placing limits on individual harvests, the regulations make it difficult for a successful hunter to provide for his extended family. One Native from Kobuk in northwest Alaska commented:

> Sometimes, it [ADF&G] gives us three caribou for a season, and look how much that lasts with a big family. It don't last. In the springtime, when we try to go hunt ducks and geese, we have to hide out like the ducks and geese from the Fish and Games, so they don't catch us. (in Berger, 1985: 60)[3]

Although current limits are higher, the idea of individual limits is only workable if most family members can get out and hunt. Because this is often not the case, the regulations are ineffective to the extent that they do not allow local residents to provide for their needs and the needs of their community.

The problem of seasons and bag limits came to a head in 1989 when the federal district court for Alaska ruled in *Bobby v. State* that the hunting seasons and bag limits for moose and caribou that applied to the Athabascan community of Lime Village in southwest Alaska were arbitrary and inadequate. Limiting seasons did not allow for the customary opportunistic hunt of moose throughout the year, and bag limits did not allow hunters to provide for other members of the community. While not invalidating all seasons and bag limits for subsistence hunting, the court criticized the Board of Game for failing to accommodate customary and traditional uses of game:

> the Board of Game must in the future proceed with scrupulous care and caution in imposing seasons and bag limits on subsistence hunting. Bag limits and seasons are game management tools which have seen extensive use in Alaska

and nationally. These restrictions have typically, if not universally, been used to regulate sport hunting. In this case, bag limits and seasons are being applied to a very different type of game use. . . .

If bag limits and seasons are imposed on subsistence hunting, there must be substantial evidence in the record that such restrictions are not inconsistent with customary and traditional uses of the game in question. It must be clear in the record that subsistence uses will be accommodated, as regards both the quantity or volume of use and the duration of the use. . . . The standard is the customary and traditional use of game. (*Bobby v. State of Alaska*, 1989: 777, 778)

This ruling applies only to the residents of Lime Village, but other villages are likely to take similar action in court. Although the *McDowell* decision has changed the way in which subsistence regulations are set, *Bobby v. State* could lead to regulations which better reflect the patterns and uses of game in the Native community while continuing to protect the viability of animal populations.

Methods and means restrictions, which prohibit some common practices in northern Alaska, can also inhibit the ability of hunters to provide for their needs. Some of the restrictions that Schaeffer *et al.* (1986) found inappropriate have been changed, such as the use of rimfire rifles to hunt swimming caribou. Others have not been changed, such as the use of CB radios from boats while hunting and the prohibition on taking game from mechanized vehicles. The use of snowmachines while hunting caribou, for example, is controversial. While some Iñupiaq elders criticize the practice of driving caribou because the stress of the chase taints the meat,[4] many hunters interviewed in the course of a regulation review in the Kotzebue area stated that sometimes it was necessary to chase caribou with snowmachines, especially if the caribou were skittish (e.g., Dau and Larsen, 1989; Larsen and Dau, 1989; Ramoth and Georgette, 1989). If providing food is the goal of the hunt, the most efficient method of harvest is the best one. Restrictions that affect only the esthetic quality of the hunt, and not the game stock or the end result, are unnecessary and ineffective in northern Alaska.

Another class of provisions of the hunting regulations concerns the use and handling of game once it has been taken. Schaeffer *et al.* (1986) found that the regulations did not accommodate many local practices. The requirement that meat not be left in the field is contrary to the practice of making meat caches. The frustration of local residents is evident in Schaeffer *et al.*'s comments about another restriction on the use of game:

The prohibition against the feeding of game meat to dog teams provides an example of one of the great ironies in the wildlife regulatory system. On one hand, biologists tend to view the use of snowmachines as somehow illegitimate, and have done everything possible to make it difficult to use snowmachines legally. On the other hand, the same biologists have deemed it illegal to feed game meat to dog teams, apparently expecting hunters from northwest Alaska to airfreight Purina dog chow to their camps. How is it that village hunters are supposed to meet their needs if they cannot use either snowmachines or dog teams legally? (1986: 23)

Seemingly pointless or discriminatory regulations do little to improve local willingness to cooperate with management agencies. Either the ability of local residents to provide for their needs is diminished or hunters suffer the stigma of breaking the law, and the worry that they will be caught.

Another conflict between regulations and practices concerns brown bears. Legally, a hunter must take the skull and hide of a brown bear with him from the field, to be sealed by an ADF&G representative. However, most local hunters are interested more in the meat than in the hide, and have no use for the skull. If there is room to bring the hide back, they will do so, but not at the expense of meat (Loon and Georgette, 1989; Georgette, 1989). In addition, the requirement that tags must be bought before hunting bears conflicts with the Iñupiaq belief that the bears must be treated with respect. Loon and Georgette write:

Many Iñupiaq residents . . . have strongly held beliefs about the proper manner in which to treat brown bears. Perhaps foremost among these is the prohibition on speaking openly about brown bears. Hunters should not "act big," brag about their bear hunting abilities, or even speak of their intentions to hunt. Brown bears are believed to have keen hearing, and to retaliate against hunters who violate these rules. Requiring local hunters to purchase a tag before hunting brown bear, and thereby deliberately make their intentions known, is incompatible with traditional Iñupiaq hunting practices. The concept that a person must pay extra to hunt a particular species, even if that animal is being taken for food, is peculiar and unfamiliar to many Iñupiaq hunters. (1989: 49)

It is small wonder that only 14 to 19 percent of the estimated brown bear harvest in Game Management Unit 23 (the Kotzebue region) in 1987 was reported to ADF&G, and that this is high compared with neighboring areas (*ibid.*: 17–18). When regulations conflict with traditional hunting practices, management efforts suffer.

Another part of the regulatory system is the hunting license. Licenses provide both information on the number of hunters and revenue for the state management system. However, they are not popular in northern Alaska. Schaeffer *et al.* write:

The committee received two general categories of comments regarding hunting licenses. In some cases, hunters have no disagreement with the act of obtaining a hunting license. These hunters commented that hunting licenses were necessary and had no fundamental objection to obtaining one. This first group of hunters was in the minority. Most hunters objected to hunting licenses. This second group of hunters commented that they and their families had hunted and lived off the land all their lives. They felt that they did not need anybody's permission or license to practice what they felt was a fundamental cultural prerogative. (1986: 3)

This is also evident in the fact that only 15 to 25 percent of northern and northwest Alaska hunters purchase licenses (*ibid.*; Geoff Carroll, pers. comm., 1990). Enforcement is minimal, so the incentive to purchase a license is low. Also, the administrative hassle of obtaining the license discourages many hunters, particularly in small villages where the proper forms are not always available when they are needed.

Schaeffer *et al.* describe another reason for disaffection with licenses:

> The committee believes that the relatively low level of compliance with licensing is an indicator of the degree to which northwest Alaska hunters have been "brought into" the state game regulatory system. There exists little feeling of ownership in the system, and there exists a great deal of antagonism toward the system. The hunting licenses are seen to be a symbol of having to comply with an undesirable system. (1986: 3–4)

In this view, hunting licenses are not in thems elves a problem but are the symptom of distrust felt by local residents towards the state system. Since enforcement is so low and compliance follows suit, the requirement to purchase a hunting license can hardly be a hindrance to northern Alaska hunters.

Similar observations could be made about the role of most hunting regulations in northern Alaska. If they are widely ignored by local hunters, who continue to hunt as they need to, then the regulations do not prevent local people from providing for their needs. This argument circumvents the issue of why hunting regulations are needed at all and what is to take their place if they are brushed aside in common practice. The chief aim of hunting regulations is to ensure that animal populations remain healthy. To do this, harvests are limited by bag limits, closed seasons, and restrictions on the methods and means of hunting, as well as on the use of game that has been taken. The chief aim of local hunters is to put food on the table and to obtain other products such as skins, antlers, and sinew. Where hunting regulations conflict with subsistence needs, compliance is likely to suffer. This is especially true if the regulations as a whole are perceived to be inappropriate.

Conclusions

The state management system, administered by the Alaska Department of Fish and Game, has tried to accommodate the needs of local people. This effort has been partly successful, but some conflicts and problems still exist between local practices and regulatory requirements. The shortcomings of the system can be found in these conflicts. Four points can be taken from the examination of the state management system to help understand how subsistence hunting can be effectively managed in northern Alaska:

1. *The system must be responsive to local concerns.* Early regulatory attempts had little evident concern for local interests and practices, fostering distrust and alienation among local people. If hunting regulations prohibit certain customary practices, or make it difficult to satisfy local needs, there is great incentive to ignore the regulations. This produces either fear of enforcement by the regulatory agency or contempt for its efforts to manage wildlife stocks. Neither is productive in the long term.

2. *Local people must participate in the system.* Part of the burden for providing effective management rests with the local hunters. Only by participating in management efforts can hunters make their interests clear so that the system can respond accurately, and only in this way can a true sense of ownership in the system be achieved. The mechanism for participation exists in the local advisory committees, but this is not altogether satisfactory. Meetings require time and may conflict with other community events or with time spent hunting. Also, for participation to be worthwhile it must produce good results. Submitting proposals to the Board of Game is meaningless unless some of those proposals are accepted.

3. *Local people must be included in the system.* This follows from the first point. When local hunters must participate in the system, the system in turn must make full use of that participation to ensure that local concerns are taken into account. If the system is perceived as one that is designed to control local people, it will be an unpopular imposition. If it is designed to incorporate local values for wildlife and wildlife use and to enhance local interests, then the system may be regarded as worthwhile, perhaps even beneficial. On an individual level, this is occurring with certain managers and hunters or trappers in northern and northwest Alaska. As an institution, ADF&G has not yet shown its usefulness to some of the hunters of northern Alaska.

4. *Local people must be involved in research and gathering information.* Schaeffer *et al.* comment:

> There is a great deal to be learned from the eyes of the hunter, and certainly a single biologist cannot spend as much time in the field as a whole population of hunters. (1986: 14)

The information returned on Larsen's questionnaires about trapping bears this out. The other side to this point is that the information gathered should be returned in a useful form so that local people can see how it is used and can see if any corrections are needed. This type of direct participation in the activities of the researchers and managers is worth more than a public meeting, because it is a cooperative venture to produce mutually beneficial results.

To be truly effective in providing for the needs of northern Alaskans, the state system requires substantial changes to both management practices and to regulatory requirements. I have concentrated on management practices in the belief that the regulatory requirements follow the sensitivity of the actions of the managers. Not all of the necessary changes are within the authority of the Board of Game, and so for ADF&G's role to become more consistent with the needs of northern Alaska the state legislature must amend certain provisions of its laws. Because the state plays a far more active role in wildlife management than federal agencies, the changes it must make are more extensive and difficult. The alternative, however, is ineffective management and the continued disaffection of local hunters.

Notes

1. At the Rural Alaska Community Action Program and Alaska Federation of Natives Subsistence Conference, Anchorage, October 16–17, 1989.
2. At the meeting of the Arctic Regional Council, June 13, 1990, Barrow, Alaska.
3. Note that the U.S. Fish and Wildlife Service, not ADF&G, has authority over migratory birds such as ducks and geese. This statement reflects the fact that rural residents often do not distinguish between the various management agencies.
4. Jakie Koonuk, at the North Slope Borough Fish and Game Management Committee meeting, April 4, 1990, Anchorage, Alaska.

6

Local management: the North Slope Borough

Federal and state agencies have authority over the harvests of animals in northern Alaska. The local government retains no regulatory authority. Nonetheless, the North Slope Borough (see Figure 6.1) has a Department of Wildlife Management, a Fish and Game Management Committee, and a Science Advisory Committee. These help promote and conduct research and other programs on wildlife and wildlife use. This chapter examines the extent to which these three bodies are able to promote both local interests and effective management.

The Department of Wildlife Management

The North Slope Borough's Department of Wildlife Management is primarily concerned with conducting and promoting scientific research into issues and species of local interest in northern Alaska. No other local government in Alaska has such a department. Established under the control of the North Slope Borough, and without any regulatory authority, its goals are outlined in its mission statement:

> The primary goal of the Department shall be to provide a factual basis for strong local participation in the management of wildlife resources within the Borough by means of:
> 1. Documenting the importance to the citizenry of subsistence use resources.
> 2. Documenting the natural history of these wildlife resources.
> (North Slope Borough Department of Wildlife Management, n.d.).

This section examines the department's work and the extent to which local control is reflected in the nature of the department's projects.

Local management: the North Slope Borough

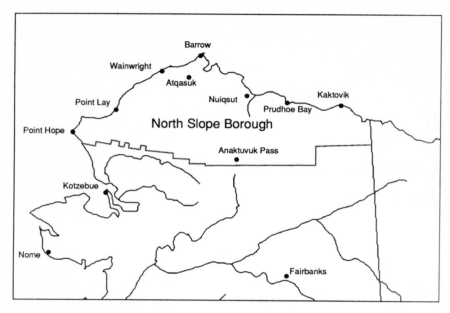

Figure 6.1 Map of the North Slope Borough showing the region's eight villages and the Prudhoe Bay oil and gas complex.

The department is able to pick its projects. Since it has a research staff of only six people, it cannot take on all studies that need to be done on the North Slope; instead, it works on those that are most important and necessary to local residents. It sponsors and helps provide support for other research (including this study), and cooperates with federal and state agencies on such work as caribou censuses with the Alaska Department of Fish and Game and marine mammal tissue studies with the National Oceanic and Atmospheric Administration. The advantage of this is that the department's work is heavily oriented toward local concerns. There are no other constituents for the department to satisfy, so it can direct its resources to the issues most in need of research. From the local perspective, the department's work should be effective.

The most substantial and significant of the department's projects is the bowhead whale census. The census was originally conducted by the National Marine Fisheries Service, but was turned over to the borough in 1982. Under the administration of the department, the estimate for the bowhead population has increased substantially, due to better census methods, including use of acoustic monitoring of whale migrations (Albert, 1988). Since the bowhead whaling issue is the most important single issue in the nine whaling villages, five of which are in the North Slope Borough, the census work is prominent and its success has brought the department much credit from both the Native and the scientific communities.

While some distrust remains among the borough's residents, most acknowledge the utility of using sound scientific research to promote local interests (*ibid.*). The department is able to bridge the gap between local knowledge and scientific rigor, making use of the depth of understanding that the Iñupiat have acquired. For example, acoustic work on the bowhead whale census provided scientific evidence that the whales will migrate through heavy pack ice, just as the Native whalers had said. Through the department's work, science has become a powerful ally for the borough's residents in their efforts to protect both subsistence and local control of resource use.

The main limitation to the department's effectiveness is its small size. Though the borough is not able to support a wildlife department on the scale of the Alaska Department of Fish and Game, the projects it does undertake are valuable not only to local residents but to other researchers as well. The department has been conducting several fish surveys over the past few years, to assess fish stocks in the Barrow area. Some work has been done previously, but much basic research still needs to be carried out. The department has also recently hired an ornithologist, planning to extend its work to other areas of wildlife research.

The success of the Department of Wildlife Management stems from its focus on local issues and interests. Since it is working for the people of northern Alaska under the direction of the local government, the department shows what can be accomplished by cooperation with local hunters. The reasons for the lack of success of some federal and state managers compared to the relative success of the borough's department is that the latter has the institutional commitment to working for and with local people. Thus the focus has shifted from personal trust in a particular manager to trust in the idea and institution of scientific wildlife management.

The Science Advisory Committee

The Science Advisory Committee (SAC) of the North Slope Borough operates under the authority of the Mayor. It was established in 1980 to help the Alaska Eskimo Whaling Commission, but soon broadened to cover other issues of interest to the North Slope Borough. Its relationship to the borough was made formal in 1982. The SAC defines its mission as follows:

1. Advise the North Slope Borough on the scope and structure of research

programs needed to evaluate and/or mitigate environmental impacts associated with resource development within the Borough.
2. Provide peer review for research proposals and research results as pertains to studies supported by the North Slope Borough.
3. Provide peer review of studies (research proposals and results) supported by others that may affect the North Slope Borough.
4. Provide peer review of various technical documents whose findings and/or interpretations may affect the North Slope Borough.

(North Slope Borough Science Advisory Committee, 1989: 33)

Like the Department of Wildlife Management, the SAC is under local control and its work can be directed to issues of special interest or significance to the North Slope Borough. Its work is more technical than that of the Wildlife Department, its primary interactions being with other researchers and their projects, rather than directly with the local people or the local environment.

Maintaining a Science Advisory Committee is a luxury. The North Slope Borough can afford a high level of participation in research and oversight. Although it has no regulatory authority over wildlife, such participation enables the borough to represent the interests of its residents in the scientific arena. The SAC gives a voice to local concerns about the health of wildlife stocks and about potential interferences with subsistence use of those stocks. Without this, scientific research would remain the province of outside agencies, beyond the control of the borough, and focused on other interests than local ones. By taking control of part of the scientific process, the borough shows that the principles of scientific management can be used in ways beneficial to local interests. In addition to overseeing the research of others, the SAC is a means of promoting the ideas and the quality of scientific research generally, and of making sure that research promotes local interests in addition to outside interests (Albert, 1988).

Like the Department of Wildlife Management, the SAC has an institutional commitment to local concerns and interests. Since it has little direct contact with the residents of the borough, the SAC by itself cannot enhance local participation in management. The activities of the SAC are more a reflection of the effectiveness of the North Slope Borough in promoting local interests rather than a reflection of the inherent value of scientific oversight. Nonetheless, the point to be taken from the SAC is that scientific management can be beneficial from the local perspective if it is directed to local concerns and has the institutional commitment to pursue that course.

The Fish and Game Management Committee

The North Slope Borough Fish and Game Management Committee (FGMC), composed of one representative from each of the borough's eight villages plus one at-large member, is designed to link village residents with managers and researchers. The Department of Wildlife Management's mission statement points out:

> Since this committee has a representative from each village it is a valuable means for: 1) bringing village concerns to the attention of the Department, and 2) assisting in the local coordination of wildlife studies and management programs. (North Slope Borough Department of Wildlife Management, n.d.)

In principle the FGMC can bring local concerns to the attention of re-searchers and managers, while assisting the researchers by providing local knowledge and cooperation. In practice, while this occurs, the FGMC is hindered by a lack of autonomy and the lack of a clear mandate for its role.

The FGMC's greatest success so far is the polar bear agreement it entered into with the Inuvialuit Game Council of Inuvik, Northwest Territories (see Chapter 7, pages 130–33). This agreement calls for a voluntary limit on the harvest of the Beaufort Sea population of polar bears. Although the agreement has no enforcement authority in Alaska, it represents the commitment of the people of the North Slope to responsible use of local resources. Because it is a local initiative, prompted by the Inuvialuit in Canada but completed with the FGMC, local hunters are far more receptive to the idea than they would be to a similar plan originating from the federal government. Local investment of effort leads to local commitment to the goals of the agreement.

The FGMC meets every three months to discuss management and regulatory issues and to hear presentations from representatives of federal, state, and local government agencies and from other researchers. The researchers and managers can keep the committee members up to date on their activities, and the committee can express its concerns or opinions about projects and proposals. The Bureau of Land Management sent a representative to the FGMC to discuss the proposal to transplant musk-oxen to a spot near Anaktuvuk Pass, since the BLM recognized that the project could not succeed without local support[1] (see Chapter 4, page 76).

In response to concerns of the U.S. Fish and Wildlife Service about the health of certain walruses, Jakie Koonuk of Point Hope pointed out that some solitary walruses can be thin and unhealthy, and that this does not mean that there is a widespread problem.[2] Local knowledge, particularly of animal behavior, is often far more detailed than that of professional biologists and managers. Providing a means of sharing such knowledge is a useful step in showing both managers and hunters that their understanding of wildlife is often complementary and that cooperation can yield far better results than working alone.

While these meetings can help the useful exchange of information, their effectiveness is hampered by a lack of clear direction for the work of the committee. Members of the FGMC have expressed frustration that the committee is often overruled by the North Slope Borough Law Department on matters concerning participation in planning and regulation of activities on the North Slope. William Leavitt, Chairman of the FGMC, said: "We need an attorney at our next meeting to interpret our role for us. If we just sit and talk, there's no point in meeting." Nolan Solomon, the committee member from Kaktovik, expressed his concern that oil companies were not coming to the FGMC, meaning the FGMC has no say in development issues that are crucial to wildlife management.[3]

Without a clear mandate, the committee's role is limited. As an institution created and controlled locally, it has the potential to provide local expertise and cooperation in wildlife management. Unlike the subsistence resource commissions of the National Park Service or the regional councils and local advisory committees of the Alaska Department of Fish and Game, the FGMC is not under the auspices of the federal or state government. Although it does not have regulatory authority, it can fill the gap left by other management agencies by giving coherent and consistent voice to local concerns. One possibility is that the FGMC could provide harvest data for the North Slope to other agencies, greatly enhancing its role and its profile (John C. George, pers. comm., 1991).

If the FGMC can represent North Slope wildlife interests to outside agencies as well as to North Slope residents, then it will be an effective player in the management of wildlife and wildlife use in northern Alaska. If by interference from other branches of the North Slope Borough government, or by its own inability to reach a consensus about its role, the FGMC cannot provide coherent representation, then it will not contribute to the effectiveness of northern Alaska wildlife management and regulation.

Conclusions

The North Slope Borough government can afford to take an active financial role in wildlife management within its boundaries. That it has done so reflects the importance of wildlife and wildlife use to borough residents. The borough has no regulatory authority for setting seasons or bag limits, which limits the borough's institutions to a research and advisory role. Because the Department of Wildlife Management, the Science Advisory Committee, and the Fish and Game Management Committee are all under local control, it is not surprising that they are more attentive to local concerns than government agencies with broader constituencies. Although their effectiveness is limited by their size and lack of authority, between the three bodies there is the potential for significantly improving the effectiveness of management in northern Alaska.

Three points can be drawn from the North Slope Borough's management efforts:

1. *Research must be oriented to local concerns.* The Department of Wildlife Management conducts valuable research and sponsors or supports a great deal more. This research is directed to issues of local importance, making sure that local concerns are adequately addressed scientifically. As a branch of the local government, the department is also more likely to gain the cooperation of local hunters than are outside agencies. Based in Barrow, the department can be more attuned to local concerns and issues, enhancing its responsiveness. It has shown the benefits to local residents of sound research in management. The Science Advisory Committee extends the efforts of the department by providing thorough review of research plans and reports, ensuring that the research that is conducted both by the Borough and by other researchers represents local concerns and issues adequately and accurately.

2. *A clearly defined role is necessary for a regime to function effectively.* The Fish and Game Management Committee lacks that role, and is caught without a mission. Its potential is great, but there can be little motivation for a body that, in William Leavitt's words, just sits and talks. The FGMC has the local control missing from committees and councils established by the state and federal governments, but it is powerless without the autonomy to represent its constituents. The Department of Wildlife Management and the SAC have clearer research roles, and so are better able to carry out their missions than the FGMC.

3. *Local control can be effective, but by itself it accomplishes little.* The FGMC suffers, in part, from too much local control. If its actions are hampered by the North Slope Borough itself, then the idea that local control will solve the imbalances of the regulatory system is absurd. There must be a commitment on the part of local leaders to allow the FGMC to represent the hunters. Local representation on a body without a clear goal is of little help to local interests. The Department of Wildlife Management and the SAC are not representative bodies, and are expected to be under the control of the borough administration. Because their role is research-oriented, local control enhances their effectiveness.

While the North Slope Borough's commitment to wildlife management has proved effective, it is unlikely to be duplicated in most regions of the state for the simple reason of cost. What it has shown, however, is the gap that state and federal agencies have left. The ability of the North Slope Borough to find and fill that gap should be an example to other management agencies of the possibilities that exist for enhancing existing management practices and developing new ones.

Notes

1. Meeting of the North Slope Borough Fish and Game Management Committee, January 24, 1990, Barrow, Alaska.
2. Meeting of the North Slope Borough Fish and Game Management Committee, April 4, 1990, Anchorage, Alaska.
3. Meeting of the North Slope Borough Fish and Game Management Committee, April 5, 1990, Anchorage, Alaska.

7

Cooperative management in northern Alaska

Since management by agencies of the federal and state governments has often proved inadequate (Usher, 1986; Osherenko, 1988; Pinkerton, 1989), many cooperative and user management regimes have been established as alternatives in northern regions since the late 1970s. By involving local hunters in at least some aspects of the management process, these regimes attempt to foster better understanding between hunters and managers at an institutional level. Managers benefit because increased cooperation means better harvest data and greater adherence to hunting regulations and recommendations. Hunters benefit because their views are taken into account, helping to ensure that regulations and enforcement are appropriate to the local situation.

Characteristics of cooperative regimes vary depending upon the agencies involved, the nature of the hunt, and whether other users exist. It should be noted that cooperative management regimes do not necessarily include all interested parties. Conservation groups like the Sierra Club are wary that bodies like the Eskimo Walrus Commission are designed to avoid more formal – and legally more cumbersome – regulation, and thus do not attempt to involve members of the public (Jack Hession, pers. comm., 1990). Some organizations of hunters from outside the local area feel that the interests of their members are ignored and that cooperative management in the interests only of local subsistence hunters does not permit maximum use of the resource in the long run (Bud Burris, pers. comm., 1990).

Valid though these concerns are, the chief aim of cooperative regimes is to provide for long-term productivity and use of the resource when other attempts to do so have failed. Cooperative management is not a perfect solution, but an attempt to improve a poor situation. If decades of mistrust can be overcome by cooperation, cooperative management has achieved a noteworthy success and perhaps laid the foundation for better management and allocation practices in the future.

This chapter examines six cooperative regimes, establishing the features that successful regimes have in common.

The Alaska Eskimo Whaling Commission

The hunt for the bowhead whale has been for centuries the culturally and spiritually defining activity of coastal Iñupiat and St. Lawrence Island Yupik peoples. In 1977 the International Whaling Commission (IWC) ended the aboriginal exemption that allowed Alaska Eskimos to continue to hunt the bowhead (IWC, 1978b). The Eskimos fought to regain the right to whale, creating the Alaska Eskimo Whaling Commission (AEWC) to represent the interests of the nine whaling villages in Alaska (see Figure 7.1). It was the first time that representatives of all nine villages had come together, and the first time that a group of Alaska Native hunters had organized themselves to protect their hunting interests.

In 1977 the estimated population of bowheads was between 600 and 1,800 animals (IWC, 1978a: 67). Between 1910 and 1969, the period between the end of commercial whaling and the economic boom following the discovery of oil on the North Slope, the average harvest was 11.7 whales. Between 1970 and 1977, the average harvest was 32.4 whales (Marquette and Bockstoce, 1980). These figures do not include animals struck but lost. The harvest in 1976 had been 48 whales landed and a further 43 struck but lost, with unknown mortality (Alaska Consultants Inc., with Stephen R. Braund, 1984: 28). The figures from 1977 were even more alarming: 29 landed and 82 struck but lost (*ibid.*). Coupled with the low population estimates, this trend worried many whale scientists and managers (IWC, 1978a, 1980; McVay, 1979) and led to the IWC's ban.

The Eskimo whalers did not share the concern over low population estimates – believing them inaccurate – and instead viewed the ban as an attack on their culture. They formed the AEWC in September 1977, giving them an institution with which to battle the IWC and others who wished to end their whaling. There appeared little promise of cooperation between the whalers and the managers, as is apparent in the statements of the AEWC at the time. The whalers were outraged at the U.S. government, which in their eyes had done nothing to protect the Eskimos' interests:

> By October 24 the United States must decide whether to preserve the Eskimo's historic right to hunt the bowhead whale or whether to abide by the abrupt and culturally genocidal actions of the IWC. (AEWC, 1977: 1)

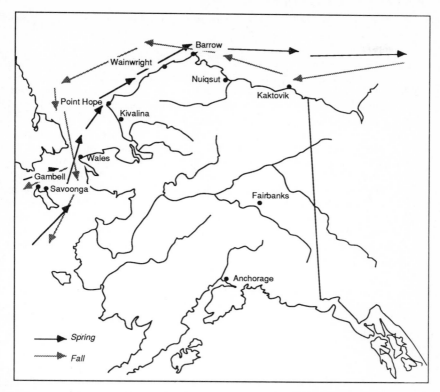

Figure 7.1 Map of the migration route of the bowhead whale, *Balaena mysticetus*, in Alaska with Alaska Eskimo whaling villages (Gambell, 1983; NOAA, 1988).

Jacob Adams, the first Chairman of the AEWC, described the battle as follows:

> The struggle to convince the U.S. government to object to the action taken by the IWC was an uphill battle because we found that the U.S. delegation was dominated by the left-wing conservationist who knew nothing about Eskimo culture and its relationship to the bowhead whale. . . . Remaining firm and strong has gotten the Eskimos through what is probably the toughest assault ever on any culture in the world. (J. Adams, 1982: 10, 13)

With emotions running high, finding a compromise looked nearly impossible.

The U.S. delegation did not formally object to the IWC decision, an action which would have exempted the U.S. from compliance with the ban. Instead, the U.S. placed the question of a bowhead quota on the agenda for the IWC special meeting in December 1977. In the *Federal Register* on November 25, 1977, the National Oceanic and Atmospheric Administration (NOAA) stated:

> The bowhead has been determined to be depleted and, therefore, regulations are being proposed for the taking of that species . . . all taking will be prohibited unless the IWC takes further action prior to the 1978 hunt. In order to provide for a controlled subsistence hunt by the Eskimos which would preserve the central elements of their culture and which would protect the bowhead stock, the United States has developed a comprehensive scientific research program and a conservation regime for bowheads. The scientific research program and the conservation regime will be presented to the IWC Scientific Committee meeting on November 21–25, 1977, and to a special meeting of the IWC December 6–7, 1977. The United States will seek an exemption from the Convention for an Alaskan Eskimo bowhead whale hunt on the basis of the U.S. implementation of the scientific research and conservation programs and consistent with the regulations proposed herein. . . . The total number of bowhead whales authorized to be taken in calendar year 1978 shall not exceed 30 struck or 15 landed, whichever comes first. (1977: 60185–6)

NOAA was finally recognizing the Eskimos' interests and seeking a compromise, although the idea of a quota was not favored by the Eskimos. The IWC agreed to the quota but reduced the numbers to 18 struck or 12 landed (IWC, 1979a) This was later raised by two whales to allow for the 1978 fall hunt (IWC, 1979b).

Relations between the whalers and the government representatives remained strained because the whalers felt that they were not being adequately represented at the IWC. The Eskimos filed two lawsuits, one designed to force the U.S. to file an objection to the IWC ruling, the other arguing that the IWC had no jurisdiction over aboriginal whaling and therefore its decisions could not be implemented by the U.S. government (*Adams v. Vance*, 1977; *Hopson v. Kreps*, 1979, 1980). Both suits were unsuccessful.

Although the Eskimos threatened to ignore the quota in the fall hunt of 1978 and during the 1979 spring hunt, the weather prevented the whalers from taking many whales. The IWC noted that "The catch appeared to be limited by the weather more than by the quota" (IWC, 1980: 104). The Eskimos had hoped that the quota would be increased as a result of their willingness to abide by the quota in the spring of 1978. Jacob Adams stated:

> Despite the good faith efforts of Eskimo whalers to abide by an unjust quota of 12 landed or 18 struck whales during 1978, the IWC ignored the proposal of the United States to permit a hunt at a level to meet nutritional and cultural needs. The IWC ignored the advice of people who know most about the bowhead whale and who are most interested in its conservation. (Arctic Coastal Zone Management Newsletter, 1978[13]: 6)

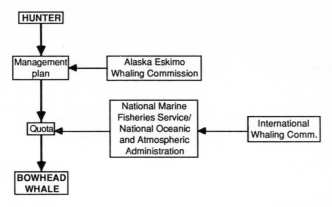

Figure 7.2 Simplified schematic diagram of bowhead whale management. Note that the quota is beyond the control of the AEWC, and that the National Marine Fisheries Service/National Oceanic and Atmospheric Administration only implements the quota established by the International Whaling Commission.

The whalers felt that the only reasonable course was to exercise self-regulation through the AEWC.

In 1980 the issue came to a head. Allegations of over-quota hunting led to a grand jury investigation by the federal district attorney in Anchorage. In Alaska many people in addition to the whalers were outraged by the probe. Senator Ted Stevens called it a "despotic attempt to intimidate Arctic Slope Eskimos" (in Abbott, 1980). Any feelings of cooperation between the whalers and the federal government evaporated. It seemed that a stalemate had been reached.

In March of 1981, a major breakthrough was achieved. The AEWC and NOAA negotiated a cooperative agreement under which NOAA delegates responsibility for managing Eskimo whaling to the AEWC (see Chapter 4, pages 65–7). While the IWC still sets the quota, the administration and management of the quota are left to the AEWC, removing any visible federal presence during whaling and allowing the Eskimos to deal with violations of the AEWC management plan in their own way (see Figure 7.2). The Arctic Coastal Zone Management Newsletter heralded the agreement as "The first U.S. commitment of the management of a subsistence resource to the subsistence users" (1981[34]: 3).

Since 1981 the AEWC has been responsible for keeping track of the number of landed and struck-but-lost whales and reporting this to NOAA. In addition, the AEWC has worked to increase the efficiency of the harvest by improving whaling weapons and by conducting whaling workshops. The success of these programs is clear from the improvement in efficiency following the creation of the AEWC. For the period 1973–77, 41.3 percent of strikes were landed (Alaska Consultants Inc., with Stephen R. Braund

& Associates, 1984: 29). For the period 1978–91, the overall harvest efficiency was 61.9 percent (*ibid.*; AEWC files). The pressure of the quota undoubtedly plays a role in forcing the whalers to make the most of all strikes.

Under AEWC administration, compliance with the quota has been almost total. The exception has been one whaler who hunted over the Barrow village quota in 1985 and again in 1988. In 1985 the AEWC fined him a total of $20,000 and suspended him from whaling for five years. NOAA considered this to be appropriate and declined the AEWC's request that NOAA should take further action.[1] When the whaler hunted over the quota again in 1988, the Barrow Whaling Captains Association expelled him and the AEWC followed suit. This time NOAA referred the case to the federal courts, where the whaler was found guilty, fined $3,000, and sentenced to three months confinement, to be served during the following whaling season (*Barrow Sun*, 1989). While the AEWC by itself could not control this whaler, recourse to NOAA and the federal courts made enforcement possible.

The quota has increased substantially since 1978. The block quota for 1989–91 is 44 struck or 41 landed per year, with a maximum carry-over of three unused strikes from one year to the next. This increase is partly a result of extensive research, supported in part by the AEWC, showing the bowhead population to be around 7,500 whales (IWC, 1991), much higher than the IWC's 1977 estimate of 800–1,600 animals.

In addition, an estimate of the need for bowhead whales in the nine whaling villages was made by Braund *et al.* (1988), who compared the number of landed whales with village populations between 1910 and 1969, and used present populations for the villages to extrapolate a current need of 41 whales per year. This unusual method for determining the harvest quota for a whale stock tackles the problem from the perspective of the whalers. If current need can be safely taken from the existing stock, it is not necessary to determine the maximum possible harvest. If subsistence need can be provided for, then there is no reason to hunt additional whales.

There are two drawbacks to this method of management, however. First, the need is calculated as an average. Since due to weather and ice conditions 41 whales cannot be landed in every year, the average harvest will be less than the average need. Second, the establishment of a quota also works as a target if the whalers feel that they need to catch the full number of whales to preserve the quota allocation for future years (Charlotte Brower, pers. comm., 1990).

The advantage of the need-based quota is that it ensures that the local people have the opportunity to harvest what they need. As long as the needed number of whales does not exceed the harvest level that the stock can sustain, this can be an effective management device.

The AEWC's success has been to apply the idea of management and regulation of subsistence hunting in a manner that is acceptable to the Eskimo whalers. While the quota itself is still unpopular, the idea of sound and responsible management has taken hold. AEWC Chairman Eddie Hopson stated:

> Man's first responsibility is his dominion over animals given by God. That means management, not wastefulness. Management agencies like the AEWC, the Alaska Department of Fish and Game, the National Marine Fisheries Service, the International Whaling Commission – they are all doing the job given to us by the Creator, so I do not object to them.[2]

Such appreciation of the legitimate role of management and regulation has been hard won in northern Alaska. It has only been achieved through the efforts of both managers and whalers to cooperate on the shared goals of preserving a healthy population of bowheads while allowing the Eskimos to harvest what they need.

The effectiveness of the AEWC's management relies primarily upon four things. First, the whalers themselves administer the management regime. With the exception of setting the quota, there is no outsider/insider conflict during the management process. Second, the quota attempts to reflect the communities' need for whales, ensuring that those needs will be provided for. Third, whaling is a communal activity with a strong traditional basis. The pressure to cooperate is much higher than when hunting other species. Fourth, the goals of the AEWC have always been clear, and the battle with an outside authority has helped the whalers form a cohesive group. By averting the threat to Eskimo culture, the AEWC proved its usefulness, earning the pride and respect of the whalers.

The main limitation of the AEWC is that it does not set the quotas itself and is not even directly a participant in the process of setting them. The final effectiveness of its management is subject to the actions of the IWC; not even the federal government can alter the bowhead quota (see Chapter 4, page 52). The AEWC has fulfilled the purpose for which it was established, and has provided far more effective management than any outside agency could have done. In the process, the AEWC proved the merits of cooperative management, leading the way for several regimes based on similar themes of involving hunters and managers in a cooperative effort.

The Eskimo Walrus Commission

For several thousand years, the aboriginal people of the Bering and Chukchi coasts have hunted the Pacific walrus (see Figure 7.3). The extent of their reliance was tragically demonstrated in the late 1800s when the commercial whalers, finding bowhead whales scarce, shot thousands of

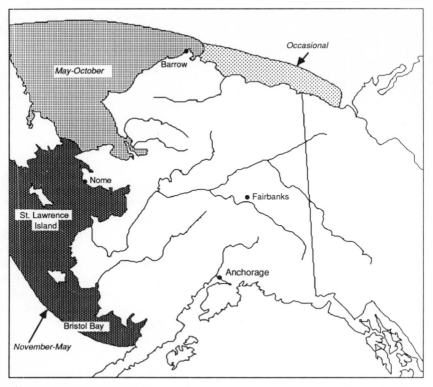

Figure 7.3 Map of the range of the Pacific walrus, *Odobenus rosmarus divergens*, in Alaska (NOAA, 1988)

walrus for their ivory. Without walrus to eat, 1,000 of the 1,500 residents of St. Lawrence Island perished in the winter of 1878–9 (Bockstoce, 1986: 139). Today, walrus provide villages in the Bering Strait region with up to three-quarters of their meat (Alaska Consultants Inc., with Stephen R. Braund & Associates, 1984). In Barrow, walrus account for as much as 11 percent of subsistence production (Stephen R. Braund & Associates and Institute of Social and Economic Research, 1989a).

Commercial harvesting of walrus was prohibited in Alaska waters by the federal government in 1909, and in 1937 the Department of Commerce banned non-Native walrus hunting (Sease and Chapman, 1988). In 1941 Congress followed suit in passing the Walrus Act, which also banned non-Native hunting of walrus. The law provided for no limit or other regulation of the hunt, although it did ban the export of raw ivory from the Territory of Alaska (Fay, 1957; Burns, 1965). This act was amended in 1956 to allow for the sale and export of walrus hides and for guided sport hunting by non-

Natives. Biologists working with walrus at this time saw the amendment as a positive step. Fay commented:

> This regulation was designed to help minimize waste and encourage bull hunting, for trophies and hides are both exclusive products of older males. It is expected that the particular group of Eskimos who practice ivory hunting will recognize the financial advantage provided them, for the income from guiding fees and sale of hides has a potential value greatly exceeding that of raw ivory. (1957: 440–441)

Kenyon observed that guiding would also keep hunters occupied with a client, not with pursuing walrus for themselves. From the first authorization of sports hunting until the end of 1959, only sixteen licenses were issued and only six animals taken by sport hunters.

It is hard to say whether walrus hunting would have gained in popularity under this system, for in 1960 the State of Alaska took over management of walrus, and, in addition to imposing hunting restrictions for the first time, permitted non-Natives to participate in the hunt (Burns, 1965). A bag limit was established, limiting the harvest of females and sub-adults to seven per year, while imposing no limit on the harvest of males. Females and sub-adults are preferred for food, and seven animals were deemed sufficient to avoid causing hardship (*ibid.*). In fact, the following year the number was reduced to five. Allowing unrestricted harvests on bulls ensured that no economic hardship would result, while minimizing the effect of the harvest on walrus population levels.

Despite concerns about head hunting and dire warnings of the imminent demise of the Pacific walrus in both the popular press and scientific journals (e.g., Buckley, 1958; *Geographical Magazine*, 1968), walrus populations increased steadily throughout this period. In 1972 the Marine Mammal Protection Act (MMPA) once again limited the harvest to Natives, again removing any limits on the harvest unless the species was shown to be depleted (see Chapter 4, pages 55–8). The introduction of limits by the State of Alaska in the 1960s had caused some conflicts with the Natives over closed seasons and inadequate harvest levels (Langdon, 1989). The return of unrestricted harvests may have pleased the Natives, but the U.S. Fish and Wildlife Service, which was given jurisdiction over walrus as well as over sea otter and polar bears, worked to return management to the state as soon as possible, an action provided for in the MMPA (*ibid.*: 157).

This transfer occurred in 1976. With it came a federally-imposed limit on the total harvest. To ensure that all communities would have an opportunity to harvest walrus within the total harvest limit, state regulations imposed limits on the total catch at each village. Although the limits imposed in some cases exceeded the averages of past harvests, they did not allow for the yearly fluctuations that occur in nearly all Native harvests. For example, Savoonga's quota was 450, while the ten-year average between 1964 and 1973 was 320.7. During that time however, the village had three times exceeded 450 animals per year, reaching a maximum of 543 (Bureau of Indian Affairs, 1977: 147). In addition, the allocated village quotas totalled 2,240 animals, while the statewide quota was 2,300. An additional 50 animals were reserved for the western Bristol Bay area, and 100 further permits were issued for non-traditional users (Alaska Department of Fish and Game, 1977: 108–14; 1978: 143). The system clearly did not provide a long-term solution for walrus management.

In response to this situation, and to reports in the press that head hunting was increasing, hunters from the villages of Gambell, Savoonga, Nome, Wales, Shishmaref, and Diomede gathered in 1978 to form the Eskimo Walrus Commission (EWC). Langdon notes:

> The EWC can be seen, in part, as an adaptation of the successful example of the Alaska Eskimo Whaling Commission (AEWC), formed the previous year, to walrus. Several founders of the EWC had participated in the formation of the AEWC and there is a substantial degree of overlap between the communities which harvest bowhead whale and walrus. (1989: 169)

> The EWC was reacting more to a potential threat than to an actual ban on walrus hunting. It is significant that the desire for responsible management and for clearing the Eskimos from the media charges of wasteful ivory hunting were among the motivating factors in the creation of the EWC (Langdon, 1984: 59).

Perhaps because of the lack of definite crisis in walrus management and harvesting – at this point the main population concern was that it might be too high – the EWC concentrated on establishing the baseline data needed for sound management of walrus stocks. In 1979, the federal government resumed management of walrus (see Chapter 4, page 57). Since this meant that once again there were no limits on the harvest and no regional quotas, the Eskimos had no need of short-term advocacy of walrus hunting and could take the longer-term view towards eliminating ivory hunting and promoting management based on sound biological information.

With a cooperative agreement enforced by no law or regulation (see Figure 7.4), the EWC relies on an annual appeal to the hunters, both by letter and by public service announcement in the local media (e.g., Qausagniq, 1990). This appeal stresses the dangers of adverse media publicity about walrus hunting, which might result in the re-establishment of a quota system for walrus or an amendment to the Marine Mammal Protection Act changing the Native exemption. Also, it reminds hunters that FWS agents will be conducting spot checks in the villages to ensure that the hunting is not wasteful (Tokeinna, 1987; Nageak, 1990). The FWS's annual enforcement plan outline states:

Agreements made several years ago between hunters and Fish and Wildlife

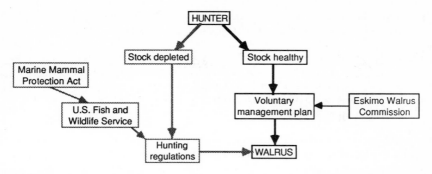

Figure 7.4 Schematic diagram of walrus management. The shaded portion (left side) takes effect only if the stock is determined to de depleted. Compare to polar bear management (Figure 7.9 page 133).

> Service Agents require the hunters to return with at least the heart, liver, flippers, . . . and some red meat of each walrus killed. . . . If only the ivory is brought back, the hunter could be cited into court, and would face seizure of the ivory. (U.S. Fish and Wildlife Service, 1990)

In addition to the threat of prosecution, the letters to the hunters conclude with an appeal to the long-term interests of the hunters, such as "Your cooperation will benefit all hunters in the future" (Tokeinna, 1987).

To the hunters, the primary perceived threat is from the portrayals of wasteful hunting that continue to appear in the media. *Newsweek* carried an article on June 5, 1989, entitled "Off with their heads." According to Walter Stieglitz, Regional Director of the FWS,

> this article focused on events which are the exception and not the rule. The situation as presented by the article inflicts an injustice upon those Native Alaskans exercising their right to legitimately take walrus as provided for by the Marine Mammal Protection Act. The picture painted by the article is distorted, inflammatory, and is counterproductive to cooperative management programs on which the U.S. Fish and Wildlife Service and the Native community have embarked upon in Alaska. (Stieglitz, 1989)

Such negative portrayals and further concern over ivory hunting in the wake of the ban on trade in elephant ivory have put the hunters on the defensive. Because walrus hunters are in a highly visible position, the EWC must continue to demonstrate its commitment to eliminating illegal ivory hunting while maintaining a viable, efficient subsistence harvest. For this, the cooperative plans mentioned by Stieglitz are essential.

The institutional commitment of the EWC, the Alaska Department of Fish and Game (ADF&G), and the FWS to cooperating to protect and understand walrus stocks is perhaps the best legacy of the EWC. In 1980 the Pacific Walrus Technical Committee was formed, with representation from the EWC, the FWS, and ADF&G. Its objectives are:

> to review and comment on all phases of research and management studies, and on the impacts of proposed resource development; to identify needs for studies; to facilitate the exchange of information and different viewpoints; and to recommend and review management strategies and regulations. (Pacific Walrus Technical Committee, 1988)

In practical terms the Technical Committee exists both as a meeting ground for the three groups, and as a distinct body dedicated to working on and solving the problems faced by all those concerned with the management of the Pacific walrus. The advantages of such a body are its cooperative nature and its ability to place collective benefits above the individual interests of the constituent groups.

In order to provide for cooperation in research and management, the FWS, ADF&G, and the EWC signed a Memorandum of Agreement in 1987 (U.S. Fish and Wildlife Service *et al.*, 1987). The essence of this approach is cooperative management. The success of the Cooperative Agreement between the National Oceanic and Atmospheric Administration (NOAA) and the AEWC had shown that sharing management authority with the hunters can lead to better management practice; by working together on areas of mutual concern and establishing an institutional means of settling differences, the FWS and the EWC should be able to achieve greater success than would be possible if one or the other had sole authority.

The Yukon-Kuskokwim Delta Goose Management Plan

Hunting of migratory birds in northern Alaska is an important part of the annual subsistence cycle. Ducks are often the first fresh meat caught in the spring. Sites where ducks migrate over narrow spits of land as they travel along the coast in the spring and fall, such as the one near Barrow known as Duck Camp or Piquniq (in the archaeological record as "Birnirk"), have been continuously used for centuries (Thompson and Person, 1963). Geese comprise over two percent of Barrow's total subsistence production, or 14 pounds of edible meat per household per year (Stephen R. Braund & Associates and Institute of Social and Economic Research, 1989a: 156).

The 1916 Migratory Bird Treaty with Canada (United States and Great Britain, 1916) and the subsequent Migratory Bird Treaty Act of 1918 (U.S. Congress, 1918b) prohibited hunting of most species of migratory birds between March 10 and September 1 of each year. Game regulations for the Territory of Alaska in 1925, the first year such regulations were issued, allowed hunting by Natives, explorers, prospectors, and travellers when in "absolute need" (Alaska Game Commission, 1925). In 1961 government wildlife agents began enforcing a strict definition of "absolute need" (Langdon, 1984; Thompson and Person, 1963). Following the arrest in Barrow of one hunter for illegally shooting a duck, nearly 150 residents presented themselves to the game warden, each carrying a duck and demanding to be arrested. Known as the "Barrow Duck-In," the incident led to tolerance of non-wasteful hunting (Blackman, 1989; Worl and Smythe, 1986) (see Chapter 2, page 28 and Chapter 3, page 42).

In the mid-1970s the State of Alaska attempted to stop the subsistence harvest of birds, successfully prosecuting a hunter in southwest Alaska in 1975 (Langdon, 1984: 54). Further enforcement efforts, including citations, led to confrontations between Native organizations and state Fish and Wildlife Protection agents. Langdon wrote in 1984:

> At present the State defers to Federal action, although they are unsatisfied with the policy of non-enforcement and their perception of Federal law. (*ibid.*)

While northern Alaska has been fairly quiet since the Barrow Duck-In, management efforts have been intensive in the Yukon-Kuskokwim Delta region of Alaska. That region is the major breeding ground for many species of waterfowl, including four species of geese which by the early 1980s had suffered drastic declines in population (see Figure 7.5). In the absence of management activities on the North Slope, I examine the cooperative efforts that led to the creation of the Yukon-Kuskokwim Delta Goose Management Plan in 1984.

In the late 1970s bird hunters from California, represented by the California Waterfowl Association (CWA), became concerned with declining populations of several species of geese (Charles Hunt, pers. comm., 1990). Fearing that hunting and taking of eggs on the breeding grounds – illegal under the treaty with Canada – was responsible for at least some of the decline, representatives of the CWA travelled to Bethel to ask Yup'ik hunters to refrain from hunting the geese. A trip for Yup'ik elders and leaders to the wintering grounds was arranged in 1978, allowing the Alaskan hunters to see what conditions were like in the south. A second visit in 1984 allowed the Alaska Natives to go hunting with the sportsmen. This allowed both parties to see the similarities in their hunting and to realize their common desire to protect the stocks for future hunting (Charles Hunt, pers. comm., 1990; Charles D.N. Brower, pers. comm., 1990).

In addition to the hunters from Alaska and California, government agencies were involved in the talks. The Alaska Department of Fish and Game (ADF&G), the California Department of Fish and Game, and the U.S. Fish and Wildlife Service (FWS) were all active in attempting to find a viable solution to the problem of declining goose populations. The initial stages of planning produced accusations and counter-accusations. Charles

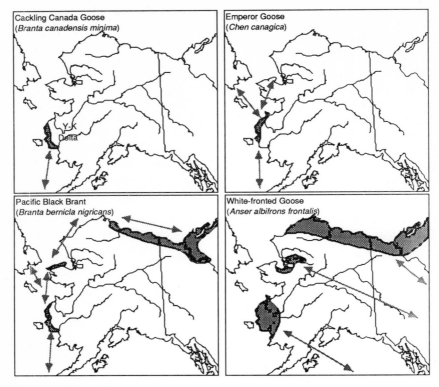

Figure 7.5 Summer range of the four species of geese included in the Yukon-Kuskokwim Delta Goose Management Plan, showing migratory routes and areas of major concentration (NOAA, 1988; U.S. Fish and Wildlife Service, 1988e)

Hunt, a Yup'ik employed as Native Liaison in Bethel by the FWS, was the translator during many of the village meetings. In a speech to a conference on subsistence sponsored by the Rural Alaska Community Action Program and the Alaska Federation of Natives, Hunt noted that "as interpreter, it wasn't easy to keep things tactful."[3] He pointed out that as a result of enforcement conflicts in the 1960s and 1970s, it is not easy for the Natives to overcome their mistrust of the government agencies, and vice versa.

Regardless of the initial relationship between the parties, the problem was becoming extreme. Populations of four species of geese had become critically low (see Table 7.1). In 1984 the parties involved signed the Hooper Bay Agreement, named after the village in the Yukon-Kuskokwim Delta where the meetings were held. This agreement called for reductions in the harvest of white-fronted geese and black brant and their eggs by both sport and subsistence hunters. For cackling Canada geese, hunting and egging were prohibited entirely (Langdon, 1984).

In 1985 the agreement was extended to include emperor geese and re-named the Yukon-Kuskokwim Delta Goose Management Plan (U.S. Fish and Wildlife Service *et al.*, 1985). A significant feature of the Goose Management Plan is the establishment of threshold populations for geese. Since these levels are stated in advance, and since the responses to populations above or below the threshold levels are known to all parties, there is no question about what will happen in response to changing populations. The population estimates used for this purpose are three-year averages, minimizing the effects of poor census conditions in a particular year. If a given population falls below its target level, all hunting and egging is prohibited, so that the effects of low populations affect all hunters together (see Figure 7.6).

Although the plan is named after the summering region of the geese, the Yukon-Kuskokwim Plan supports protection and acquisition of wintering habitat. The California Department of Fish and Game and the California Waterfowl Association, both signatories to the Yukon-Kuskokwim Plan, are involved in one such scheme, the Central Valley Habitat Joint Venture Implementation Plan. Participants in this plan include other hunters' organizations, conservation groups, and the U.S. Fish and Wildlife Service (National Audubon Society *et al.*, 1990).

Upon being informed of these efforts, Danny Karmun, an Iñupiaq elder from Nome, commented:

> I'm hearing something I've never heard before. Other states are having conser-vation measures imposed upon them. I'd always thought Alaska was singled out. I'm glad to hear that other states are working to protect the geese, too.[4]

Karmun's comment highlights an important aspect of the Yukon-Kuskokwim Plan. Unlike co-management plans for marine mammals, which involve only Native hunters and government agencies, the Goose Plan unites different types of hunters who, in fact, may have reason to feel that they are competing with one another for a limited resource. The essence of preserving such cooperation is sharing both the benefits and the costs of preserving the resource.

Table 7.1 Population levels of four species of geese in the Yukon-Kuskokwim Delta (U.S. Fish and Wildlife Service, [1989])

Species	1965	1975	1985	Management Plan threshold population
Black brant	170,000	130,000	144,800	120,000
Cackling Canada Goose	385,000	220,000	32,100	80,000
Emperor Goose	140,000 (in 1964)	(no data)	58,800	60,000
White-fronted goose	300,000	170,000	93,900	95,000

Cooperative management in northern Alaska

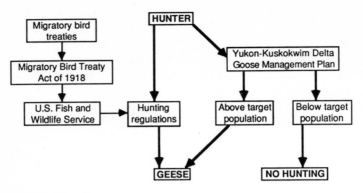

Figure 7.6 Schematic diagram showing the role of the Yukon-Kuskokwim Delta Goose Management Plan in goose management. Because the migratory bird treaties forbid hunting between March 10 and September 1, spring hunting is not legal under existing hunting regulations.

Karmun's comment also points out another obstacle to achieving cooperation and sound management. Although he is from Nome, outside the Yukon-Kuskokwim Delta region, and might not be familiar with the details of the plan, there are doubtless many hunters within the region who are unaware of the plan's provisions. Getting the word out to the villages is not an easy task, especially since many people have had bad experiences with wildlife management plans and agents in the past.

The FWS established a system of Refuge Information Technicians to go to the villages and spread the word about the plan. These people must be bilingual in English and Yup'ik, and they keep village residents informed about the plan and the population status of the four species of geese (Charles Hunt, pers. comm., 1990). A comprehensive education program has also helped emphasize the need for conservation of geese. This has been done through radio and television shows, booklets about geese and the Goose Management Plan in comic-book format, informative posters, pamphlets, and a calendar of contest-winning drawings by schoolchildren on the theme of goose conservation. Hunt (*ibid.*) stresses that:

> the most important and effective method is the village meetings in which Yup'ik Eskimos spoke face to face with officials of the U.S. Fish and Wildlife Service. For the past six years, we have had Yup'ik elders and leaders from the villages visit our [FWS] waterfowl biological camps where they observed for themselves how studies and research are accomplished on ducks and geese.

Since some Yup'ik hunters have expressed concern that the biological studies on the breeding grounds – especially those involving neck collars on geese – could themselves be the cause of the population declines,[5] these visits can go a long way to producing better understanding between the hunters and the researchers.

Despite the successes of the Yukon-Kuskokwim Plan, management of migratory bird hunting in Alaska is still constrained by the Migratory Bird Treaty Act of 1918 (MBTA)(see Chapter 4, pages 49–52). In 1984 the Alaska Fish and Wildlife Conservation Fund filed suit against the FWS and the ADF&G, arguing that the Hooper Bay Agreement allowed Natives to hunt in illegal violation of the MBTA. Though they were turned down in 1986, their argument was upheld on appeal in 1987. In the opinion to the case, Judge Otto Skopil wrote:

> A decision not to enforce a law is generally committed to an agency's absolute discretion. However, an agency's failure to act is reviewable where the substantive statute has provided guidelines for the agency to follow in exercising its enforcement powers. . . . The Secretary of the Interior is authorized to issue regulations permitting subsistence hunting, but only to the extent that the regulations are in accord with all four [migratory bird] treaties. (*Alaska Fish and Wildlife Federation v. Dunkle*, 1987)

In other words, the FWS is not allowed to permit subsistence hunting in the spring.

FWS is, however, allowed discretion in how it enforces the law. According to a policy statement in the *Federal Register*, FWS policy "concentrates enforcement efforts on violations that have the most serious impacts on the resource and focuses special attention on four diminished populations of geese" (U.S. Fish and Wildlife Service, 1988c). While this allows the FWS to overlook most personal-use hunting of migratory birds (Jerald Stroebele, pers. comm., 1990), it still means that most subsistence hunting is technically illegal.

Strict enforcement will only antagonize the hunters yet again. Explicit tolerance of "illegal" hunting undermines the credibility of management regulations. Uhl and Uhl write, in regard to migratory bird hunting:

> The fact that international treaties are involved and are immutable has been the usual official response to concerned citizens seeking a legal spring open season. Practical subsistence living has therefore brought about a traditional disregard for the law that has over the years penetrated very deeply in the philosophy by which contemporary people live. This has affected both those who are subsistence people and those who are charged with managing different species. It is hoped that someone with Solomon-like wisdom might present a plan to resolve this unhealthy situation with equanimity. (1977: 66)

A long-term solution must certainly include a change in the treaty with Canada, which is the most restrictive of the four treaties governing migratory birds. An amendment permitting Native harvests was signed in Ottawa in 1979, but has not yet been ratified. For now, the Yukon-Kuskokwim Delta Goose Management Plan succeeds admirably in reconciling different parties and creating a cooperative means of protecting a shared resource.

The Alaska and Inuvialuit Beluga Whale Committee

When the International Whaling Commission (IWC) moved to stop bowhead whaling in Alaska in 1977, mobilizing the Eskimo whalers against the ban was relatively straightforward. There were nine whaling villages, the whaling captains were well known, and some of the villages already had whaling captains associations. There was also a definite need to act quickly to formulate a management plan and to establish the Alaska Eskimo Whaling Commission. For the beluga whale (see Figure 7.7) there is no such precipitating crisis. However, noting how the lack of both a management plan and of detailed scientific knowledge had exacerbated the crisis over bowhead whaling, the North Slope Borough Department of Wildlife Management moved in December 1987 to create an Alaska beluga whale committee, following the example of the AEWC. In a letter to potential participants, Director Benjamin Nageak wrote:

> The bowhead whale controversy and the response of the Alaska Eskimo Whaling Commission (AEWC) to this threat to the bowhead subsistence hunt provide two very good lessons about wildlife management: 1) a lack of information can lead to a serious problem, and 2) a local user group *can* effectively participate in the management of a marine mammal species. . . .
> In view of the bowhead whale "example," it would be wise to initiate an effective cooperative management program for belukha whales before a crisis develops. (Nageak, 1987)

The impetus for the formation of the beluga whale committee was the desire to ensure that beluga stocks remained healthy and to forestall IWC involvement, or at least to minimize its impact on the subsistence hunt. Following the moratorium on commercial whaling that began in 1986, there was concern that the IWC might turn its attentions to small cetaceans. Nageak also noted:

> Some conservation groups are becoming concerned because of reports of large numbers of belukhas being entrapped by ice in Siberian waters,[6] declining numbers of belukha whales being seen in Kotzebue Sound, and because belukha whales are a popular animal among the general public. (*ibid.*)

The Alaska and Inuvialuit Beluga Whale Committee is the result of this concern. Although it is still in its formative stages – the management plan is in draft form and the committee is not yet well known in the hunting villages – the AIBWC is an example of applying the experiences of other cooperative management regimes to a species that has not been actively managed. Several of the members of the committee have had extensive

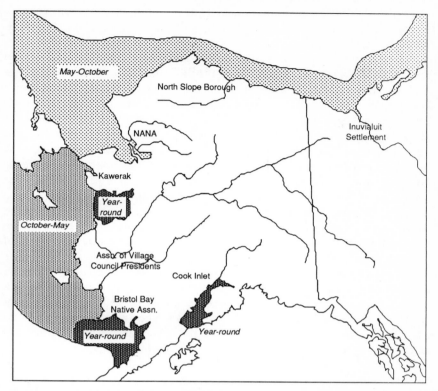

Figure 7.7 Range of beluga whales, *Delphinapterus leucas*, in Alaska, with areas of representation for the Alaska and Inuvialuit Beluga Whale Committee (NOAA, 1988; AIBWC, 1989a).

experience with the Alaska Eskimo Whaling Commission, the Eskimo Walrus Commission, and the Yukon-Kuskokwim Delta Goose Management Plan.

While the bowhead hunt takes place in only nine villages, the Alaska beluga harvest extends from Cook Inlet in the south of Alaska around the western and northern coasts to Kaktovik, near the border with Canada. The Bering Sea population of belugas appears to be divided into at least four stocks (Lowry *et al.*, 1989), one of which migrates to Canada each summer and is hunted by residents of the Mackenzie Delta in the Northwest Territories. Dozens of villages are involved in hunting belugas and there are several different hunting methods in use. Some of the hunts are not collective village efforts and so are difficult to monitor and record. It is believed that harvests declined by as much as 50 percent from the early 1960s to the mid-1970s as a result of replacing meat-eating dog teams with gasoline-powered snowmachines (Sergeant and Brodie, 1975; Seaman and

127

Burns, 1981). Although some beluga meat is sold in Native food stores in Anchorage and elsewhere, there is no significant market for beluga products outside the villages.

The first meeting of the Alaska Belukha Whale Committee was held in Fairbanks on March 4, 1988. (The name and spelling were changed at the next meeting to the Alaska and Inuvialuit Beluga Whale Committee.) Discussions focused on the need for management and research. John Burns, a biologist from Fairbanks, observed that although villagers are often reluctant to give out information in the belief that it may be used against them, the knowledge gained from that information is also necessary to promote the hunters' interests. Also, the committee could help facilitate the gathering and distribution of information so that the communities would know what is being done with information they provide (Alaska Belukha Whale Committee, 1988). Formulating the objectives of the committee was postponed until the following meeting, so that the village representatives could consult the hunters to determine what the goals of the committee should be.

The AIBWC by-laws were adopted in March 1989. They stress the need to "facilitate and promote wise conservation, management, and utilization of beluga whales based on the best available information and socio-economic considerations" (AIBWC, 1989b). The by-laws state that the purposes of the committee also include gathering harvest data, promoting research, improving hunting proficiency, developing a management plan, and initiating or continuing other activities to enhance the understanding of belugas and their use. Unlike any other such committee, the AIBWC includes government representatives from the National Marine Fisheries Service, the Alaska Department of Fish and Game, and the Fisheries Joint Management Committee in Canada. The hunting communities are represented regionally by hunter representatives, local government, or other institutions involved in management – North Slope Borough, Northwest Arctic Native Association, Kawerak, Association of Village Council Presidents, Bristol Bay Native Association, Cook Inlet, and the Inuvialuit Settlement Region of the Northwest Territories (AIBWC, 1989a) (see Figure 7.7). To ensure that regulatory control rests with the hunters the by-laws state that "Only representatives of beluga-hunting communities shall vote on matters relating to hunting" (AIBWC, 1989b).

The next stage is to develop a management plan for belugas in Alaska. The Fisheries Joint Management Committee, a co-management body in Inuvik, Northwest Territories, comprised of the Canadian federal government and the local hunters, has drafted a management plan for the Canadian harvest. To ensure that overharvesting would not endanger the future health of the beluga population, the Canadian plan establishes a total allowable catch, equal to 5 percent of the population (AIBWC, 1989a). The difficulty comes in estimating the population and in determining reproductive rates and natural and harvest mortality levels. Although the Canadians are very concerned with the lack of harvest limits in Alaska, since the same stock is hunted in both countries, the draft management plan of the AIBWC concentrates on harvest efficiency and utilization of animals that are taken – in other words, preventing loss and waste.

In Alaska there are four common techniques for hunting belugas: they may be shot or harpooned from the ice edge in the spring, hunted from boats, netted, or herded into shallow water where they cannot escape and can be easily shot. The management plan of the AIBWC concentrates on ensuring that adequate gear to recover the animals is used, that hunters make sure to take only what they need, and that they can properly take care of the meat and maktaak (skin and blubber) from the animals that are caught (AIBWC, 1990). Geoff Carroll, then a biologist for the North Slope Borough, noted at the March 1989 meeting that taking only the maktaak and leaving the meat, which often occurs, is a big concern at the IWC. The management plan has as another goal that "Belugas shall be used as fully as possible in a non-wasteful manner" (AIBWC, 1990).

Getting word out to the hunters, both about the AIBWC and about the need for research and management, is a problem that has yet to be resolved. A newsletter describing the AIBWC and the management plan has been distributed to post office boxholders in the hunting villages. Drawing on the experiences of other co-management groups, several suggestions have been made, such as preparing a video presentation or a comic book similar to those used in the Yukon-Kuskokwim Delta Goose Management Plan (AIBWC, 1989c). Funding and staff are not available at present to produce such products.

Meetings of the AIBWC are funded by the Bureau of Indian Affairs, the North Slope Borough, and the government agencies that belong to the committee. While the Marine Mammal Commission and the National Marine Fisheries Service support the idea of the committee and NMFS sends a representative to the meetings, they have no money available to help finance its activities (AIBWC, 1988). It is clear that beluga whale management is not a priority of any federal agency at this time. Studies have been done in connection with oil and gas exploration on the outer continental shelf, but these concentrate on the natural history of the belugas and potential impacts of industrial activity (e.g., Frost *et al.*, 1983; Stewart *et al.*, 1983; Hazard, 1988).

In summary, the Alaska and Inuvialuit Beluga Whale Committee, initiated by the North Slope Borough Department of Wildlife Management, is working on developing a management plan for the beluga whale. The committee fills a gap in the management of marine mammals in Alaska (see Hazard, 1988): it provides the ability to monitor harvests, to help improve hunting efficiency and harvest utilization, and to promote research on the beluga whale. Already, the committee has obtained the

Cooperative management in northern Alaska

best beluga harvest data ever for Alaska (Kathy Frost, pers. comm., 1990). The degree of local involvement is critical to the success of the AIBWC, but because its members also include representatives of government agencies the AIBWC promises to facilitate cooperation between hunters, managers, and researchers. The challenges for the committee will be communicating with the hunters and developing and instituting the management plan.

The management agreement for polar bears in the southern Beaufort Sea

Although polar bears have provided only a minor material role in Inuit culture, they hold a dominant place in imagination and folklore (Randa, 1986). Polar bears are also prominent in the public imagination, as symbols of the wilds of the Arctic. It is hardly surprising that polar bears have been the subject of considerable international attention, including the first multilateral agreement between the five circumpolar nations (Fikkan, 1990).

Although there was some commercial take of polar bears during the commercial whaling era in Alaska, until the 1940s the harvest was primarily by Natives for subsistence. In the late 1940s guided sport hunting from aircraft started (Amstrup and DeMaster, 1988), and increased substantially in the 1950s and 1960s. In Alaska the hunt centered in Kotzebue, the self-proclaimed "Polar Bear Capital of the World." The Alaska take of bears between 1961 and 1972 averaged 260 (*ibid.*: 47). In Canada, the annual kill peaked in 1967 at 726, the year before quotas were introduced (Urquhart and Schweinsburg, 1984). In 1969, an estimated 1,300 polar bears were taken worldwide, at a time when the world population was estimated at 10,000 (Fikkan, 1990).

The resulting concern about polar bear populations led to the International Agreement on Conservation of Polar Bears and Their Habitat, signed in 1973 by Canada, Denmark (Greenland), Norway, the Soviet Union, and the United States. Fikkan (1990) observes that the political climate at the time was conducive to a non-military, circumpolar accord. It was nonetheless the "first international agreement based on ecological principles" (*ibid.*: 32). Stirling comments:

> from a biological standpoint . . . the agreement is remarkably sound scientifically; it is not simply a protectionist document contributing solely to the welfare of bears and of little substance to related environmental issues. (1986: 167)

In Alaska, however, hunting regulations for polar bears had already taken a different tack.

In 1971 the State of Alaska limited residents to taking three polar bears each per year, and offered a limited number of permits for sport hunting. On June 30, 1972, the State ended aerial hunting of polar bears, promoting instead hunting by snowmachine and dog team, guided by Native hunters (Lentfer, 1976). This was superseded on December 18 of that year by the signing of the Marine Mammal Protection Act (MMPA), limiting the take of polar bears to Native subsistence hunters and forbidding the sale of polar bear hides. This led to a sharp decline in the annual kill of polar bears in Alaska, although the·actual harvest figures are unknown since there was no requirement to report the harvest (Amstrup, 1984; DeMaster, 1980). However, since there is no hunting regulation at all for Natives and thus no regulatory protection of females and cubs, current U.S. management practice is not in accordance with the recommendations of the International Polar Bear Specialist Group established under the International Polar Bear Agreement (Lentfer, 1974, 1976: 55; Amstrup and DeMaster, 1988: 50) (see Chapter 4, page 53–4).

The southern Beaufort Sea population of polar bears (see Figure 7.8), numbering around 2,000 (Treseder and Carpenter, 1989), ranges between Wainwright, Alaska, and Paulatuk, Northwest Territories, and thus is managed under two different systems. In the Northwest Territories quotas were started in 1968 and are assigned on a village-by-village basis, currently administered in the Beaufort Sea by local hunters and trappers associations and local game councils established under the Inuvialuit Final Agreement. Out of a total quota of 617 bears for the Northwest Territories in 1988 (Northwest Territories Department of Renewable Resources, 1990), approximately 38 are allocated from the shared population (Inuvialuit Game Council and North Slope Borough Fish and Game Management Committee [IGC-NSB], 1988).[7] Since sustainable harvest levels are determined by the number of females in a population, the Northwest Territories Polar Bear Management Plan seeks to reduce the harvest of female bears (Northwest Territories Department of Renewable Resources, 1990).

While the southern Beaufort Sea population is believed to be fairly stable (Amstrup and DeMaster, 1988: 44), it is also believed that the annual take of females is near the maximum that can be sustained (IGC-NSB, 1988). Although the average reported take of southern Beaufort bears in Alaska averaged 34, the Inuvialuit Game Council (IGC) of Inuvik, Northwest Territories, feared that the lack of regulation on the Alaska side of the border might jeopardize management efforts in Canada. To express these concerns, the IGC initiated talks with the North Slope Borough Fish and Game Management Committee in 1985 (Treseder and Carpenter, 1989). In September 1986 the latter passed a resolution that Alaska hunters should not shoot cubs or females with young (Amstrup and DeMaster, 1988).

On January 29, 1988, representatives of the two bodies signed an agreement entitled "Polar Bear Management in the Southern Beaufort

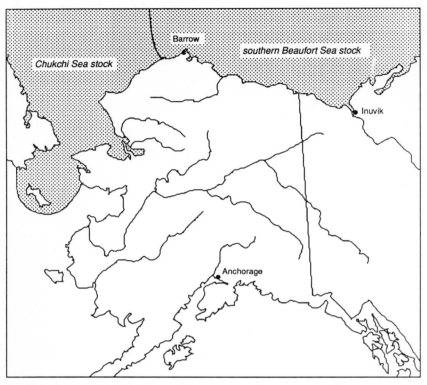

Figure 7.8 Range of polar bear, *Ursus maritimus*, in Alaska, showing division of stocks (NOAA, 1988; IGC-NSB, 1988)

Sea" (see Figure 7.9). Objectives of the agreement include the following:

to maximize protection for female bears,
to manage bears on a sustainable yield basis,
to minimize habitat disruption, and
to encourage collection of management-related information.

To publicize the agreement and its objectives, the North Slope Borough and the Inuvialuit Game Council have broadcast radio messages and printed and distributed glossy posters with a picture of a bear and the words "A resource to share; a gift to our children." In the reporting year from July 1, 1988, to June 30, 1989, 58 bears were taken in the southern Beaufort Sea by Alaska hunters, well in excess of the target of 38.[8] During the spring of 1990, however, hunters in Barrow were aware of the number that had been taken and the number in the guidelines (author's observations).[9]

In October 1988 the U.S. Fish and Wildlife Service (FWS) issued

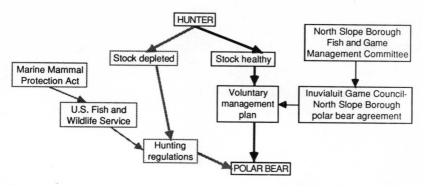

Figure 7.9 Schematic diagram of polar bear management in the southern Beaufort Sea. The shaded portion (to left) takes effect only if the stock is determined to be depleted. Compare to walrus management (Figure 7.4, page 119).

regulations requiring that all polar bear kills must be reported and that all hides and skulls must be tagged. This will help keep track of the numbers and sex ratios of bears killed in the entire state, since the NSB-IGC agreement covers only the western half of the North Slope.

While the agreement has no legal authority, and so constitutes only a guideline or recommendation for North Slope residents, it is nonetheless a means of promoting the values of wise use and sound management. Since it was initiated at the local level by representatives of the hunters themselves, the agreement is an appeal to local interests and customs, not an imposition from an outside authority. The U.S. FWS gave the North Slope Borough its highest award, the Director's "Outstanding Contribution Award," for the polar bear agreement. The agreement is only beginning to be well known in Alaska, and so it is difficult to say how well it will work. With the growing success of cooperative management practices in northern Alaska, however, FWS's optimism appears to be well founded.

Cooperative management of caribou

The first five organizations discussed in this chapter developed at least in part as responses either to a lack of active governmental management (the AIBWC and the polar bear agreement), or to a threat to traditional use of a resource (the AEWC, the EWC, and the Goose Management Plan). Now I consider the possibilities of cooperative management for a species for which there is active governmental management, and for which continued traditional use is not directly threatened.

Caribou provide the major food source for the Kutchin Athabascan

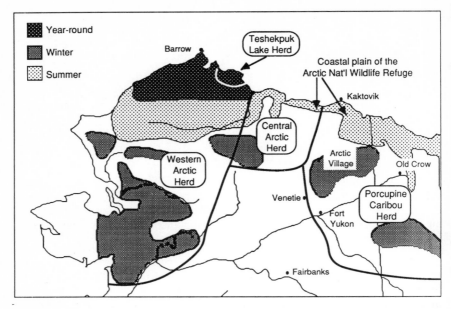

Figure 7.10 Range of caribou, *Rangifer tarandus*, in northern Alaska, with approximate ranges of individual herds. Villages dependent on the Porcupine Caribou Herd are shown as is the location of the coastal plain of the Arctic National Wildlife Refuge (NOAA, 1988).

villages of Arctic Village, Fort Yukon, and Venetie in Alaska, and Old Crow in the Yukon Territory. They are also a significant part of the subsistence production of the Iñupiat village of Kaktovik, Alaska (Langdon, 1984; Alaska Consultants, Inc., with Stephen R. Braund, 1984). These villages all lie within the range of the Porcupine Caribou Herd (PCH). Since the late 1970s, proposals to develop the coastal plain of the Arctic National Wildlife Refuge in northeast Alaska, primary calving grounds of the PCH, have caused much concern among traditional users of the caribou (see Figure 7.10).

Various lobbying efforts attempted to induce the governments of Canada and the United States to sign a treaty providing for joint protection of the PCH's habitat in Alaska and Canada. These efforts were delayed due to the opposition of the State of Alaska and the Yukon Government to federal actions that would encroach upon their authority as managers of caribou (Langdon, 1984: 65–6). In 1982, while efforts at the federal and state/territorial levels were still at a standstill, Natives on both sides of the border formed the International Porcupine Caribou Commission (IPCC), with the primary objective of getting an international treaty signed (*ibid*.: 67).

While these efforts were underway, some of the affected villages decided to take matters into their own hands. The village council of Arctic Village adopted rules limiting residents to five caribou per person and specifying how the meat was to be cared for. Pedersen and Caulfield write:

> Preliminary reports indicate that village councilmembers have taken it upon themselves to enforce these rules on several occasions.
>
> In general it appears that village discussions pertaining to the enactment of an international convention on migratory caribou has had a positive spin-off in terms of educating local residents about the broad range of factors influencing the Porcupine herd – including the effects of habitat modification and human harvest. (1981: 8)

Despite being a unilateral move by one village, these rules were nonetheless an example of culturally appropriate user management, arising from concern about the future of a valuable resource (Langdon, 1984: 69–70).

In Canada in 1985 the Porcupine Caribou Management Agreement was signed by the governments of Canada, the Yukon Territory, and the Northwest Territories, and by the Council for Yukon Indians, the Inuvialuit Game Council, and the Dene Nation and Métis Association of the Northwest Territories. The objectives of this agreement were to coordinate management of the herd within Canada to provide for the needs of Native users, to improve communications between the interested parties, and to provide for Native participation in management of the PCH. The agreement also established the Porcupine Caribou Management Board, with representatives from each of the signatories, to carry out the mandate of the agreement. To date the Board has been involved in many activities, including efforts to educate users and to promote international coordination (Porcupine Caribou Management Board, 1989a). It has also produced a detailed Interim Management Plan for the PCH extending from 1989 to 1993 (Porcupine Caribou Management Board, 1989b).

In 1987 the governments of the United States and Canada signed an agreement on the conservation of the PCH (see Chapter 4, page 54). Among the objectives of the treaty are:

> To ensure opportunities for customary and traditional uses of the Porcupine Caribou Herd [by traditional users as defined in each country]; [and]
> To enable users of Porcupine Caribou to participate in the international coordination of the conservation of the Porcupine Caribou Herd and its habitat. (in Porcupine Caribou Management Board, 1989a)

The agreement establishes the International Porcupine Caribou Board to carry out the terms of the treaty. It is too early to determine what effect this will have on the management of the caribou herd in Alaska, since the Alaska Department of Fish and Game (ADF&G) retains control over hunting regulations and habitat preservation is a long-term project.

To date, cooperative efforts concerning the PCH have centered on habitat preservation and coordination between different management authorities. Since the concern over habitat disruption began in the 1970s, the population of the PCH has been increasing (Urquhart, 1983). Management during a population crisis, however, is a different matter. In Alaska, with no cooperative management of terrestrial mammals, one can only ask how cooperative management might have helped during, for example, the apparent crash of the Western Arctic Herd in the 1970s. The apparent crash in the late 1970s of the Beverly and Kaminuriak caribou herds of the Northwest Territories, Saskatchewan, and Manitoba led to the formation of a cooperative regime for those herds. This regime is worth examining for the insight it gives to management on the North Slope of Alaska.

The Beverly and Kaminuriak caribou herds range across the barrens of the southern part of the District of Keewatin, Northwest Territories, and into the northern parts of the provinces of Saskatchewan and Manitoba. Between 1968 and 1980 the population estimate for the Kaminuriak herd had declined from 70,000 to 39,000. Between 1974 and 1980 the Beverly herd had gone from 170,000 animals to 94,000 (*Caribou News*, 1982b; 1985;1986).[10] Also, the herd was no longer seen in parts of its range, including northern Manitoba (*Caribou News*, 1981). The Caribou Management Group, representing the governments of Canada, the Northwest Territories, Manitoba, and Saskatchewan, realized it could not manage the herds effectively by itself. Failure to reverse the population decline would have been a political disaster, so there was considerable pressure on the governments to find an effective means of managing the herds (Don Gordon, pers. comm., 1991). To achieve this, the Caribou Management Group was replaced by the Beverly and Kaminuriak Caribou Management Board, with eight Native user representatives and five government representatives (Osherenko, 1988; *Caribou News*, 1985).

Some organizations viewed this with misgivings for opposing reasons. The Keewatin Wildlife Federation, comprised of the presidents of the local hunters and trappers associations, had reservations about whether the board would do all they wanted it to do. The Canadian Wildlife Federation, a conservation organization, felt that the Natives shouldn't be given management responsibility, but did not specify whether this was because of inability or conflict of interest (*Caribou News*, 1982a). Breaking down the barriers of mistrust and suspicion was the first step towards effective management (Don Gordon, pers. comm., 1991).

In any event, the Caribou Management Board directed its attentions to developing a comprehensive management plan for each herd, as well as an education program, an information program, and other related activities to enhance management and understanding of the caribou herds by all concerned parties (*Caribou News*, 1985). Increases in the population estimates of both herds, in part because of better census methods, have given the

Board time to develop its management plans without the pressure of a crisis. Under the new regime, harvest reporting has increased dramatically (Osherenko, 1988). A measure of the acceptance of the new regime can be seen in a 1984 survey conducted in Eskimo Point, Northwest Territories, one of the villages in the region. Gordon (1985) found that while three-quarters of the people surveyed had heard of the board and slightly less than half knew its goals and activities, 85 percent of respondents supported either the concept of management or a management body.

Although the Board has only advisory power, the governments have followed its advice on species management issues. The board has been successful in proving to government agencies that involving users can facilitate management by allowing for direct input and by increasing the likelihood of acceptance by hunters, while users have been shown that cooperation can yield positive returns (*Caribou News*, 1985).

Given the contentious nature of management in Alaska, a new Native or local-hunter board seems unlikely to gain much authority. But there is certainly room for cooperation. ADF&G's "Western Arctic Caribou Herd strategic management plan," written in 1984, states:

> The reported harvest from the WAH [Western Arctic Herd] has always been a small fraction of the actual harvest, and the failure of rural residents to report their take is in part due to a lack of understanding of hunting regulations and reasons for the reporting requirement.
>
> . . . The success of these [management] efforts will, to a large extent, depend upon the Department's ability to develop and improve communications with rural residents and leaders in northern and western Alaska. (Alaska Department of Fish and Game, 1984)

Institutional involvement of rural residents has been a cornerstone of the success of Canadian efforts at cooperative management of caribou and of other cooperative efforts in Alaska. The institutions already exist in the form of local advisory committees and regional councils under the ADF&G Division of Boards. Imaginative use of those bodies might help to achieve the goals of education and understanding between all those concerned with caribou management.

Conclusions

Osherenko (1988) found four criteria for successful cooperative management:

1 The regime must have strong support from and a link to the villages.
2 Public authorities must grant indigenous users a decision-making role in shaping and operating the regime from research design to enforcement.

3 Governments must provide adequate funding for the regime.
4 Cultural and linguistic barriers to Native user participation must be removed.

For a cooperative regime to be necessary and respected, it also needs a definite goal towards which both parties can work. In the case of the AEWC, that goal is meeting the quota while trying to get better scientific information with which to argue for an increase in the quota. For the Yukon-Kuskokwim Delta Goose Management Plan, population goals have been established for the four species of geese. With an explicit and objective target (despite the vagaries of census data) and known responses to population levels above or below the targets, participants in the agreement can work toward increasing the numbers of geese.

These two examples suggest another feature of successful regimes – reaction to a crisis (see also Pinkerton, 1989). While establishing procedures and regulatory systems before a crisis develops would be good, it is hard to get and keep the attention of people without a source of strong external pressure. While Eskimo whalers may have had concerns about excessive numbers taken in the 1970s, it took the IWC action in 1978 to precipitate the formation of the AEWC. The Beverly and Kaminuriak Caribou Management Board was established when the government-only group could not deal effectively with the population crisis in 1980. The AIBWC and EWC have not managed to establish themselves so forcefully, largely because they have not had a crisis to spur their members and constituents into action.

Osherenko's criteria are useful for understanding the workings of an existing regime. In a broader context, other factors are necessary, too:

1. *The regime must be legal.* Court challenges have been made concerning whaling, walrus regulation, goose hunting provisions, as well as the operation of regulatory bodies such as the Alaska Board of Game. Since such challenges seem almost inevitable in controversial issues, regimes must be prepared to withstand close legal scrutiny.
2. *The regime must be ecologically relevant.* While the need of the users is important, the long-term health of the stock must be the first priority. Conversely, harvest restrictions that have no ecological reason behind them should be avoided. Although difficult to quantify, ecological concerns are a place of common ground for all parties involved in hunting and management and form a sound basis for establishing common goals.
3. *The regime should have explicit goals and predictable responses to population and other changes.* The Y-K Delta Plan and the Beverly-Kaminuriak caribou management plan have populations targets, and the former has its responses established in advance. While censuses of other animals may be too imprecise for setting numerical goals, consistent principles should be established, unlike the early years of the

bowhead quota when the biological basis for the quota varied from year to year.

4. *There must be a clear understanding of the limitations of the regime.* The AEWC has limited direct enforcement and thus had to expel a captain and let the government prosecute him for hunting over the quota. The polar bear agreement has no legal authority in Alaska and can only establish hunting guidelines. Without a clear understanding of the limitations of the regime, such issues as these could cause frustration and distrust because it would be difficult to resolve problems to the satisfaction of all concerned parties. If the limitations are understood, problems outside the scope of the regime can be recognized and alternative means of resolution can be sought.

These criteria are similar to those needed in government management regimes, although the degree of cooperation required is by definition greater in cooperative management regimes. Cooperative regimes have shown themselves on the whole better able to provide effective management of subsistence hunting. In part this is because they are usually oriented to a specific problem and can focus closely on that. Also, cooperative regimes are able to take into account local concerns and can adapt themselves to accommodate the needs of subsistence hunters better than established government management regimes.

Notes

1. Letter from Anthony J. Calio, NOAA, to Lennie Lane, Chairman, AEWC, June 28, 1985.
2. At the AEWC Whaling Captains' convention, Barrow, Alaska, February 27, 1990.
3. Conference held in Anchorage, Alaska, October 16–17, 1989.
4. North American Waterfowl Management Plan meeting, Barrow, Alaska, June 11–12, 1990.
5. e.g., Paul Gregory speaking at the Rural Alaska Community Action Program and Alaska Federation of Natives subsistence conference, Anchorage, Alaska, October 16–17, 1989.
6. Although ice entrapments of small numbers of beluga whales happen occasionally (Hill, 1968), between December 1984 and February 1985, some 2,500 to 3,000 belugas were reported trapped in the ice of Senjavin Strait near Arakamchechen Island. Although ice breakers reportedly freed most of the whales, 506 were taken for subsistence purposes and a further 500 were believed to have died (Armstrong, 1985; Ivashin and Shevlagin, 1987). Out of a total estimated Bering Sea population of 13,500 to 18,000 (Lowry, *et al.*, 1989), this entrapment understandably caused great concern.
7. The village of Paulatuk has a quota of 17, six of which are estimated to come from the southern Beaufort Sea population.
8. Scott Schliebe, U.S. Fish and Wildlife Service, presentation to the North Slope Borough Fish and Game Management Committee, Barrow, Alaska, January 25, 1990.
9. According to Lloyd Lowry, Marine Mammals Coordinator for the Alaska Department of Fish and Game, the Canadians had not expected instant adherence by the Alaska

hunters, since their own system had not won instant acceptance either (pers. comm., 1990).

10. Subsequent dramatic increases in numbers for each herd – including a five-fold increase for the Kaminuriak herd between 1980 and 1982 – make it likely that census data was greatly in error (Freeman, 1989; *Caribou News*, 1982c).

8

Conclusions

The last four chapters have examined federal, state, local, and cooperative regimes, noting the interconnections between them and drawing specific conclusions from examples of each class of regime. In this chapter I create a comprehensive list of criteria that facilitate successful interaction between a management regime and local subsistence hunters. As stated in Chapter 1, this study has focused on only that aspect of resource management. The criteria are aimed at improving the ability of management regimes to satisfy the two goals of effective management that I have proposed for this sector: protecting animal stocks and allowing local people to provide for their needs.

The criteria describe the interaction of the management regime and the local hunters. This interaction is expressed in two forms: First, in the provisions of the management regime – such as hunting regulations or research priorities – that involve local hunters or the animals they hunt. Second, in the actual contact between managers and hunters, such as local advisory councils or public meetings and hearings. Each criterion may apply to both types of interaction, and I will not try to separate them in this discussion. It is important to remember that the criteria apply to the interaction between management regimes and local hunters. In this way, the criteria can be used to analyze the roles of management regimes with different goals, different structures, and different responsibilities.

The relative importance of each criterion may vary widely depending upon which regime is being examined. For example, facilitating successful interaction between the Alaska National Interest Lands Conservation Act of 1980 (ANILCA) and local subsistence hunters may depend more on promotion of local involvement and less on ecological relevance. The effectiveness of the Minerals Management Service (MMS) may depend less on local involvement and more on ecological relevance. In the former case, local residents need a means of involvement in the planning process for

Conclusions

land use mandated by ANILCA, while ecological considerations are more the responsibility of other regimes. In the latter case, local involvement in planning offshore development is not so important as making sure that MMS's decisions are based upon sound ecological considerations and will not adversely affect the marine environment. In both cases, the important thing is to identify how the regime–hunter interaction can be improved to facilitate effective management.

In assessing the effectiveness of various regimes in the terms that I have proposed, I have applied an absolute standard irrespective of other factors affecting the function of the regime. The function of a management regime is woven with many threads of interaction between the regime and its constraints and constituents. In order to develop an understanding of that particular aspect of management, I have separated one strand to see how it alone might be strengthened. Following this analysis, however, one faces the problem of how to put these ideas into practice. The other threads of interaction limit the extent to which a regime can concentrate on the one which attaches it to local subsistence hunters. In some regimes, subsistence is a minor consideration, while in others it is of primary importance. Three types of factors limit the ability to improve the effectiveness of the inter-action between a management regime and local subsistence hunters:

1. *Factors that are external to the regime and to the hunters.* These include characteristics of the resource being managed, constitutional and legal limits on the actions of the regime, the regime's mandate and its funding. These factors are beyond the direct control of either the regime or the hunters, but may profoundly constrain the ability of the regime to meet the demands local subsistence hunters place upon it. Legal challenges may result in changes to the last three factors listed, but the authority to make such changes rests with the courts, not with the management agency or the hunters.
2. *Factors that involve either the management regime or the hunters, but are external to the regime–hunter interaction.* These include subsistence demand by local hunters for the resource, and the demands of other interest groups on the regime. Depending on the extent of the subsis-tence demand and the share of the resouce that this involves, the former may complicate or simplify the task of management. Other interest groups include other hunters, conservationists, and developers. Having more interested groups quickly leads to conflicts of interest, and the relative political strength of each group will have a large impact on the action that the regime undertakes. The regime's mandate may be predicated to one group's interests, limiting its ability to provide for the other groups' demands.
3. *Factors that are internal to the regime–hunter interaction.* These include enforcement, orientation of relevant research, the means of gathering

and distributing information, and opportunities for local involvement in the regime's activities. These are the factors toward which this study has been directed. They are addressed by the criteria and are explored in detail below.

It is clear that the first and second types of factors will greatly limit the ability of a regime to address and improve the factors in the third category. While a regime might, by the absolute standards I have been using, have significant shortcomings, it is possible that it is in practice achieving the best result that it can with the limitations placed upon it. For example, management under the migratory bird treaties (see page 49) is fixed by the legal and constitutional constraints that control amendments to the treaties. This factor is external to the regime and to the hunters. Amending the treaties would affect many other interests than just the regime–hunter interaction. The fact that the proposed amendment to the treaty between the U.S. and Canada has yet to be ratified twelve years after it was signed suggests that such an amendment may not be politically feasible. From that perspective management under the migratory bird treaties may be as effective as is possible. From the perspective of the regime–hunter interaction, however, its effectiveness remains poor (see p. 146).

Although other factors may inhibit the ability of a regime to adapt to improve effectiveness in terms of the regime–hunter interaction, I do not mean to suggest that such changes in management strategy necessarily have an adverse impact on some other aspect of management. Improving one aspect of management reduces variability in the overall task of management by reducing the guesswork involved in making decisions about at least one aspect of management strategy. Changing the regulations concerning brown bear hunting to reflect Native needs may result in better reporting of the harvest, enabling managers to monitor populations more accurately, perhaps enhancing opportunities for sport hunters and for wildlife viewers. In other cases the gains to other interests may be negligible, but the losses may also be minimal. Amending individual bag limits to allow for sharing by successful hunters, providing harvest levels did not increase as a result, would have little effect on other users while greatly enhancing the ability of hunters to provide for the needs of their communities.

My analysis of the regime–hunter interaction is divided into three parts. First, I list and briefly discuss the eight criteria that I have developed. Second, I test their relevance by turning them back on ten of the regimes examined in this study. Collectively the criteria identify the strengths and weaknesses of the regimes and suggest areas of possible improvement. Finally, I use the criteria to analyze the effectiveness of current management of walrus, caribou, geese, polar bears, and bowhead whales. Since the local hunter is concerned primarily with the species he is hunting,

Conclusions

rather than with the regime under which the animal or land is managed, this approach rephrases the question from a perspective more relevant to the local hunter.

The criteria

The concluding sections of the four chapters on management regimes draw a number of points necessary for effective management. From these points I have established eight criteria for testing and analyzing regimes that manage local use of wildlife:

1. *The regime and its provisions must be legal.* This may seem unnecessary, but the number of lawsuits concerning wildlife issues is high. It is central to the regime–hunter relationship because legality directly defines the parameters of that interaction and because changes brought about by the courts undermine the dependability of the relationship and increase the uncertainty of provisions made by either hunters or managers. Nine of the regimes examined in this study have been subject to a lawsuit at least once. The effects of a decision can be profound, as with the *McDowell* decision in 1989 (see page 30). Not only must the regime itself be legal, but its actions must also satisfy close legal scrutiny. Actions of the Alaska Board of Game have been declared invalid in the cases *Bobby v. State* and *Kwethluk IRA Council v. State.* Unfortunately, the only certain way to test whether a regime or its actions are legal is to defend it successfully in court. Given the divisive nature of wildlife issues in Alaska, it is likely that many regimes or provisions will face that test, especially in the chaotic wake of the *McDowell* decision.
2. *The regime must be based on ecologically sound principles.* Ecological relevance is the strongest basis for wildlife management. It is also the point of common interest for hunters, managers, and others concerned with the health of game populations. Seasons and bag limits are but a means of achieving the biological aim of avoiding excessive harvests. Limited access on non-biological or culturally inappropriate grounds causes great frustration and dissatisfaction for hunters. Conversely, there is little point to a regime that does not concern itself with the long-term health of the animal stocks. While there are too few data for complex scientific management of most species used in northern Alaska, existing information should be used wherever possible.
3. *The regime must be culturally appropriate.* If the regime contains provisions that contradict certain patterns, customs, or beliefs in the local community, the regime will not be accepted and will have defeated out of hand the idea of effectiveness through providing for local needs. Not only must its regulations and management policies be appropriate, but

the decision-making process must also be consistent with local custom. For a regime to be effective and appropriate, it must be developed in an appropriate manner. Even if its provisions are sound, a regime that is imposed from the outside without local input in the development phase will not receive the support it needs to succeed.

4. *The regime must be flexible and predictable in its responses to changes in ecological and other conditions.* Conditions change, and regulations and management practices must change with them. If a population falls, hunting may have to be reduced until the stock recovers. Local hunting patterns or levels may change due to changes in resource availability. For a regime to be effective in providing for local uses, it must be flexible to accommodate changing conditions. It must also have predictable responses, like the Yukon-Kuskokwim Delta Goose Management Plan, so that all parties know what to expect when changes do occur. To allow for effective response, the regime must be capable of responding before a crisis occurs.

5. *The regime must be adaptable in its responses to local concerns and changes.* If there is particular local concern over the health of a certain animal stock, or over a related action such as the transplantation of muskoxen, the regime must respond to that concern. If changes in game distribution or populations mean that new areas must be used for hunting, or that animals must be hunted at a different time of year, then the regime must be flexible enough that local needs can still be satisfied.

6. *The regime must include local hunters in all phases of its activity, and it must avoid any cultural or linguistic barriers to such participation.* The entire idea of formal management regimes is alien to Native societies in Alaska. As long as such regimes remain an imposition from the outside, they will remain ineffective. To be successful, a regime must impart a sense of ownership through effective participation. Cultural and linguistic barriers must be removed so that Natives are fully included in the regime. Local hunters must be involved in all phases of the management process, from research to formulation and implemention of regulations. The process must also be oriented towards local issues, so that its relevance to local concerns enhances the sense of ownership.

7. *The regime must clearly define its role and its limitations.* Without a clear role, a regime can impart little sense of purpose, and can provide little evidence of its success. Without an awareness of its limitations, a regime will be unsure of the extent of its role, or of the potential with which it has to work. Without such clear definitions, the regime will suffer from uncertainty on the inside and confusion on the outside.

8. *The regime must have the ability to implement its provisions.* This need not be the legal power to enforce regulations. Since so many regulations and laws are widely ignored by residents of northern Alaska, legal authority would seem to have little relevance. Instead, this ability is a

Conclusions

combination of a sense of ownership in the regulatory provisions, a belief in the relevance of those provisions, and the desire to achieve goals that are shared by hunters and managers.

Analyzing the regimes

To test the usefulness of the eight criteria, I have used them to analyze the regimes that are examined in this study. Figure 8.1 compiles the results graphically for ten of the regimes, with an estimate of overall effectiveness for each one. They are listed in the order in which they are discussed in Chapters 4–7. This section discusses these ten regimes in detail and is an example of how I apply the criteria to different classes of regimes. The ten were chosen both for their relative importance in overall wildlife management in northern Alaska and for the light they shed on the issue of effectiveness. Some of the criteria are more relevant to certain regimes than others. This is particularly apparent when contrasting treaties or legislative acts with the agencies that must implement them.

1. *Migratory bird treaties.* Rigid, culturally inappropriate, and difficult to change, the migratory bird treaties – in particular the one with Canada – are among the least effective management regimes in northern Alaska. As Figure 8.1 shows, the treaties satisfy only two of the criteria. The only point in their favor is that they are not enforced, although that is due to the policy of the U.S. Fish and Wildlife Service and not to the treaties themselves. I include them here primarily because they are such a poor example of management strategy. This fact is recognized by most who have examined the issue, but unfortunately that recognition has not translated into ratification of the amendment necessary to legalize the spring hunt. In this case, the criterion of local participation is not as important in the treaty as it is in the implementing agency. The treaty could demand local participation in management planning, but it is far more important that the agency establishes an institutional commitment to local involvement. To allow for flexible responses to changes, and for adaptability to local conditions, treaties should concentrate on achieving stable populations rather than fixing rigid means such as closed seasons.

2. *Marine Mammal Protection Act of 1972.* This allows for unrestricted Native harvests of marine mammal stocks that are not depleted. Local hunters who are not Native are not allowed to hunt any marine mammal for any purpose, so the Act does not provide for the needs of those residents. For the Natives, the MMPA places no restrictions on their harvests, and so allows local hunters to satisfy their needs in a culturally appropriate way. While the stock remains healthy, this is

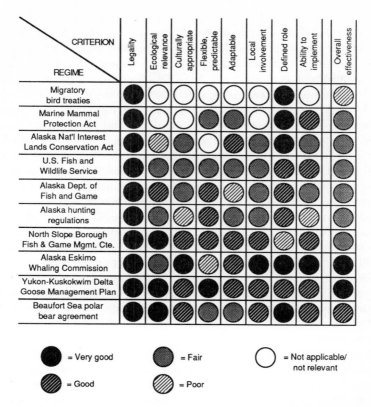

Figure 8.1 Analysis of ten management regimes in northern Alaska and the extent to which each satisfies the eight criteria. Overall effectiveness is judged separately, not as an average of the effectiveness of the criteria.

fine. Should the stock become depleted, the MMPA makes little provision for local participation in management and regulation. Also, the standard of "depleted stocks" as the management threshold makes response to population changes highly insensitive and unwieldy. Without local cooperation and participation in management, marine mammal populations could fluctuate dramatically. Once a species is declared depleted, the process for removing the animal from the list is likely to be difficult, especially since conservation groups are likely to fight to retain the species's protected status.

Thus, the MMPA is not particularly relevant to the ecology of marine mammals. With walrus in northern and western Alaska, and with sea otter on the southern coast, the MMPA has failed to resolve problems of appropriate use and sustainable harvests. While granting sole harvest rights to Native Alaskans has some merits, the failure to provide for any form of effective management is a significant drawback to the MMPA. Cooperative agreements can help to overcome that, but they have arisen primarily in response to the inability of the MMPA to direct the relevant federal agencies to provide effective management.

3. *The Alaska National Interest Lands Conservation Act of 1980.* ANILCA intended to resolve the issues of local wildlife use by creating a subsistence priority for rural residents and by ensuring that local residents participate in the formulation of regulations concerning hunting. This has had some success, but on the whole ANILCA has not fulfilled its promise. In part this is because the agencies responsible for implementing ANILCA have not carried out the intent of the Act. However, ANILCA itself contains some inherent problems with management. The system of advisory councils is culturally inappropriate in northern Alaska (see Chapter 5, page 87). Also, while the Act establishes such councils, it does not determine the way in which regulations will be created from such advice. The system is no more flexible and predictable in its responses than it was before ANILCA. To a certain extent, local participation is enhanced by the Act, but responsiveness to that participation is not improved. Although it responds to the need to preserve "traditional" patterns of society and culture, ANILCA has proved difficult to implement.

4. *U.S. Fish and Wildlife Service.* The FWS has responsibility for migratory birds, some marine mammals, the national wildlife refuge system, and, after *McDowell*, managing subsistence on federal lands. Its effectiveness varies with each of these, as does its ability to meet the eight criteria. The FWS's most successful effort so far is its participation in the Yukon-Kuskokwim Delta Goose Management Plan (see item 9 below). However, FWS management on its own has significant shortcomings. Between the MMPA, ANILCA, and the migratory bird treaties, the FWS is constrained on many sides. However, it is up to the FWS to ensure that its actions are culturally appropriate, that its regulations are flexible and predictable, and that it encourages a high level of local participation. It has yet to do so effectively. The FWS has not made the institutional effort to seek cooperation from the hunters and in return to give priority to the needs and concerns of the hunters.

5. *The Alaska Department of Fish and Game.* The various divisions of ADF&G attempt to fulfill different management criteria. The Division of Boards attempts to ensure that local participation is high and that local concerns are responded to in the regulatory process. The Division of Wildlife Conservation makes sure that harvest levels are not excessive and that the regulations are ecologically sound. To promote regulations which are appropriate to local conditions, the Division of Subsistence examines patterns of game use and the cultural

role of hunting. To a certain extent, these efforts succeed. However, success by one division does not necessarily translate into success by another division. For example, the existence of local advisory committees within the Division of Boards does not produce local participation in population research by the Division of Wildlife Conservation. Overall, ADF&G has not shown the institutional commitment to local hunters that is needed to gain the respect of those hunters. Individual managers may have succeeded in working effectively with local residents, but on the whole ADF&G's actions are often culturally inappropriate, and it has struggled to adapt to local conditions and concerns. Because of this, ADF&G has been unable to implement many of its programs, such as harvest reporting schemes.

6. *Alaska hunting regulations.* Schaeffer *et al.* (1986) found that overall the state's hunting regulations were inappropriate in northwest Alaska. Analysis using the eight criteria leads to the same conclusion for northern Alaska. Too many regulations – such as individual bag limits, closed seasons, limitations on use of game, and restrictions on treatment of game – are culturally inappropriate to the area. The regulations can change in response to changes in game populations and other natural factors, but it is difficult to predict what specific changes the Board of Game will make. The regulations are adapted with great difficulty to local patterns, conditions, and concerns in northern Alaska, so that cultural inappropriateness seems a permanent fixture of the system. Local participation is encouraged both by the local advisory committees and by individual proposals to the Board of Game, but this is only moderately successful in producing the desired changes in the regulations. The hunting regulations have a well-defined role, but they are poorly implemented because there is limited enforcement capability in northern Alaska. Without the cooperation of the hunters, there is little hope that the regulations will ever be implemented effectively.

7. *North Slope Borough Fish and Game Management Committee.* As a local body designed to fill the gap left by federal and state agencies, the FGMC should show the way to greater cultural awareness and more effective local participation. Unfortunately, this is overshadowed by the fact that the FGMC has a poorly defined role. The North Slope Borough's Department of Wildlife Management and Science Advisory Committee both are able to act at the direction of the local government and can advise and assist the FGMC. But the FGMC has yet to make the most of its potential. The agreement between the Inuvialuit Game Council and the FGMC concerning Beaufort Sea polar bears (item 10 below) is an example of what the FGMC can achieve. Although it has no authority to enforce such an agreement, community awareness of the importance and relevance of the agreement is likely

to lead to good compliance with the hunting guidelines. Without a sense of purpose, the FGMC will remain an ineffectual group meeting and discussing, but achieving little. With a mandate to participate fully in all levels of management, the FGMC could be a great asset to the cause of effective management in northern Alaska.

8. *The Alaska Eskimo Whaling Commission.* As the first co-management group in northern Alaska, the AEWC has provided inspiration for the move toward greater hunter involvement in management. Such inspiration has come mainly from the fact that the AEWC has been successful in achieving its goals of protecting whaling and, with the exception of setting the quota, keeping management activity within the whaling communities. Since it is regarded as an example of the potential of co-management, how does it match up to the eight criteria? Two failings stem from the problem of following the IWC's quota. First, the biological relevance of the quota is debatable. The quota is based now upon the historical need for whales within the whaling villages, not upon an estimate of the level of harvest the stock can sustain. Second, the regime is not flexible or predictable in its responses to changes in ecological conditions, simply because the AEWC has no authority to change the quota. A third weakness also reflects the limits of the AEWC's authority. The AEWC is willing to adapt itself to the extent of including other communities, such as Little Diomede Island, but the decision to allow whaling in other villages can only be made by the National Marine Fisheries Service. The AEWC satisfies the other five criteria.

9. *The Yukon-Kuskokwim Delta Goose Management Plan.* According to the criteria analysis, the Y-K Delta Plan has no weak spots. It is the only regime with population thresholds to determine management responses, so that all parties know in advance what the reaction will be should the population fall below or climb above that threshold. The primary goal of the plan is to ensure that the geese populations remain healthy, and so the plan is ecologically relevant and designed to benefit all users of geese. A substantial effort has been made to inform local residents about the plan and its goals and to involve local people in planning and designing both the features of the plan and the publicity promoting it. Some distrust still exists, with some hunters blaming the population crises on scientists working on the breeding grounds. However, the plan has succeeded in getting sport hunters from California and Native hunters from the Y-K Delta to cooperate. The fact that the plan allows for spring hunts of geese, in violation of the migratory bird treaty with Canada, led to a lawsuit filed by Alaska sport hunters claiming the plan was invalid. Although this was upheld by the court, the opinion stated that the FWS retains wide discretion in its enforcement and so can continue to ignore Native subsistence

harvests if it so chooses. Clearly it would be better if the treaty were amended, but within the limitations the treaty imposes the Y-K Delta Goose Management Plan has been very effective.

10. *The Inuvialuit Game Council–North Slope Borough Fish and Game Management Committee Management Agreement for Polar Bears.* Although the polar bear agreement has no enforcement authority in Alaska, it can be implemented because it makes sense to local hunters. It is based on biological grounds, originates from a local institution, and takes local concerns and customs into account. Compliance with the agreement may take time to achieve, but local hunters are well aware of the agreement and its goals. The agreement explicitly acknowledges its limitations in Alaska, since it has no authority to enforce or implement any of its provisions. Recognizing this removes any unrealistic expectations about its capacity to achieve its goals. In a sense this may seem counterproductive, but the failure to deliver what is promised has given local hunters poor impressions of many management regimes. The polar bear agreement has not existed long enough to judge it fully, but it has the potential to provide effective management of the Beaufort Sea harvest.

An analysis by species

Managers work through individual regimes, and changes to management practices or policies must come from those regimes. For the hunter, the unit of reference is not the regime but the animal he is hunting. A species may be subject to several regimes, and so the individual effectiveness of each regime may be different from the overall effectiveness of the management of a particular animal. Figure 8.2 uses the eight criteria to analyze the management of five animal species or types. They are listed in order of increasing effectiveness. This section discusses the application of the criteria to the overall management of a given animal.

1. *Walrus.* Under the Marine Mammal Protection Act, walrus hunting cannot be restricted unless the species is depleted. When the species is not depleted, as at present, the only limits on hunting are voluntary ones taken under the auspices of the Eskimo Walrus Commission. Unlike other animals of northern Alaska, walrus have considerable commercial value because of their ivory. The incentive exists to hunt for the ivory, taking numbers of walrus far in excess of the actual need for walrus meat and other locally used products. Effective walrus management must take this into account, and to date there has been little ability to implement restrictions on taking walrus only for ivory. The EWC has been successful in helping to reduce the take of female walrus, giving a

SPECIES \ CRITERION	Legality	Ecological relevance	Culturally appropriate	Flexible, predictable	Adaptable	Local involvement	Defined role	Ability to implement	Overall effectiveness
Walrus									
Caribou									
Geese									
Polar bears									
Bowhead whales									

Figure 8.2 Analysis of the management of five species or types of game, using the eight criteria.

biological basis to some of its management efforts. The EWC has also concentrated on providing culturally appropriate guidelines for hunting and use of walrus. The weakest point of walrus management is its implementation. While the cooperative agreement between the EWC and the U.S. Fish and Wildlife Service has succeeded in reducing the take of female walrus by 25 percent, both the incentive for and the fact of ivory hunting still exist. For walrus management to be truly effective, it must be able to limit the potential for destruction caused by illegal ivory hunting. Overall, walrus management is moderately effective, since at present local hunters can take what they need. If the population of walrus drops, this will change.

2. *Caribou.* Until the *McDowell* decision in 1989, management of caribou hunting was solely the responsibility of the Alaska Department of Fish and Game. Access to federal lands was and is controlled by the relevant federal agency, adding another layer of management to the system. After *McDowell*, subsistence hunting on federal lands is controlled by the Federal Subsistence Board, although the State of Alaska may try to regain management authority for all lands within the state. At present in northern Alaska, caribou populations are high, as are bag limits. Other restrictions on methods of capture and treatment of game are inappropriate and have not been adapted to reflect local conditions and concerns. The system is moderately flexible in regard to ecological changes and allows for some degree of local participation, although

both of these are difficult to implement effectively. Like regulations concerning geese, most regulations about caribou are widely ignored in northern Alaska at the moment. Overall the system is moderately effective, although in the event of another population crash it is difficult to predict what would happen. During the crash of the Western Arctic herd in the 1970s, the State was able to enforce the ban on hunting fairly effectively but at a cost of considerable frustration and distrust on the part of local residents.

In terms of land access, the most restrictive regulations are those of the National Park Service. The subsistence resource commissions are able to influence NPS policy to a certain extent, but the very idea of limiting access is inappropriate in a region where lands traditionally had no owners and were controlled only by the local villages. In terms of caribou, as a representative land animal, land management by different agencies is confusing at best, especially where boundaries are not marked and hunting areas have been traditionally used for far longer than federal agencies have been present. When coupled with different hunting regulations depending upon which agency's land the hunter is on, the overall system becomes far too unwieldy to be effective. The burden does not lie with the local hunter to figure out the details of the system, it lies with the managers to concentrate on the goals of management and to achieve them in the way that has the least impact on the local hunter.

3. *Geese*. The Yukon-Kuskokwim Delta Goose Management Plan is an effective regime, but the overall picture of goose management in Alaska is not so rosy. For other types of waterfowl, management is even less effective because there is no counterpart to the Y-K Delta plan for other birds or in other parts of the state. The migratory bird treaties prohibit any management strategy that involves legalizing the spring harvest. This outlaws the traditional spring hunt, rendering goose management culturally inappropriate and making adaptation to local conditions impossible. Only the Y-K Delta plan is ecologically relevant and responsive to changes in population levels. The provisions of the bird treaties are not implemented, so local hunters can in fact get the animals they need, but this does not help to promote sound management of the resource. Unless the bird treaties are amended – ideally by removing the closed season altogether and concentrating on an ecological basis for achieving stable populations – goose management in northern Alaska will remain ineffective.

4. *Polar bears*. The management situation for polar bears is similar to that for walrus, with two significant differences: the commercial incentive to hunt polar bears is not as great, and the local agreement for polar bear management is more precise than the cooperative agreement for walrus management. The former makes management policies easier to im-

plement for polar bears, and the latter means that the role of the polar bear agreement between the Inuvialuit Game Council and the North Slope Borough Fish and Game Management Committee is better defined. In practice, the management of polar bears is more effective than the management of walrus; in Figure 8.2, I have placed it in the same category of effectiveness as bowhead whale management.

Although the domestic side of polar bear management may not be as developed or as effective as the Alaska Eskimo Whaling Commission, there is no international body setting quotas for the Alaska polar bear harvest. The recommendations of the International Agreement on Conservation of Polar Bears and Their Habitat are not followed in Alaska, since the Marine Mammal Protection Act preempts regulating the Native harvest if the stock is not depleted. The IGC-NSB agreement should be capable of limiting the take of female polar bears, reducing the risk of damage to the Beaufort Sea stock. The biological relevance of polar bear management is low only because the Marine Mammal Protection Act makes little provision for biological considerations if a species is not depleted. Since the MMPA is still the governing legislation for polar bear management, the IGC-NSB agreement is capable only of limited improvement of the situation and only in the area east of Wainwright. Other criteria are satisfied to the same extent as for walrus.

5. *Bowhead whales*. The main hindrance to effective management of bowhead whales is the International Whaling Commission quota. While the quota spurred the whalers to form the Alaska Eskimo Whaling Commission and to begin to manage themselves, it now remains as an obstacle. Because the harvest level is controlled by outsiders, it is not adaptable to local changes. Local participation exists within AEWC management but not beyond. Similarly, AEWC management is culturally appropriate and adaptable to local changes, while the IWC quota is not. The quota is also not based on biological grounds, but on the historical need for whales in the nine villages. In one sense this is a victory for the whalers and a fulfillment of the goal of providing for local needs. On the other hand, it raises the question of why a quota is needed at all, especially since a high quota may function more as a target than as a limit. The quota and the AEWC management plan are both well implemented. Overall, bowheads are well protected and the local need for whales is satisfied. The only drawback to the system is the nature of the quota.

Conclusion

Effective management of local hunting in northern Alaska requires intensive local involvement. At present, cooperative regimes best provide this.

By involving local hunters in all phases of management, cooperative regimes ensure responsiveness to local concerns and instill in local hunters a sense of ownership in the regime. Although tensions continue to exist between the parties involved in cooperative regimes, there is a shared commitment to the ideas of local use and of resource conservation.

Cooperative management is not a panacea for all management problems. Federal and state agencies have well-defined management and regulatory roles which often do not permit delegation of authority to cooperative regimes. However, mechanisms for local involvement already exist in several agencies, although they are often not used as fully as possible. While cooperative regimes have made the most of their management role, federal and state agencies have had difficulty in accommodating local input in the form of subsistence resource commissions or local advisory committees.

The future effectiveness of all regimes, whether federal, state, local, or cooperative, depends on the ability to gain and use the full cooperation and involvement of local hunters. Improving the relationship between hunters and managers will increase the effectiveness of management in regard to both local subsistence hunting and to the wider goals of each management regime.

References

Abbott, J. 1980. Eskimo whalers probed. *Anchorage Daily News*, October 23.

Adams v. Vance. 1977. 570 *Federal Reporter*, 2nd Series 950–7. St. Paul, Minnesota: West Publishing Co.

Adams, J. 1982. History and function of the Alaska Eskimo Whaling Commission. In: Alaska Eskimo Whaling Commission. 1982. *Proceedings of the first conference on the biology of the bowhead whale*, Balaena mysticetus: *population assessment*. 25–9 January 1982, Anchorage, Alaska. Barrow, Alaska: Alaska Eskimo Whaling Commission. pp. 9–13.

Alaska and Inuvialuit Beluga Whale Committee. 1988. Minutes of meeting, 22, 23 September, Fairbanks, Alaska. Alaska and Inuvialuit Beluga Whale Committee, Barrow, Alaska. 11p.

Alaska and Inuvialuit Beluga Whale Committee. 1989a. Minutes of meeting, 22, 23 March, Fairbanks, Alaska. Alaska and Inuvialuit Beluga Whale Committee, Barrow, Alaska. 10p.

Alaska and Inuvialuit Beluga Whale Committee. 1989b. *By-Laws*. Alaska and Inuvialuit Beluga Whale Committee, Barrow, Alaska. 9p.

Alaska and Inuvialuit Beluga Whale Committee. 1989c. Minutes of meeting, 7, 8 November, Fairbanks, Alaska. Alaska and Inuvialuit Beluga Whale Committee, Barrow, Alaska. 9p.

Alaska and Inuvialuit Beluga Whale Committee. 1990. Draft management plan. Alaska and Inuvialuit Beluga Whale Committee, Barrow, Alaska. 6p.

Alaska Belukha Whale Committee. 1988. Minutes of meeting, March 4, Fairbanks, Alaska. Alaska and Inuvialuit Beluga Whale Committee, Barrow, Alaska. 9p.

Alaska Consultants, Inc. with Stephen R. Braund & Associates. 1984. *Subsistence study of Alaska Eskimo whaling villages*. Prepared for the U.S. Department of the Interior.

Alaska Department of Fish and Game. 1960. *Alaska game regulations, 1960*. Game Regulatory Announcement No. 1. Juneau: Alaska Department of Fish and Game.

Alaska Department of Fish and Game. 1963. *Alaska game and guiding regulations*. Game and Guiding Regulatory Announcement No. 4. Juneau: Alaska Department of Fish and Game. 50p.

Alaska Department of Fish and Game. 1977. *Alaska hunting regulations, 1977–78*. No. 18. Juneau: Alaska Department of Fish and Game. 127p.

Alaska Department of Fish and Game. 1978. *Alaska hunting regulations, 1978–79*. No. 19. Juneau: Alaska Department of Fish and Game. 159p.

Alaska Department of Fish and Game. 1984. *Western Arctic Caribou Herd strategic management plan.* Approved by the Board of Game, April 1984.

Alaska Department of Fish and Game. 1989. *Abstracts: technical paper series.* Juneau: Alaska Department of Fish and Game, Division of Subsistence. iii + 57p.

Alaska Department of Fish and Game. 1990. *Alaska state hunting regulations, July 1, 1990–June 30, 1991.* No. 31. Juneau: Alaska Department of Fish and Game, Alaska Board of Game. 47p.

Alaska Eskimo Whaling Commission. 1977. *You will not bury our hearts (at Wounded Knee or anywhere else).* Statement of the commissioners concerning the banning of the subsistence hunting of the bowhead whale by the International Whaling Commission. October.

Alaska Fish and Wildlife Federation v. Dunkle. 1987. 829 *Federal Reporter*, 2nd Series 933–45. St. Paul, Minnesota: West Publishing Co. (1988.)

Alaska Game Commission. 1925. *Alaska Game Law and regulations and federal laws relating to game and birds in the territory.* Service and Regulatory Announcements. Washington, D.C.: U.S. Department of Agriculture.

Alaska Game Commission. 1939. *Regulations relating to game and fur animals, and birds in Alaska, 1939–40.* Circular No. 17. Washington, D.C.: U.S. Department of Agriculture.

Alaska Game Commission. 1943. *Regulations relating to game and fur animals, birds, and game fishes in Alaska.* Circular AGC-21. Washington, D.C.: U.S. Department of the Interior, Fish and Wildlife Service.

Alaska Game Commission. 1947. *Regulations relating to game and fur animals, birds, and game fishes in Alaska, 1947–48.* Regulatory Announcement 20. Washington, D.C.: U.S. Department of the Interior, Fish and Wildlife Service.

Alaska Game Commission. 1948. *Regulations relating to game and fur animals, birds, and game fishes in Alaska, 1948–49.* Regulatory Announcement 23. Washington, D.C.: U.S. Department of the Interior, Fish and Wildlife Service.

Alaska Game Commission. 1949. *Regulations relating to game land fur animals, birds, and game fishes in Alaska, 1949–50.* Regulatory Announcement 26. Washington, D.C.: U.S. Department of the Interior, Fish and Wildlife Service.

Alaska Game Commission. 1954. *Regulations relating to game land fur animals, birds, and game fishes in Alaska, 1954–55.* Regulatory Announcement 43. Washington, D.C.: U.S. Department of the Interior, Fish and Wildlife Service.

Alaska Oil Spill Commission. 1990. *Spill: the wreck of the* Exxon Valdez. Final Report, February 1990. Juneau: State of Alaska. xii + 224p.

Albert, T.F. 1988. The role of the North Slope Borough in Arctic environmental research. *Arctic Research of the United States*, 2: 17–23.

Amoco Production Company, *et al.* 1988. *Petition for the promulgation of regulations and issuance of letters of authorization pursuant to Section 101(a)(5) of the Marine Mammal Protection Act and Sections 7(b)(4) and 7(o) of the Endangered Species Act.* Submitted to National Oceanic and Atmospheric Administration, National Marine Fisheries Service.

Amstrup, S.C. 1984. Polar bear research in Alaska, 1980–2. In: International Union for Conservation of Nature and Natural Resources. 1984. *Proceedings of the technical workshop of the IUCN Polar Bear Specialists Group, 16–18 February 1983.* Gland, Switzerland: IUCN. Appendix 5.

Amstrup, S.C., and D.P. DeMaster. 1988. Polar bear, *Ursus maritimus.* In:

References

Lentfer, J.W. 1988. *Selected marine mammals of Alaska: species accounts with research and management recommendations.* Washington, D.C.: Marine Mammal Commission. p. 17–38.

Andersen, D. 1989. Pass it on: a young hunter's first moose. *Alaska Fish & Game,* 21(6): 37.

Anderson, D.D. 1970. Microblade traditions in northwestern Alaska. *Arctic Anthropology,* 7(2): 2–16.

Anderson, D.D. 1972. An archaeological survey of Noatak Drainage, Alaska. *Arctic Anthropology,* 9(1): 66–117.

Anderson, D.D. 1988. Onion Portage: the archaeology of a stratified site from the Kobuk River, northwest Alaska. *Anthropological Papers of the University of Alaska,* 22(1–2): xi + 163p.

Arctic Coastal Zone Management Newsletter. 1978. Issue 13. Barrow, Alaska: North Slope Borough.

Arctic Coastal Zone Management Newsletter. 1981. Issue 34. Barrow, Alaska: North Slope Borough.

Armstrong, T. 1985. White whales trapped in sea ice. *Polar Record,* 22(140): 552.

Arundale, W.H., and W.S. Schneider. 1987. *Quliaqtuat Iñupiat nunaniññiñ: the report of the Chipp-Ikpikpuk River and Upper Meade River oral history project.* Barrow, Alaska: North Slope Borough. xii + 100p.

Bandi, H.G. 1969. *Eskimo prehistory.* Translated from German by A.E. Keep. London: Methuen. xii + 226p.

Barrow Sun. 1989. The Nusunginya sentencing (transcript excerpts). *Barrow Sun,* 6(2): 6–8. March 17.

Berger, T.R. 1985. *Village journey.* New York: Hill and Wang. xiii + 200p.

Birket-Smith, K. 1936. *The Eskimos.* London: Methuen. xiv + 250p.

Bjorklund, I. 1988. Sámi reindeer pastoralism as an indigenous resource management system in northern Norway – a contribution to the common property debate. In: Freeman, M.M.R., and L.N. Carbyn, eds. 1988. *Traditional knowledge and renewable resource management in northern regions.* Occasional Paper No. 23. Edmonton: Boreal Institute for Northern Studies. pp. 48–54.

Blackman, M.B. 1989. *Sadie Brower Neakok: an Iñupiaq woman.* Seattle: University of Washington Press. xviii + 274p.

Bobby v. State of Alaska. 1989. 718 *Federal Supplement* 764–815. St. Paul, Minnesota: West Publishing Co.

Bockstoce, J.R. 1986. *Whales, ice, and men.* Seattle: University of Washington Press.

Bockstoce, J., ed. 1988. *The journal of Rochfort Maguire, 1852–1854.* London, Hakluyt Society. xiv + 584p. (2 vols.)

Bockstoce, J.R., and D.B. Botkin. 1980. *The historical status and reduction of the Western Arctic bowhead whale* (Balaena mysticetus) *population by the pelagic whaling industry, 1848–1914.* Report to the National Marine Fisheries Service by the Old Dartmouth Historical Society.

Braund, S.R.; S. Stoker; and J. Kruse. 1988. *Quantification of subsistence and cultural need for bowhead whales by Alaska Eskimos.* Anchorage: Stephen R. Braund & Associates.

Brewster, K.N. 1987. *Subsistence in Alaska: a case study for cultural and environmental planning.* Unpublished B.A. thesis, University of California, Santa Cruz.

vii + 158p.

Bromley, R.G. 1988. Waterfowl of the Northwest Territories: the extent and management of a world class resource. *Occasional Papers of the Prince of Wales Northern Heritage Center*, 3: 53–73.

Brower, C. 1942. *Fifty years below zero.* New York: Dodd Mead.

Bruce v. Director, Department of Chesapeake Bay Affairs. 1971. 276 *Atlantic Reporter*, 2nd Series 200. St. Paul, Minnesota: West Publishing Co.

Buckley, J.L. 1958. *The Pacific walrus: a review of current knowledge and suggested management needs.* Special Scientific Report – Wildlife No. 41. Washington, D.C.: U.S. Fish and Wildlife Service. iv + 29p.

Burch, E.S. 1974. Eskimo warfare in northwest Alaska. *Anthropological Papers of the University of Alaska.* 16(2): 1–14.

Bureau of Indian Affairs. 1977. *Gambell, its history, population and economy.* Billings, Montana: Bureau of Indian Affairs. vii + 255p.

Bureau of Land Management. 1989a. *Recreation 2000: Alaska.* Anchorage: U.S. Department of the Interior, Bureau of Land Management. May 1989. iii 100p.

Bureau of Land Management. 1989b. *Utility Corridor: proposed resource management plan and final environmental impact statement.* Fairbanks: U.S. Department of the Interior, Bureau of Land Management.

Bureau of Land Management. 1989c. *Muskox reintroduction: environmental assessment.* Fairbanks: U.S. Department of the Interior, Bureau of Land Management. 31p.

Bureau of Land Management and Defenders of Wildlife. 1990. *Watchable wildlife.* Washington, D.C.: U.S. Department of the Interior, Bureau of Land Management. 14p.

Burns, J.J. 1965. *The walrus in Alaska: its ecology and management.* Federal Aid in Wildlife Restoration Project Report. Juneau: Alaska Department of Fish and Game. 48p.

Busiahn, T.R. 1989. The development of state/tribal co-management of Wisconsin fisheries. In: Pinkerton, E., ed. 1989. *Cooperative management of local fisheries.* Vancouver: University of British Columbia Press. pp. 170–85.

Caribou News. 1981. 1(1).

Caribou News. 1982a. 2(1).

Caribou News. 1982b. 2(2).

Caribou News. 1982c. 2(3).

Caribou News. 1985. 5(2).

Caribou News. 1986. 6(6).

Case, D.S. 1989. Subsistence and self-determination: can Alaska Natives have a more "effective voice"? *University of Colorado Law Review*, 60(4): 1009–35.

Caulfield, R. 1988. The role of subsistence resource commissions in managing Alaska's new national parks. In: Freeman, M.M.R., and L.N. Carbyn, eds. 1988. *Traditional knowledge and renewable resource management in northern regions.* Occasional Paper No. 23. Edmonton: Boreal Institute for Northern Studies. pp. 55–64.

Chance, N.A. 1966. *The Eskimo of north Alaska.* New York: Holt, Rinehart and Winston. xii + 107p.

Cohen, F.G. 1989. Treaty Indian tribes and Washington State: the evolution of tribal involvement in fisheries management in the U.S. Pacific Northwest. In:

References

Pinkerton, E., ed. 1989. *Cooperative management of local fisheries*. Vancouver: University of British Columbia Press. pp. 37–48.

Cumming, D.H.M. 1990. *Communal land development and wildlife utilisation: potential and options in northern Namibia*. Harare, Zimbabwe: EarthAfrica and Southern Africa Foundation for Economic Research. 47p.

Dau, J., and D. Larsen. 1989. Memorandum to Regulation Review Subcommittee. Subject: Kiana & Noorvik notes. April 14, 1989. Unpublished report. Kotzebue: Alaska Department of Fish and Game. pp. 33–42.

DeMaster, D.P. 1980. Polar bear research and management in Alaska, 1977–1978. In: International Union for Conservation of Nature and Natural Resources. 1980. *Proceedings of the seventh working meeting of the IUCN Polar Bear Specialist Group*. Gland, Switzerland: IUCN. pp. 86–92.

Donovan, G.P., ed. 1982. Aboriginal/subsistence whaling (with special reference to the Alaska and Greenland fisheries). *Reports of the International Whaling Commission*, Special Issue 4. 86p.

Doubleday, N.C. 1989. Co-management provisions of the Inuvialuit Final Agreement. In: Pinkerton, E., ed. 1989. *Cooperative management of local fisheries*. Vancouver: University of British Columbia Press. pp. 209–27.

Fay, F.H. 1957. History and present status of the Pacific walrus population. *Transactions of the Twenty-Second North American Wildlife Conference*. Washington, D.C.: Wildlife Management Institute. pp. 431–45.

Fay, F.H.; B.P. Kelly; and J.L. Sease. 1989. Managing the exploitation of Pacific walruses: a tragedy of delayed response and poor communication. *Marine Mammal Science*, 5(1): 1–16.

Fikkan, A. 1990. Polar bears – hot topic in a cold climate. *International Challenges*, 10(2): 32–8.

Fischer, V. 1975. *Alaska's constitutional convention*. Fairbanks: University of Alaska Press. xiv + 277p.

Ford, J.A. 1959. Eskimo prehistory in the vicinity of Point Barrow, Alaska. *Anthropological Papers of the American Museum of Natural History*, 47(1): 272p. + 13 plates.

Frank v. State of Alaska. 1979. 604 *Pacific Reporter*, 2nd Series 1068–76. St. Paul, Minnesota: West Publishing Co. (1980.)

Freeman, M.M.R. 1985. Appeal to tradition: different perspectives on Arctic wildlife management. In: Brøsted, J., *et al.*, eds. 1985. *Native power: the quest for autonomy and nationhood of indigenous peoples*. Oslo: Universitetsforlaget. pp. 264–281.

Freeman, M.M.R. 1986. Renewable resources, economics and Native communities. In: Alberta Society of Professional Biologists. 1986. *Native people and renewable resource management*. Edmonton: Alberta Society of Professional Biologists. pp. 29–37.

Freeman, M.M.R. 1989. Graphs and gaffs: a cautionary tale in the common-property resources debate. In: Berkes, F., ed. 1989. *Common property resources*. London: Belhaven Press. pp. 92–109.

Frost, K.J.; L.F. Lowry; and R.R Nelson. 1983. Investigations of belukha whales in coastal waters of western and northern Alaska, 1982–83: marking and tracking of whales in Bristol Bay. In: Outer Continental Shelf Environmental Assessment Program. 1986. *Final Reports of Principal Investigators*, Volume 43:

461–585.

Gambell, R. 1983. Bowhead whales and Alaskan Eskimos: a problem of survival. *Polar Record*, 21(134): 467–73.

Geographical Magazine. 1968. Walrus hunters on the Bering Sea. 40(15): 1288–93.

Georgette, S. 1989. Left-handed bears: how *Kuuvangmiit* see the grizzly. *Alaska Fish & Game*, 21(6): 8–10.

Giddings, J.L. 1967. *Ancient men of the Arctic*. New York: Alfred A. Knopf. xxxi + 391p.

Giddings, J.L., and D.D. Anderson. 1986. *Beach ridge archeology of Cape Krusenstern*. Washington, D.C.: U.S. Department of the Interior, National Park Service. xxviii + 386p. + 174 plates.

Gordon, D.M. 1985. *Caribou management and the Caribou Management Board: Eskimo Point perspectives*. Unpublished master's thesis, Natural Resources Institute, University of Manitoba. viii + 143p.

Gunn, A.; G. Arlooktoo; and D. Kaomayok. 1988. The contribution of the ecological knowledge of Inuit to wildlife management in the Northwest Territories. In: Freeman, M.M.R., and L.N. Carbyn, eds. 1988. *Traditional knowledge and renewable resource management in northern regions*. Occasional Paper No. 23. Edmonton: Boreal Institute for Northern Studies. pp. 22–30.

Hall, E.S., Jr. 1975. *The Eskimo storyteller*. Knoxville, University of Tennessee. xi + 491p.

Hazard, K. 1988. Beluga whale, *Delphinapterus leucas*. In: Lentfer, J.W., ed. 1988. *Selected marine mammals of Alaska: species accounts with research and management recommendations*. Washington, D.C.: Marine Mammal Commission. pp. 195–235.

Hill, R.M. 1968. Observations on white whales trapped by ice in the Eskimo Lakes during the winter of 1966–7. *Arctic Circular*, 17(3–4): 28–36.

Holdsworth, W.S. 1922. *A history of English law*. Vol. 1. Third edition. London: Methuen. xlv + 706p.

Hopson v. Kreps. 1979. 462 *Federal Supplement* 1374–83. St. Paul, Minnesota: West Publishing Co.

Hopson v. Kreps. 1980. 622 *Federal Reporter*, 2nd Series 1375–82. St. Paul, Minnesota: West Publishing Co.

Huffman, J.L., and G.C. Coggins. 1986. The federal role in natural resources management in the United States. In: Saunders, J.O., ed. 1986. *Managing natural resources in a federal state*. Toronto: Carswell. pp. 52–72.

Hughes, C.C. 1965. Under four flags: recent cultural change among the Eskimos. *Current Anthropology*, 6(1): 3–69.

Huntington, H.P. 1989. *The Alaska Eskimo Whaling Commission: effective local management of a subsistence resource*. Unpublished M.Phil thesis, Scott Polar Research Institute, University of Cambridge, United Kingdom. 71p.

International Agreement on Conservation of Polar Bears and Their Habitat. 1973.

International Convention for the Regulation of Whaling. 1946.

International Whaling Commission. 1950. *First Report of the Commission*.

International Whaling Commission. 1978a. Report of the Scientific Committee. *International Whaling Commission Reports*, 28: 66–7.

International Whaling Commission. 1978b. Chairman's report of the twenty-ninth meeting. *International Whaling Commission Reports*, 28: 22.

References

International Whaling Commission. 1979a. Chairman's report of the special meeting, Tokyo, December 1978. *International Whaling Commission Reports*, 29: 2.

International Whaling Commission. 1979b. Chairman's report of the thirtieth meeting. *International Whaling Commission Reports*, 29: 26.

International Whaling Commission. 1980. Report of the sub-committee on protected species and aboriginal whaling. *International Whaling Commission Reports*, 30: 103–4.

International Whaling Commission. 1982. Report of the cultural anthropology panel. *Aboriginal/subsistence whaling*. Cambridge: International Whaling Commission. pp. 34–49.

International Whaling Commission. 1991. [In press]. *International Whaling Commission Reports*, 41.

Inuvialuit Game Council and North Slope Borough Fish and Game Management Committee. 1988. Polar bear management in the southern Beaufort Sea: an agreement. January 29, 1988. [Inuvik and Barrow: Inuvialuit Game Council and North Slope Borough.] 13p.

Ivashin, M.V., and K.V. Shevlagin. 1987. The white whale (*Delphinapterus leucas Pallas*, 1776): entrapment and escape in the ice of Senjavin Strait, USSR. *Report of the International Whaling Commission*, 37: 357–9.

Jacobson, M.J., and C. Wentworth. 1982. *Kaktovik subsistence; land use values through time in the Arctic National Wildlife Refuge area*. Fairbanks: U.S. Fish and Wildlife Service.

Jenness, D. 1962. *Eskimo administration: I. Alaska*. Arctic Institute of North America, Technical Paper No. 10. 64p.

Kapel, F.O., and R. Petersen. 1982. Subsistence hunting – the Greenland case. In: International Whaling Commission. 1982. Aboriginal/subsistence whaling. *Reports of the International Whaling Commission*, Special Issue 4. Cambridge: International Whaling Commission. pp. 51–73.

Katelnikoff v. U.S. Department of the Interior. 1986. 657 Federal Supplement, 659–68. St. Paul, Minnesota: West Publishing Co. (1987.)

Kelly, B.P. 1988a. Ringed seal, *Phoca hispida*. In: Lentfer, J.W., ed. 1988. *Selected marine mammals of Alaska: species accounts with research and management recommendations*. Washington, D.C.: Marine Mammal Commission. pp. 57–75.

Kelly, B.P. 1988b. Bearded seal, *Erignathus barbatus*. In: Lentfer, J.W., ed. 1988. *Selected marine mammals of Alaska: species accounts with research and management recommendations*. Washington, D.C.: Marine Mammal Commission. pp. 77–94.

Kelly, B.P. 1988c. Ribbon seal, *Phoca fasciata*. In: Lentfer, J.W., ed. 1988. *Selected marine mammals of Alaska: species accounts with research and management recommendations*. Washington, D.C.: Marine Mammal Commission. pp. 95–106.

Kelso, D.D. 1981. *Technical overview of the state's subsistence program*. Technical Paper Number 64. Alaska Department of Fish and Game, Division of Subsistence. 34p.

Kelso, D.D. 1982. *Subsistence use of fish and game resources in Alaska: considerations in formulating effective management policies*. Technical Paper No. 65. Juneau: Alaska Department of Fish and Game, Division of Subsistence. 28p.

Kenaitze Indian Tribe v. State of Alaska. 1988. 860 *Federal Reporter*, 2nd Series

312–21. St.Paul, Minnesota: West Publishing Co. (1989.)

Kevin Waring Associates. 1988. *A demographic and employment analysis of selected Alaska rural communities. Volume II (northern communities)*. Technical Report No. 137. Submitted to Minerals Management Service, U.S. Department of the Interior. xxvii + 424p.

Kilmarx, J.N. 1986. Archaeological and ethnohistorical evidence for material acculturation in Barrow, Alaska. *Etudes Inuit Studies*. 10(1–2): 203–31.

Kruse, J. 1986. Subsistence and the North Slope Inupiat: the effects of energy development. In: Langdon, S.J., ed. 1986. *Contemporary Alaska Native economies*. Lanham, Maryland: University Press of America. pp. 121–52.

Kwethluk Ira Council v. State of Alaska. 1990. United States District Court for the District of Alaska. Preliminary injunction filed April 4, 1990. 7p.

Langdon, S. 1984. Alaska Native subsistence: current regulatory regimes and issues. *Alaska Native Review Commission*, XIX. Anchorage: Alaska Native Review Commission. 100p.

Langdon, S.J. 1986. Contradictions in Alaska Native economy and society. In: Langdon, S.J., ed. 1986. *Contemporary Alaska Native economies*. Lanham, Maryland: University Press of America. pp. 29–46.

Langdon, S.J. 1989. Prospects for co-management of marine mammals in Alaska. In: Pinkerton, E., ed. 1989. *Cooperative management of local fisheries*. Vancouver: University of British Columbia Press. pp. 154–69.

Larsen, D., and J. Dau. 1989. Memorandum to Regulation Review Subcommittee. Subject: Ambler visit. June 7, 1989. Unpublished report. Kotzebue: Alaska Department of Fish and Game. pp. 49–59.

Larsen, H., and F. Rainey. 1948. Ipiutak and the Arctic Whale Hunting culture. *Anthropological Papers of the American Museum of Natural History*, 42: 276p. + 101 plates.

Lentfer, J. 1974. An agreement on conservation of polar bears. *Polar Record*, 17(108): 327–30.

Lentfer, J.W. 1976. Polar bear management and research in Alaska, 1972–74. In: International Union for Conservation of Nature and Natural Resources. 1976. *Polar bears: proceedings of the fifth working meeting of the Polar Bear Specialist Group. 3–5 December 1974*. Morges, Switzerland: IUCN, Survival Service Commission. pp. 53–60.

Lewis v. State of Arkansas. 1913. 161 *Southwestern Reporter* 154. St. Paul, Minnesota: West Publishing Co. (1914.)

Lobdell, J.E. 1986. The Kuparuk pingo site: a Northern Archaic hunting camp of the Arctic Coastal Plain, north Alaska. *Arctic*, 39(1): 47–51.

Lonner, T.D. 1980. *Subsistence as an economic system in Alaska: theoretical and policy implications*. Technical Paper Number 67. Juneau: Alaska Department of Fish and Game, Division of Subsistence. 37p.

Lonner, T.D. 1981. *Perceptions of subsistence and public policy formation in Alaska*. Technical Paper Number 68. Juneau: Alaska Department of Fish and Game, Division of Subsistence. 14p.

Loon, H. 1989. Sharing: you are never alone in a village. *Alaska Fish & Game*, 21(6): 34–6.

Loon, H., and S. Georgette. 1989. *Contemporary brown bear use in northwest Alaska*. Technical Paper Number 163. Kotzebue: Alaska Department of Fish

References

and Game, Division of Subsistence. iv + 58p.

Lowry, L.F.; J.J. Burns, and K.J. Frost. 1989. Recent harvests of belukha whales, *Delphinapterus leucas*, in western and northern Alaska and their potential impact on provisional management stocks. *Report of the International Whaling Commission*, 39: 335–9.

Lund, T.A. 1980. *American wildlife law*. Berkeley: University of California. ix + 179p.

McCandless, R.G. 1985. *Yukon wildlife*. Edmonton: University of Alberta. xvii + 200p.

McDonald, M. 1988. Traditional knowledge, adaptive management and advances in scientific understanding. In: Freeman, M.M.R., and L.N. Carbyn, eds. 1988. *Traditional knowledge and renewable resource management in northern regions*. Occasional Paper No. 23. Edmonton: Boreal Institute for Northern Studies. pp. 65–71.

McDowell v. State of Alaska. 1989. 785 *Pacific Reporter*, 2nd Series 1–19. St. Paul, Minnesota: West Publishing Co. (1990.)

McVay, S. 1979. Another perspective. *Orca*, 1(1): 13–15.

Madison v. Alaska Department of Fish and Game. 1985. 696 *Pacific Reporter*, 2nd Series 168–178 . St.Paul, Minnesota: West Publishing Co.

[Magdanz, J.] 1988. Northwest Alaska game regulation review: a discussion paper. November 1988. Kotzebue: Alaska Department of Fish and Game. Unpublished report.

Manwood, J. 1598. *A treatise and discourse of the laws of the forest*. London: Thomas Wight and Bonham Norton.

Marks, S.A. 1984. *The imperial lion*. Boulder, Colorado: Westview Press. xv + 196p.

Marquette, W.M., and J.R. Bockstoce. 1980. Historical shore-based catch of bowhead whales in the Bering, Chukchi and Beaufort Seas. *Marine Fisheries Review*, 42(9–10): 5–19.

Minerals Management Service. 1987. *Chukchi Sea oil and gas lease sale 109: final environmental impact statement*. Anchorage: U.S. Department of the Interior, Minerals Management Service. 2 vols.

Minerals Management Service. 1988. *Beaufort Sea sale 97: final environmental impact statement*. Anchorage: U.S. Department of the Interior, Minerals Management Service. 2 vols.

Minerals Management Service. 1989. *Alaska regional studies plan*. Anchorage: U.S. Department of the Interior, Minerals Management Service.

Minerals Management Service. 1990. *Beaufort Sea planning area oil and gas lease sale 124: draft environmental impact statement*. Anchorage: U.S. Department of the Interior, Minerals Management Service. 2 vols.

Mitchell, E., and R.R. Reeves. 1980. The Alaska bowhead problem: a commentary. *Arctic*, 33(4): 686–723.

Moore, G.D. 1980. *Report on the special caribou season for Buckland, Alaska, December 5, 1979–February 4, 1980*. Technical Paper No. 8. Alaska Department of Fish and Game, Division of Subsistence. 22p.

Morgan, L. 1988. *Art and Eskimo power*. Fairbanks: Epicenter Press. xi + 258p.

Nageak, B.P. 1987. Letter to potential members of beluga whale committee. December 16, 1987. North Slope Borough, Department of Wildlife Management,

Barrow, Alaska. 3p.

Nageak, B.P. 1990. Letter to hunter. April 18, 1990. North Slope Borough Department of Wildlife Management, Barrow, Alaska.

Nash, R. 1982. *Wilderness and the American mind.* Third Edition. New Haven: Yale University Press. xvii + 425p.

National Audubon Society, U.S. Fish and Wildlife Service, The Nature Conservancy, Waterfowl Habitat Owners Alliance, California Department of Fish and Game, California Waterfowl Association, The Trust for Public Land, Defenders of Wildlife, and Ducks Unlimited, Inc. 1990. Central Valley habitat joint venture implementation plan. [N.p.] 102p.

National Oceanic and Atmospheric Administration. 1977. Bowhead whales: taking by Indians, Aleuts, or Eskimos for subsistence purposes. *Federal Register*, 42(227): 60149–50.

National Oceanic and Atmospheric Administration. 1988. *Bering, Chukchi, and Beaufort Seas: coastal and ocean zones strategic assessment data atlas.* Washington, D.C.: U.S. Department of Commerce, National Oceanic and Atmospheric Administration.

National Oceanic and Atmospheric Administration and Alaska Eskimo Whaling Commission. 1981. Cooperative agreement. March 26, 1981.

National Park Service. 1986a. *Cape Krusenstern National Monument, Alaska.* Washington, D.C.: U.S. Department of the Interior, National Park Service. xiv + 220p.

National Park Service. 1986b. *Gates of the Arctic National Park and Preserve, Alaska.* Washington, D.C.: U.S. Department of the Interior, National Park Service. xiv + 299p.

National Park Service. 1986c. *Kobuk Valley National Park, Alaska.* Washington, D.C.: U.S. Department of the Interior, National Park Service. x + 220p.

National Park Service. 1986d. *Noatak National Preserve, Alaska.* Washington, D.C.: U.S. Department of the Interior, National Park Service. xii + 228p.

National Park Service. 1991. *Draft legislative environmental impact statement on all-terrain vehicles for subsistence use in Gates of the Arctic National Park and Preserve, Alaska.* Anchorage: U.S. Department of the Interior, National Park Service. xiv + 344p.

Neakok, W.; D. Neakok; W. Bodfish; D. Libbey; E.S. Hall, Jr.; and The Point Lay Elders. 1985. *To keep the past alive: the Point Lay cultural resource site survey.* Barrow, Alaska: North Slope Borough. x + 111p.

Nelson, R.K. 1969. *Hunters of the northern ice.* Chicago: University of Chicago Press. xxiv + 429p.

Nelson, R.K. 1981. *Harvest of the sea: coastal subsistence in modern Wainwright.* A report for the North Slope Borough's Coastal Management Program.

Nelson, W. 1751. *The laws concerning game.* London: T. Waller. xvii + 255p.

North Slope Borough. 1980. *Qiñiqtuagaksrat utuqqanaat iñuuniagniŋisiqun: the traditional land use inventory for the mid-Beaufort Sea. Volume 1.* Barrow, Alaska: North Slope Borough. v + 209p.

North Slope Borough Department of Wildlife Management. N.d. *Mission statement.* Unpublished document. Barrow, Alaska: North Slope Borough Department of Wildlife Management. 3p.

North Slope Borough Science Advisory Committee. 1989. *A review of the technical*

References

plan for the 1989 Endicott Development fish monitoring program. December 1989. Barrow, Alaska: North Slope Borough Science Advisory Committee. iii + 33p.

Northwest Territories Department of Renewable Resources. 1990. Northwest Territories polar bear management plan. Yellowknife: Department of Renewable Resources, Government of the Northwest Territories. 13p.

O'Neill, D. 1989. Project Chariot: how Alaska escaped nuclear excavation. *Bulletin of Atomic Scientists*, 45(10): 28–37.

Okakok, L. 1989. Serving the purpose of education. *Harvard Educational Review*. 59(4): 405–22.

Osherenko, G. 1988. Wildlife management in the North American Arctic: the case for co-management. In: Freeman, M.M.R., and L.N. Carbyn, eds. 1988. *Traditional knowledge and renewable resource management in northern regions.* Occasional Paper No. 23. Edmonton: Boreal Institute for Northern Studies. pp. 92–104.

Pacific Walrus Technical Committee. 1988. Minutes of meeting, October 18, 1988. North Slope Borough Department of Wildlife Management, Barrow, Alaska.

Pamplin, W.L., Jr.; L.F. Lowry; and K.J. Frost. 1988. *Report and recommendations regarding the State of Alaska's role in management of marine mammals.* Alaska Department of Fish and Game, Division of Game. January 1988.

Pedersen, S. 1979. *Regional subsistence land use, North Slope Borough, Alaska.* Fairbanks and Barrow: University of Alaska and North Slope Borough. 30p.

Pedersen, S., and R.A. Caulfield. 1981. *Some elements of subsistence land and resource use within the range of the Porcupine Caribou Herd in Alaska.* Technical Paper Number 3. Alaska Department of Fish and Game, Division of Subsistence. 9p.

People of Togiak v. United States. 1979. 470 *Federal Supplement* 423–430. St. Paul, Minnesota: West Publishing Co.

Pinkerton, E., ed. 1989. *Cooperative management of local fisheries.* Vancouver: University of British Columbia Press. xiii + 299p.

Porcupine Caribou Management Board. 1989a. *Third annual report, 1988–89.* Whitehorse, Yukon: Porcupine Caribou Management Board. 39p.

Porcupine Caribou Management Board. 1989b. *Interim management plan for the Porcupine Caribou Herd in Canada, 1989/90–1992/93.* Whitehorse, Yukon: Porcupine Caribou Management Board. 23p.

Qausagniq. 1990. A reminder to hunters. *Qausagniq, A New Dawn*, 2(6): 7. Barrow: North Slope Borough.

Quakenbush, L.T. 1988. Spotted seal, *Phoca largha.* In: Lentfer, J.W., ed. 1988. *Selected marine mammals of Alaska: species accounts with research and management recommendations.* Washington, D.C.: Marine Mammal Commission. pp. 107–24.

Ramoth, M., and S. Georgette. 1989. Memorandum to Regulation Review Subcommittee. Subject: Point Hope field visit. July 7, 1989. Unpublished report. Kotzebue: Alaska Department of Fish and Game. pp. 60–8.

Randa, V. 1986. *L'Ours polaire et les Inuit.* Paris: SELAF. xviii + 324p.

Ray, D.J. 1983. *Ethnohistory in the Arctic: the Bering Strait Eskimo.* R.A. Pierce, ed. Kingston, Ontario: Limestone Press. vi + 274p.

Robinson, M.; M. Dickerson; J. Van Camp; W. Wuttunee; M. Pretes; and L.

References

Binder. 1989a. *Coping with the cash*. Prepared for the N.W.T. Legislative Assembly, Special Committee on the Northern Economy, by the Sustainable Research Development Group, Arctic Institute of North America. x + 133p.

Robinson, M.; M. Pretes; and W. Wuttunee. 1989b. Investment strategies for northern cash windfalls: learning from the Alaskan experience. *Arctic*, 42(3): 265–76.

Rural Alaska Community Action Program. 1989. Results of a survey: implementation of ANILCA's subsistence priority and advisory committee system by the State of Alaska. Rural Alaska Community Action Program, Inc., Subsistence Department. 11p.

Schaeffer, P.; D. Barr; and G. Moore. 1986. Kotzebue Fish and Game Advisory Committee regulation review: a review of the game regulations affecting Northwest Alaska. In: U.S. Fish and Wildlife Service. 1988. *Subsistence management and use: implementation of Title VIII of ANILCA*. Anchorage: U.S. Department of the Interior, Fish and Wildlife Service. B54–79.

Schroeder, R.F.; D.B. Andersen; R. Bosworth; J.M. Morris; and J.M. Wright. 1987. *Subsistence in Alaska: Arctic, Interior, Southcentral, Southwest and Western regional summaries*. Technical Paper No. 150. Alaska Department of Fish and Game, Division of Subsistence. 690p.

Seaman, G.A., and J.J. Burns. 1981. Preliminary results of recent studies of belukhas in Alaskan waters. *Report of the International Whaling Commission*, 31: 567–74.

Sease, J.L., and D.G. Chapman. 1988. Pacific walrus, *Odobenus rosmarus divergens*. In: Lentfer, J.W., ed. 1988. *Selected marine mammals of Alaska: species accounts with research and management recommendations*. Washington, D.C.: Marine Mammal Commission. pp. 17–38.

Sergeant, D.E., and P.F. Brodie. 1975. Identity, abundance, and present status of populations of white whales, *Delphinapterus leucas*, in North America. *Journal of the Fisheries Research Board of Canada*, 32(7): 1047–54.

Sherwood, M. 1981. *Big game in Alaska*. New Haven: Yale University Press. xii + 200p.

Spencer, R.F. 1959. *The north Alaskan Eskimo: a study in ecology and society*. Bureau of American Ethnology, Bulletin 171. Washington, D.C.: U.S. Government Printing Office. vi + 490p.

Stefansson, V. 1913. *My life with the Eskimo*. New York: Macmillan. ix + 527p.

Stephen R. Braund & Associates and Institute of Social and Economic Research. 1988. *North Slope subsistence study: Barrow, 1987*. Technical Report No. 133. Minerals Management Service, Alaska Outer Continental Shelf Office.

Stephen R. Braund & Associates and Institute of Social and Economic Research. 1989a. *North Slope subsistence study: Barrow, 1988*. Technical Report No. 135. Anchorage: U.S. Department of the Interior, Minerals Management Service, Alaska Outer Continental Shelf Office. viii + 193p.

Stephen R. Braund & Associates and Institute of Social and Economic Research. 1989b. *North Slope subsistence study: Wainwright, 1988*. Draft Technical Report No. 136. Minerals Management Service, Alaska Outer Continental Shelf Office.

Stephenson, C. and F.G. Marcham. 1972. *Sources of English constitutional history*. Volume I. Second edition. New York: Harper & Row. xxvii + 502p.

Steward, B.S.; F.T. Awbrey; and W.E. Evans. 1983. Belukha whale (*Delphinap-

References

terus leucas) responses to industrial noise in Nushagak Bay, Alaska: 1983. In: Outer Continental Shelf Environmental Assessment Program. 1986. *Final Reports of Principal Investigators*, Volume 43: 587–616.

Stieglitz, W.O. 1989. Letter to the Editor of *Newsweek*. June 26, 1989. (North Slope Borough Department of Wildlife Management, Barrow, Alaska).

Stirling, I. 1986. Research and management of polar bears, *Ursus maritimus*. *Polar Record*, 23(143): 167–76.

Subsistence Resource Commission for Gates of the Arctic National Park. 1987. *Subsistence management program*. Unpublished report, March 13, 1987. 16p.

Thompson, D.Q., and R.A. Person. 1963. The eider pass at Point Barrow, Alaska. *Journal of Wildlife Management*, 27(3): 348–56.

Thompson, E.P. 1975. *Whigs and hunters*. London: Allen Lane. 313p.

Thornton, H.R. 1931. *Among the Eskimos of Wales, Alaska, 1890–93*. Baltimore, Johns Hopkins.

Tober, J.A. 1981. *Who owns the wildlife?* Westport, Connecticut: Greenwood. xix + 330p.

Tokeinna, J.K. 1987. Letter to hunters. April 17, 1987. (North Slope Borough Department of Wildlife Management, Barrow, Alaska).

Trench, C.C. 1967. *The poacher and the squire*. London: Longmans. 248p.

Treseder, L., and A. Carpenter. 1989. Polar bear management in the southern Beaufort Sea. *Information North*, 15(4).

Uhl, W.R., and C.K. Uhl. 1977. *Tagiumsinaaqmiit: ocean beach dwellers of the Cape Krusenstern area subsistence patterns*. Fairbanks: University of Alaska, Cooperative Park Studies Unit. vi + 227p.

United States and Canada. 1987. *Agreement on the conservation of the Porcupine Caribou Herd*.

United States and Great Britain. 1916. *Convention for the protection of migratory birds*.

United States and Japan. 1972. *Convention for protection of birds and their environment*.

United States and Mexico. 1936. *Convention for the protection of migratory birds and game mammals*.

United States and Union of Soviet Socialist Republics. 1976. *Convention concerning the conservation of migratory birds and their environment*.

Urquhart, D.R. 1983. *The status and life history of the Porcupine Caribou Herd*. Yukon Territory Department of Renewable Resources. iii + 78p.

Urquhart, D.R., and R.E. Schweinsburg. 1984. *Polar bear: life history and known distribution of polar bear in the Northwest Territories up to 1981*. Yellowknife: Northwest Territories Renewable Resources. v + 70p.

U.S. Congress. 1918a. Hearings before the Committee on the Territories, House of Representatives, 65th Congress, 2nd Session, on H.R. 7344: To regulate the killing and sale of certain game animals in northern Alaska. Washington, D.C.: Government Printing Office.

U.S. Congress. 1918b. Migratory Bird Treaty Act.

U.S. Congress. 1934. Indian Reorganization Act.

U.S. Congress. 1941. Walrus Act.

U.S. Congress. 1969. National Environmental Policy Act.

U.S. Congress. 1971. Alaska Native Claims Settlement Act.

U.S. Congress. 1972. Marine Mammal Protection Act.

U.S. Congress. 1976. Federal Land Policy and Management Act.

U.S. Congress. 1980. Alaska National Interest Lands Conservation Act.

U.S. Fish and Wildlife Service. 1987. *Selawik National Wildlife Refuge: comprehensive conservation plan/environmental impact statement/wilderness review/wild river plan*. Anchorage: U.S. Fish and Wildlife Service. xv + 378p.

U.S. Fish and Wildlife Service. 1988a. *Federal Register*. 53: 45,788.

U.S. Fish and Wildlife Service. 1988b. *Subsistence management and use: implementation of Title VIII of ANILCA*. Anchorage: U.S. Department of the Interior, Fish and Wildlife Service.

U.S. Fish and Wildlife Service. 1988c. Policy regarding harvest of migratory birds in Alaska during the closed season. *Federal Register*, 53(92): 16877–81.

U.S. Fish and Wildlife Service. 1988d. *Arctic National Wildlife Refuge: comprehensive conservation plan/environmental impact statement/wilderness review/wild river plans*. Anchorage: U.S. Fish and Wildlife Service. xxxii + 609p.

U.S. Fish and Wildlife Service. 1988e. *The lives of geese*. Anchorage: U.S. Department of the Interior, Fish and Wildlife Service. 38p.

U.S. Fish and Wildlife Service. [1989.] Population levels in Alaska: black brant, cackling Canada geese, emperor geese, white-fronted geese. (Looseleaf graphs)

U.S. Fish and Wildlife Service. 1990. Law enforcement plan for 1990 walrus season. Anchorage: U.S. Fish and Wildlife Service – Alaska. 1p.

U.S. Fish and Wildlife Service. 1991. *Subsistence management for federal public lands in Alaska: draft environmental impact statement*. Anchorage: U.S. Department of the Interior, Fish and Wildlife Service.

U.S. Fish and Wildlife Service, Association of Village Council Presidents, Association of Village Council Presidents Waterfowl Conservation Committee, Alaska Department of Fish and Game, and California Department of Fish and Game. 1985. Yukon-Kuskokwim Delta Goose Management Plan.

U.S. Fish and Wildlife Service, Alaska Department of Fish and Game, and Eskimo Walrus Commission. 1987. Memorandum of agreement. 7p.

Usher, P.J. 1986. *The devolution of wildlife conservation in the Northwest Territories*. Policy Paper No. 3. Ottawa: Canadian Arctic Resources Committee. 193p.

VanStone, J.W. 1962. *Point Hope: an Eskimo village in transition*. Seattle: University of Washington Press. x + 177p.

Wheeler, P. 1988. State and indigenous fisheries management: the Alaska context. In: Freeman, M.M.R., and L.N. Carbyn, eds. 1988. *Traditional knowledge and renewable resource management in northern regions*. Occasional Paper No. 23. Edmonton: Boreal Institute for Northern Studies. pp. 38–47.

Wilson, J. 1903. *Regulations for the protection of game in Alaska*. Biological Survey Circular, No. 39. Washington, D.C.: U.S. Department of Agriculture. 6p.

Wilson, J. 1908. *The Alaska Game Law and regulations of the Department of Agriculture, 1908*. Biological Survey Circular, No. 66. Washington, D.C.: U.S. Department of Agriculture. 8p.

Wolfe, R.J.; J.A. Fall; V. Fay; S. Georgette; J. Magdanz; S. Pedersen; M. Pete; and J. Schichnes. 1986. *The role of fish and wildlife in the economies of Barrow, Bethel, Dillingham, Kotzebue and Nome*. Technical Paper Number 154. Juneau: Alaska Department of Fish and Game, Division of Subsistence. v + 90p.

References

Worl, R., and C.W. Smythe. 1986. *Barrow: a decade of modernization*. Technical Report No. 125. Anchorage: U.S. Department of the Interior, Minerals Management Service, Alaska Outer Continental Shelf Office.

Index

Index

Index

Index